HAWTHORNE'S

MAD SCIENTISTS

Hawthorne's Mad Scientists

PSEUDOSCIENCE AND SOCIAL SCIENCE IN NINETEENTH-CENTURY LIFE AND LETTERS

by

TAYLOR STOEHR

Archon Books 1978

First published 1978 as an Archon Book,
an imprint of The Shoe String Press, Inc.,
Hamden, Connecticut 06514

Printed in the United States of America

Library of Congress Cataloging in Publication Data

Stoehr, Taylor, 1931-
Hawthorne's mad scientists.

Bibliography: p.
Includes index.
1. Hawthorne, Nathaniel, 1804-1864—Characters—Scientists. 2. Scientists in literature. 3. Quacks and quackery in literature. 4. Social reformers in literature. 5. United States—Civilization—1783-1865. I Title.
PS1889.S7 813'.3 78-50
ISBN 0-208-01710-0

To Jonathan Bishop
and Neil Hertz

Contents

Preface

HAWTHORNE DID NOT invent "the mad scientist," nor was he the last to imagine a mysterious doctor or an evil mesmerist plotting to subjugate helpless innocents to his will. Other writers are more thoroughly identified with the stereotype. A great artist is not so easily pigeonholed, and one thinks of Hawthorne as commanding a wider range of subjects and effects than the authors of *Frankenstein* or *Dr. Jekyll and Mr. Hyde.* Nonetheless Hawthorne is the chief practitioner of science fiction in our literature, and his crazy doctors and villainous alchemists stalk through the imagination like no others—Heidegger, Aylmer, Rappaccini, Chillingworth, Maule, Westervelt, Grimshawe, Dolliver.

I have asked myself why Hawthorne should be so fascinated with these figures. Where did they come from? What models did he have? Why did they grip him so?

As it happens an enormous body of material is available to answer such questions, for the sources of Hawthorne's fascination go deep in the culture of his times, as well as in his own nature. Nineteenth-century America displayed a remarkable popular interest in science and technology, even among citizens who had little notion of the actual methods and aims of the laboratory. There simultaneously arose a whole class of what we now call pseudosciences—mesmerism, phrenology, homoeopathy, and the like—which competed successfully with more respectable doctrines for public attention. Still other systems of experiment and belief borrowed the name and prestige of science, but were really philanthropic theories—programs meant to reform society as thoroughly as applied science was to transform the material world. By the 1850s these last had begun to be called *social* sciences, with names like "sociology" and "prison discipline" as well as "associationism" and "universology." Many of these sciences straddled the fence that hindsight now sees between pseudoscience and social science—phrenology, for example, had its fingers on psychiatry and penal reform as well as the noggin. Others, like mesmerism/spiritualism, passed from one avatar to another; the transition was neither orderly nor very dignified, and professional reformers had to be quick on their feet to follow the currents.

All this ferment fed Hawthorne's conception of the mad scientist; even the shift from pseudoscience to social science may be observed in the parceling-out of strange powers and fanatical projects that complicates *The Blithedale Romance.* Plot, characterization, theme, method and genre are profoundly touched by these popular phenomena.

There are several ways of looking at this pervasive presence. To show the extent and cultural significance of these movements, I have devoted a portion of my text to a rather detailed account of the individual sciences—the mesmerism, phrenology, and so forth that I examine in succeeding chapters. On the other hand, it was Hawthorne's intimate experience of pseudoscience and social science that made him dwell on such things in his stories; therefore each discussion of a particular science is interwoven with a report of his personal encounters with its enthusiasts and lore. Sometimes this report rests on direct biographical evidence, but often I have had to fall back on the testimony of the fiction, conjecturing what cannot be known with certainty. This sort of inquiry is not expected to issue in hard facts so much as patterns of emphasis and centers of energy; I see no reason to value such results less than any other discoveries of literary criticism. Certain cruxes in the canon open up to such treatment, as does the deeper problem of Hawthorne's curiously paced and balked career.

At the same time I have tried to pinpoint the literary manner and narrative techniques that Hawthorne worked with and to show how his "scientific" materials helped sustain his habits of composition. Finally, from the perspective of literary history it has seemed worthwhile to ascertain the generic features of "mad scientist" fiction, and to attempt some formal analysis of the competing genres—especially the gothic and the utopian novel—along with their roots in nineteenth-century social change.

I suppose it would have been possible to subordinate these inquiries to one overriding concern. Indeed, the title *Hawthorne's Mad Scientists* may suggest such an emphasis, but aside from a certain heuristic illusion I have not been willing to play the critic at the expense of biography, cultural history, or literary theory. I admit to being just as interested in the trivia that went into *The Blithedale Romance* as I am in the book itself, marvel that it is. Frankly I do not see how any reader can appreciate it properly unless conversant with the riches of gossip and circumstance that saturate it, and I have therefore felt justified in indulging my own taste.

Hawthorne wrote at a time when one popular movement was replacing another, as pseudoscience made way for social science, and also at a turning point in literary history, the overlap of gothic and utopian fiction. *The Blithedale Romance* is poised on both of these thresholds, and so I have devoted most of my attention to it—all of the second half of this book. That *Blithedale* can bear such a weight of interpretation and analysis seems to me a proof of its greatness. No one but Melville could hold a candle to it.

I have also discussed many other books and authors, including some rather seedy examples. It may be objected that there is too little distinction made between Melville or Poe, for example, and Charles Webber or T.S. Arthur. This is another liability of my larger enterprise, for an account of popular culture must take its materials where they lie. I confess that I think Poe well-companioned with his friends Webber and Mary Gove. His is a vastly overrated reputation; but in any case a writer cannot mount the pedestal without leaving his place in the life of his times. Even to single out Hawthorne distorts social history.

It ought to be reiterated that no other writer so thoroughly reflects the scientific mania of his age as Hawthorne, however he may soar above it. There have been some fruitful studies of phrenology in Poe and Whitman, spiritualism in James and Twain, and so on, but these have always seemed mere illustrations of the pervasiveness of this or that fad; if my panoptic method succeeds at all, it is because Hawthorne was *immersed* in these sciences.

There are a number of fine books on Hawthorne, and also some excellent treatments of phrenology, spiritualism, and other enthusiasms of the period. While I have made use of these whenever possible, my text is already so burdened with intentions that I have resisted the temptation to weave any scholarly dialogue into the discussion. Most valuable to me have been the researches of scholars such as Randall Stewart and Norman Holmes Pearson, on whose biographical and textual work all serious study of Hawthorne must rely. I am also indebted to the more specialized textual and bibliographical achievements of Nelson F. Adkins, Edward H. Davidson, and the editors of the Centenary Edition of Hawthorne going forward at Ohio State. Marion L. Kesselring's work on Hawthorne's reading has been very helpful, as has Arlin Turner's on Hawthorne's editorship of the *American Magazine of Useful and Entertaining Knowledge.* Louise Hall Tharp's *Peabody Sisters of Salem* contains biographical material not available anywhere else. Still more directly relevant have been Elizabeth Ruth Hosmer's dissertation, "Science and Pseudo-science in the Writings of Nathaniel Hawthorne" (1948), and Francis W. Weeks' M.A. thesis, "Some Aspects of Pseudo-Sciences in Nineteenth Century American Literature" (1939), both of which do much of the spade work for my own harvest. Among scholars of pseudoscience, I owe the most to Madeleine B. Stern, whose books have thrown much light in these esoteric corners of American culture. In addition to her history of *The Phrenological Fowlers* I have found John Davies' *Phrenology: Fad and Science* instructive.

Most of the foregoing works will be found fully cited in my notes, along with a great many others of somewhat narrower application. For the reader who is further interested in these matters I can also recommend the following studies, most of which do not appear in the notes: on mesmerism and spiritualism, Emma Hardinge Britten, *Modern American Spiritualism* (New York, 1870), Slater Brown, *The Heyday of Spiritualism* (New York, 1970), and Howard Kerr, *Mediums and Spirit-Rappers and Roaring Radicals* (Urbana, 1972); on homoeopathy, Martin Kaufman, *Homoeopathy in America* (Baltimore, 1971); on associationism, John Humphrey Noyes, *History of American Socialisms* (Philadelphia, 1870) and Henry W. Sams (ed.), *Autobiography of Brook Farm* (Englewood Cliffs, N.J., 1958); on prison reform, W. David Lewis, *From Newgate to Dannemora* (Ithaca, 1965). Among innumerable useful books on American feminism—the best of which is still *The History of Woman Suffrage* (New York and Rochester, 1881-1922), edited by Elizabeth

Cady Stanton, Susan B. Anthony, and Matilda J. Gage—there is no carefully documented account of the free love wing of the movement. Hal Sears' *The Sex Radicals* (Kansas, 1977) is an excellent study of the Moses Harman circle, but free love had a greater radius than that. Sidney Ditzion's *Marriage, Morals, and Sex in America* (New York, 1953) is the closest thing to it, but must be used with caution. Alice Felt Tyler's *Freedom's Ferment* (Minneapolis, 1944) is still the best overview of the movement phenomenon and provides useful bibliographies. Modern compendiums of pseudoscience tend to be interested only in debunking, but are sometimes informative; Martin Gardner, *Fads and Fallacies in the Name of Science* (New York, 1957) is better than most.

Finally it must be said that for a reliable sense of these movements and enthusiasms, there is no substitute for familiarity with the primary documents—an undertaking I can recommend to the reader who is himself a potential enthusiast, with some years at his disposal.

Acknowledgments

HAWTHORNE LETTERS are published here with the kind permission of Mrs. Gwendolen H. Mikkelsen. I have used the typescripts edited by the late Professor Norman Holmes Pearson, to whom I am also indebted for much scholarly advice. Mr. David B. Stowe has given permission to print an unpublished letter of Harriet Beecher Stowe. The following libraries have given their permission to quote letters in their collections: The Huntington Library, San Merino, California; Berg Collection, New York Public Library, Astor, Lenox and Tilden Foundations; Clifton Waller Barrett Library, University of Virginia Library; the Pierpont Morgan Library; Trustees of the Boston Public Library; Harvard College Library; Fruitlands Museum; Schlesinger Library, Radcliffe College; Maine Historical Society. Earlier versions of two chapters—on mesmerism and on physiognomy and phrenology—were first published in the *Huntington Library Quarterly.* Parts of the chapter on associationism have been published in *The Antioch Review.*

I wish to thank Madeleine B. Stern, Louise Hall Tharp, Neal Smith of the Ohio State Center for Textual Studies, Kenneth J. Boyer of the Bowdoin College Library, Mrs. Charles A. Potter of the Essex Institute, Emily Hewitt, John Graham, and John Davies, for their generous assistance in tracking down obscure persons and events.

Zofia Drzewieniecki and Janet Wesser of the Lockwood Memorial Library at the State University of New York at Buffalo, Joan Hodgson of the library at the University of California, Santa Cruz, and Molly Matson, Janet Stewart, and Hildegarde Von Laue of the library at the University of Massachusetts in Boston performed miracles in getting the books I needed.

My research was aided by grants from the Cornell University English Department, the State University of New York at Buffalo, the University of California, Santa Cruz, and the American Council of Learned Societies.

I owe most of all to innumerable conversations with Jonathan Bishop, John Dings, Neil Hertz, Alison Lurie, Irving Massey, and Ruth Perry.

T.S.

Abbreviations

WHERE POSSIBLE I have used the Centenary Edition of *The Works of Nathaniel Hawthorne* (Columbus, Ohio, 1962-   ). For the *English Notebooks* I have used Randall Stewart's edition (New York, 1941). For the *Italian Notebooks* and a few sketches it has been necessary to rely on the Riverside Edition of *The Complete Works of Nathaniel Hawthorne,* ed. George Parsons Lathrop, 12 vols. (Boston, 1883), and for the unfinished romances I have used the exemplary editions of Edward H. Davidson, *Hawthorne's Last Phase* (New Haven, 1949), and *Hawthorne's Doctor Grimshawe's Secret* (Cambridge, Mass., 1954).

References to these sources appear in parentheses immediately following quotations in my text. Roman numerals signify volumes in the Riverside Edition, and capital letters refer to the titles of all other works, as follows:

AN	*The American Notebooks*
BR	*The Blithedale Romance*
EN	*The English Notebooks*
F	*Fanshawe*
HSG	*The House of the Seven Gables*
MF	*The Marble Faun*
MOM	*Mosses from an Old Manse*
SI	*The Snow-Image and Uncollected Tales*
SL	*The Scarlet Letter*

TTT	*Twice-told Tales*
DGS	*Hawthorne's Doctor Grimshawe's Secret*
LP	*Hawthorne's Last Phase*

I

One

Pseudoscience

In 1838 the tough-minded and sharp-tongued Harriet Martineau published her second book on America, and in it she devoted several pages to an analysis of "the fickleness and impressibleness of the Americans (particularly of the New-Englanders) about systems of science, philosophy, and morals," which, she declared, "exceed anything ever seen or heard of in the sober old country":

> When Spurzheim was in America, the great mass of society became phrenologists in a day, wherever he appeared; and ever since itinerant lecturers have been reproducing the same sensation in a milder way, by retailing Spurzheimism, much deteriorated, in places where the philosopher had not been. Meantime the light is always going out behind as fast as it blazes up round the steps of the lecturers. While the world of Richmond and Charleston is working at a multiplication of the fifteen casts (the same fifteen or so) which every lecturer carries about, and all caps and wigs are pulled off, all fair tresses dishevelled in the search after organization, Boston has gone completely round to the opposite philosophy, and is raving about spiritualism to an excess which can scarcely be credited by any who have not heard the Unknown Tongues. If a phrenological lecturer from Paris, London, or Edinburgh should go to Boston, the superficial, visible portion of the public would wheel round once more, so rapidly and with so clamorous a welcome on their tongues, that the transported lecturer would bless his stars which had guided

him over to a country whose inhabitants are so candid, so enlightened, so ravenous for truth. Before five years are out, however, the lecturer will find himself superseded by some professor of animal magnetism, some preacher of homoeopathy, some teacher who will undertake to analyze children, prove to them that their spirits made their bodies, and elicit from them truths fresh from heaven.[1]

Miss Martineau's estimate of the American "impressibleness" was as just as it was witty, though her final swipe at Bronson Alcott bordered on the malicious (his friends held her responsible for the closing of the Temple School). One might complain that America is unfairly contrasted with "the sober old country," which was itself stirring—more sedately—about mesmerism and phrenology, but after all the tone of Miss Martineau's jibes at American gullibility is not so much impassioned as amused. It was certainly mild in comparison with the vehemence of a native observer of the American scene, David Meredith Reese, a cantankerous New York physician who, also in 1838, took the *Humbugs of New-York* to task:

Every year, and indeed almost every month, brings to our city some imported mountebank; some foreign or domestic humbug; each of which in its turn is greedily swallowed while the rage of novelty lasts, until another more clamorous, or more showy, succeeds it. Meanwhile, however, each of these acquires proselytes; and as fanaticism is constitutional, the same individuals, in many instances, deliberately swallow them all. Indeed there are gentlemen and ladies in this city, who have been successively gulled by Matthias, Fanny Wright, the moon story, and the Crawcours. They have taken the pills of foreign and domestic quacks by the thousand, with Lobelia, Cayenne pepper, and vapour baths. They have swallowed Maria Monk, abolitionism, and homoeopathia; and are now equally busy in bolting down Phrenology and Animal Magnetism.[2]

Although domestic as well as the foreign brands of quackery are acknowledged by Dr. Reese, he patriotically fretted more about imported humbugs, which New Yorkers were apparently eager to embrace, "however monstrous or absurd."[3] In truth, the major fads (discounting Dr. Reese's "ultra-abolitionism," chiefly homegrown) were European imports, but only in the United States did they capture the popular imagination so thoroughly that they sometimes seemed to mirror the culture itself.

Some European proselytizers for the new sciences found the American enthusiasm rather distasteful. George Combe, the Scottish phrenologist, complained (also in 1838) of the "great numbers of 'practical phrenologists' in the United States . . . , men who examine heads and predicate characters for fees, and who are pretty extensively consulted. This practice, which to the uninitiated resembles palmistry and fortune telling, is said to have created a strong feeling of disgust against Phrenology itself, in the minds of men of science and education."[4] Yankee knowhow degenerated all too easily to mere sharp practice, 25 cents a head being a profitable return on the original investment of European intellectuals and eccentrics. The public, for its part, seemed willing to pay the price for any scientific demonstrations or treatments so long as there was something tangible to show for it, something "practical"—a cranial character reading, marked on a card like a dentist's chart, or a circumstantial account of the condition of one's liver, diagnosed by a clairvoyant who in the trance state became a sort of human fluoroscope.

Of course susceptibility to faddish delusions was not the only interesting trait of the American character revealed during the pseudoscientific craze, nor were there lacking sensible men to point out encouraging signs as well as absurdities in these enthusiasms. One obvious possiblity was that there might be some truth in the claims of Mesmer and Gall, Hahnemann and Priessnitz, and their disciples. This depended on the claims. Many scientifically trained observers sneered, like Dr. Reese, at the pseudoscientists' frequent ignorance or disregard of the facts of human anatomy. Others no less serious or skilled wondered about those facts themselves, since the evidence of success in pseudoscientific experiments often seemed at least as palpable if not so familiar as long-established truths. Perhaps there was no such thing as animal magnetism, but that did not necessarily rule out the genuineness of phenomena attributed to it. Even a skeptic might be convinced if the proof were registered in his own body. Harriet Martineau, for example, who had scoffed in 1838, was by 1844 a convert, after being cured of an ailment (prolapse of the uterus and polypous tumours) which had made her an invalid for most of the intervening years. Her recovery, achieved over a period of some months of daily treatment, was the strongest possible argument for the truth of mesmerism:

> I can describe it only by saying, that I felt as if my life were fed from day to day. The vital force infused or induced was as clear and certain as the strength given by food to those who are faint from hunger. I am careful to avoid theorizing at present on a subject which has not yet furnished me with a sufficiency of facts; but it can hardly be called theorizing to say (while silent as to the nature of the agency) that the principle of life itself—that principle which is antagonistic to diseases—appears to be fortified by the mesmeric influence.[5]

No doubt there is more theorizing here than Miss Martineau was aware of, and some of her later experiments with mesmerism (she once magnetized a cow) make one hesitant to praise her empiricism; but Dr. Reese and others might have learned at least one lesson from her—a respect for unusual and unexplained facts as well as for those more familiar and accountable to accepted theory. Miss Martineau tells us about one gentleman whose skepticism went so far that, as he said, "if he saw the incidents himself, he would not believe them; he would sooner think himself and the whole company mad than admit them."[6]

Certain practical truths of the pseudosciences have been incorporated into modern science—various hypnotic phenomena, such as Harriet Martineau experienced and as James Braid and James Esdaile researched more carefully; the localization of cortical functions of the brain, such as Gall aided with his advances in anatomical technique; the physiology of physiognomical expression of emotion and character, such as Sir Charles Bell and Charles Darwin explored; the systematic "proving" of drugs to ascertain their medicinal virtues, as the homoeopathists advocated. The anesthetic uses of the trance would alone go far toward explaining the excitement mesmerism produced in a world that had no reliable pain killer until 1846. Such useful discoveries might account for the interest in pseudoscience, but to the social philosopher of the nineteenth century more significant truths seemed to lurk behind the practical phenomena. In his "Historic Notes on Life and Letters in New England," Emerson hints at some of these further truths:

> . . . there was, in the first quarter ["second quarter" would have been more accurate] of our nineteenth century, a certain sharpness of criticism, an eagerness for reform, which showed itself in every quarter. It appeared in the popularity of Lavater's Physiognomy,

> now almost forgotten. Gall and Spurzheim's Phrenology laid a rough hand on the mysteries of animal and spiritual nature, dragging down every sacred secret to a street show. The attempt was coarse and odious to scientific men, but had a certain truth in it; it felt connection where the professors had denied it, and was leading to a truth which had not yet been announced. On the heels of this intruder came Mesmerism, which broke into the inmost shrines, attempted the explanation of miracle and prophecy, as well as creation. What could be more revolting to the contemplative philosopher! But a certain success attended it, against all expectations. It was human, it was genial, it affirmed unity and connection between remote points, and as such was excellent criticism on the narrow and dead classification of what passed for science; and the joy with which it was greeted was an instinct of the people which no true philosopher would fail to profit by. . . . There was a breath of new air, much vague expectation, a consciousness of power not yet finding its determinate aim.[7]

It was only fitting that Emerson should have welcomed the popular interest in "the newness," as it was sometimes called, for he too was part of it. An aging temperament like that of John Quincy Adams, for example, saw Emerson's own mild philosophizing as another such "rascality":

> A young man, named Ralph Waldo Emerson, a son of my once-loved friend William Emerson, and a classmate of my lamented son George, after failing in the every-day avocations of a Unitarian preacher and schoolmaster, starts a new doctrine of transcendentalism, declares all the old revelations superannuated and worn-out, and announces the approach of new revelations and prophecies. Garrison and the non-resistant abolitionists, Brownson and the Marat Democrats, phrenology and animal magnetism, all come in, furnishing each some plausible rascality as an ingredient for the bubbling cauldron of religion and politics.[8]

What appealed to Emerson in his "Historic Notes" was precisely the public enthusiasm that conservatives like Adams or David Reese found so revolting. Having outlived the controversy (he was writing after the Civil War, when only social sciences like feminism and psychology still held the field in any force), it was easier for Emerson to see the "good" in such manifestations; a long retrospect turned fad into groundswell—if not to be valued in itself, then at least something for the philosopher to "profit by."

But "revolting" is also Emerson's word here, and in 1837, a year before Miss Martineau and Dr. Reese had their say, Emerson was noting some of his own early revulsions from the pseudosciences in his journal: ". . . Animal Magnetism seems the phenomena of Disease & too fuliginous & typhoid in their character to attract any but the physician. I suppose that as the marketplace & the alleys need to be stimulated by the raw head & bloody bones of a murder or piracy with wood-cuts so our wise cotemporaries are glad to be made to wonder by something that is wonderful to the *senses.*"[9] Thirty years later "physician" has changed to "philosopher," "marketplace" and "alleys," have become "people."

These shifts of emphasis are especially instructive when we weigh them against the fact that David Reese was a physician and that he made use of the expression "Popular Delusion" in the subtitle of his book. As a medical man, Dr. Reese was interested in exploding the claims of phrenologists who knew no anatomy, of mesmeric somnambulists—"medecins endormez" he called them—who pretended to "detect and cure all manner of diseases, by *looking into the inside* of the stomach, bowels, liver, spleen, lungs, brain, or any other organ of the body, and describing the disease as well as naming the remedy."[10] Emerson in his turn was more concerned with the health of the citizenry as a whole, and one sees, following his remarks on mesmerism over the years, that his diagnosis grew steadily more "philosophical," less impatient with the "popular delusion" and more trusting of the "instinct of the people." In this swing of interest, and in the related medical facts, which we must derive from testimonies as various as Miss Martineau's and Dr. Reese's, the range of possible truths in and about the pseudosciences is spread before us.

However well-defined the pattern of Emerson's interest in these matters, the precise nature of the truths he felt behind their surfaces is left curiously unclear—"new air" and "vague expectation" might be apt phrases for the uncertainty of an observer in 1837, but given his advantage of hindsight in the "Historic Notes," one is puzzled to find the moralist yet unsure of his moral, or less sure of it than of its implications. The paradox is a familiar one in the history of pseudoscience; a characteristic of the movement was absolute conviction in the importance of truths as yet unrevealed. The resistance to formulation of these truths served only to confirm pseudoscientists in their faith that, once laid bare, their discoveries would penetrate all mysteries and solve all problems. Not that the average practitioner was as cautious as Harriet Martineau about theorizing; only that every theory, no matter how authoritatively proclaimed, was tacitly recognized as tentative and ad hoc, to be revised or reversed by the same theorizer in the following year. Recantations and confessions were regarded as advances rather than backtracking. As time went on, the pseudoscientists grew more and more comfortable with their mass of amorphous doctrine, each shift of which seemed to strengthen rather than undermine the belief in progress.

From one point of view, the most interesting feature of pseudoscience was its extreme adaptability, which made room for so many revisionists and synthesizers—bringing phrenology and animal magnetism together in phrenomagnetism, adding daguerreotypy to beget psychography, or mnemonics to produce phrenomnemotechny, yet still leaving open the possibility of further liaisons with hydropathy, chirography, phonography, grahamism, homoeopathy, not to mention social sciences such as penology, education, feminism, abolition, temperance, associationism, and so on. "Reform," was the favorite term for all these movements; "pseudoscience" was a derogation its opponents had yet to popularize. There was a moral cast to such activities, even when they amounted to nothing more than a new system of shorthand or of memorizing dates. Improvement in any area of human life was an ethical endeavor, and the pseudoscientists did not miss many opportunities to cure evil and promote good. "A physician for the cure of moral diseases" was an idea Hawthorne jotted down in his notebooks in 1842 (*AN* 235); this psychiatric notion, which finds its way, inverted, into many of his stories of evil scientists who experiment with vice, was a familiar one in the period. It lay behind the identification of the pseudosciences with more obviously social and humanitarian undertakings, and accounted for the interest of men like Horace Mann, Samuel Gridley Howe, Henry Ward Beecher, Horace Greeley, and William Cullen Bryant in phrenology, animal magnetism, and their sister sciences.

Everyone was welcome on the reforming bandwagon, which would carry America into the millenium:

> How long before the rising waters of reform and the descending icebergs of evil will rush down against these dams of conservatism with such overwhelming might as to sweep all before them, it is difficult to predict. . . . But a final break-up must come. The winter is past. The snows of antiquated institutions are fast melting before the genial rays of truth which the ascending sun of progression is pouring down upon humanity with perpetually increasing effulgence. And I opine that the grand break-up must occur within our own life time—that many of us will live to see the mighty mass of evil and misery which has thus far bound society in its relentless sheet of ice, move on in majestic grandeur toward the ocean grave of the past.[11]

This prophetic voice belonged to Orson S. Fowler, whose *American Phrenological Journal* ("Home Truths for Home Consumption") gave shelter and publicity to every fad born in America from 1838 to 1911. Fowler's accents owe something to the millenial rhetoric that was in the air during the 1840s—the Millerites, who numbered thousands by 1843, "the last year that Satan will reign in our earth;"[12] the "Perfectionists," led by John Humphrey Noyes, whose community of saints at Oneida, New York, dated from 1846;[13] or various other "Adamic" and adventist colonies and cults, Mormons, Shakers, the "Brotherhood of the New Life" that Thomas Lake Harris first established at Mountain Cove, Virginia, "the identical spot where our first parents sinned."[14]

This was the tail end of the nineteenth century's "Second Great Awakening," the work of Finney and other evangelists. In an age of moralism and progress, the secular counterpart of this fervor was the pseudoscientific reform movement itself. Often the connections between pseudoscience and religious enthusiasm were made quite explicit, as when Elder George Storrs of the Millerites explained (after the failure of the appointed last day) that the delusion he had labored under "was nothing but *Mesmerism.*"[15] In 1847 Thomas Lake Harris had been a disciple of Andrew Jackson Davis, "the Poughkeepsie Seer," and so was involved in experiments with magnetic trances before embarking on his more messianic career at Mountain Cove and other stations of the Brotherhood.[16] In general, however, the implications of pseudoscience were conceived as moral rather than mystical, even in a religious context. John Humphrey Noyes drew on phrenological terminology in formulating his theories of "Bible Communism" and "Complex Marriage," part of the Oneida experiment in communal living.[17] Emerson called George Combe's phrenological *Constitution of Man* "the best sermon I have read for some time."[18] The famous preacher Henry Ward Beecher, who had been the first to introduce Orson Fowler to phrenology (when both were undergraduates at Amherst), claimed that being without tools on a desert island would be "much the same plight that I should be [in] as a preacher if Phrenology and all that it has taught me of man, his character, his wants, and his improvement, were blotted from my mind."[19] "Improvement," "preacher," and "sermon" are the key words; they sum up the pseudoscientific contributions to piety. Nothing could be more bland or benevolent than this smiling public countenance, and if some of the professors of the new sciences were hypocrites or frauds, a far greater number genuinely intended to do the world good.

Nathaniel Hawthorne's private encounters with pseudoscience were in many ways typical of the public experience. Like Emerson and others, he soon saw that the significance of the movement was to be estimated in what it reflected of the popular imagination, not in the claims and proofs of the pseudoscientists themselves: "Be the individual theory as wild as fancy could make it," he remarked in his own voice in a sketch published in 1843, "still the wiser spirit would recognize the struggle of the race after a better and purer life, than had yet been realized on earth. My faith revived, even while I rejected all their schemes" (*MOM* 181). A decade later he had edged away from this position, though it is difficult to say how far. Clifford Pyncheon in *The House of the Seven Gables,* not a totally reliable spokesman, is allowed to say, ". . . the harbingers of a better era are unmistakeable. Mesmerism, now! Will that effect nothing, think you, towards purging away the grossness out of human life? . . . These rapping spirits . . . What are these but the messengers of the spiritual world, knocking at the door of substance?" (*HSG* 263-264)

The tone of Clifford's expostulation harkens back to "The Hall of Fantasy" quoted above, but now everything is undercut by being presented through an untrustworthy observer.

Hawthorne's own stance in an earlier chapter of *The Seven Gables* is more cautious. Speaking of old Maule's evil eye, he suggests rather tentatively: "Modern psychology, it may be, will endeavor to reduce these alleged necromancies within a system, instead of rejecting them as altogether fabulous" (*HSG* 26). Hedged round with quotation marks or undermined with "it may be," Hawthorne's attitude in these passages is very hard to pin down. Although in 1843 it seemed that a "wiser spirit" might make out the vague shape of the future from some detached vantage point, Hawthorne had not achieved that higher philosophic ground by the time of *The House of the Seven Gables.* Nor did he subsequently.

Hawthorne's considerable personal experience of the pseudosciences affected his fiction in crucial ways, but his attitude toward such materials remained hesitant and ambiguous to the end, at least so far as formal statements of opinion are concerned. Like his contemporaries, he saw the possibility that "science" might organize a good deal of uncanny experience in systematic ways, perhaps even usefully. He himself had seen mesmerism heal the sick. He himself had been "infinitesimally dosed" by homoeopathists. He knew how to read character in the face. He knew people who had seen ghosts and heard the spirits rapping, who had eaten nothing but brown bread or doused themselves inside and out according to Priessnitz's principles. Much of this experience, even when it was not firsthand, hit close to home, for he had married into a "reforming" family. He had lived at Brook Farm and invested in it. He had edited a popular magazine and had set himself to write for popular tastes. At every point of his external relations he was bound to be touched by the pseudoscientific manias of his time. Yet, so far as his public voice can be identified in his fiction, he withheld final judgment.

Of course there is no reason to suppose that the sort of didactic formulation Hawthorne forbore would have been nearly so revealing as the rendering he could and did give in his fiction, with plot and character, scene and situation. Attentive as he was to the pronouncements of "modern psychology," his own concern was with the "fabulous" in danger of being reduced to "system." The local and topical materials of his experience he adapts as metaphor for truths about his age that eluded literal and philosophic statement. The history of pseudoscience is itself largely anecdotal, and this was much of its appeal to the popular imagination. So long as sentimental and gothic forms dominated the American literary scene (until after the Civil War), novelists would turn such materials to mythic uses, expressive of the underlying fantasies of the pseudoscientific craze. No matter how confused they might get the facts and the theories, the patterns of fear and desire were delineated with unmistakeable clarity. And in this imaginative response to the spirit of the times, Hawthorne, more than any other novelist, had both personal cause and artistic skill to find and develop the plots and themes, the fictive truths, that we can "profit by."

Two

Mesmerism

MESMERISM CAME to America in two waves. The first subsided almost before Hawthorne was born and left so little trace as to be of no interest to us; the second began in the mid-1830s, reached an ultrascientific phase when it merged with phrenology as phrenomagnetism in the early 1840s, then developed an other-worldly aspect as it gradually melted into spiritualism during the 1850s. Like all the pseudosciences, mesmerism was completely overwhelmed in the tide of abolitionism and secession, but after the war it was one of the few to reappear, this time in a more explicitly religious guise as a much elaborated spiritualism, and less obviously as Christian Science.

The heyday of animal magnetism was the decade just before Hawthorne's *The House of the Seven Gables* and *The Blithedale Romance,* which borrowed heavily from it. During the 1840s the popular mind was much engrossed with the new science, whose professors offered something for everyone—diagnosis and treatment for the sick, marvels of telepathy and clairvoyance for the curious, accounts of the "Summer-Land" of eternity for those with a metaphysical turn, and feats of mind over matter for country audiences in village lyceums. Literary hacks like T.S. Arthur, George Lippard, or Edgar Allan Poe were quick to spot the possibilities for fiction, and their exploitation of the sensational side of mesmerism helped define a genre before Hawthorne came to it. Poe was especially intrigued by magnetic themes, as by all pseudoscientific phenomena, and he indulged himself in a series of hoax tales based on the trance, telepathy, clairvoyance, and the like. Of these, the most successful was "The Facts in the Case of M. Valdemar," an account of suspended animation achieved by mesmerism. The narrator reports his experience as if it were case history: called by prearrangement to the death bed of his friend, he succeeds in forestalling Valdemar's demise at the last minute by putting his patient into a deep sleep. For almost seven months his bodily decay is arrested, but finally Valdemar is allowed to awake to death. The narrator performs the required "reverse passes," whereupon the body immediately disintegrates before his horrified eyes to "a nearly liquid mass of loathsome—of detestable putridity."[1]

This gruesome fancy was widely reprinted in the mid-1840s, and readers were so eager to swallow whatever wonders a pseudoscientist might dangle in front of them that many took Poe's bold fabrication hook, line, and sinker. An English expert, Thomas South, was completely fooled by "The announcement lately made by Mr. Poe . . . of a dying man magnetised by him in *articulo mortis,* and though inevitable death did certainly supervene, yet there in his chamber and in testimony of a crowd of witnesses, for seven months consecutively lay the undemagnetised corpse, and when questioned by the magnetiser Poe, in a sepulchral voice gave utterance that he was dead, dead, and should not be disturbed. . . . This is well and publicly attested, yet few even of the faithful will believe, though one spoke from the dead."[2]

Poe of course was gratified by such reactions. Even more delectable was the response of a well-known mesmerist working out of Boston, Dr. Robert H. Collyer, who wrote a fan letter to Poe's *Broadway Journal:*

> DEAR SIR—Your account of M. Valdemar's Case has been universally copied in this city, and has created a very great sensation. It requires from me no apology, in stating, that I have not the least doubt of the *possibility* of such a phenomenon; for, I did actually restore to active animation a person who died from excessive drinking of ardent spirits. He was placed in his coffin ready for interment.
>
> You are aware that death very often follows excessive excitement of the nervous system; this arising from the extreme prostration

> which follows; so that the vital powers have not sufficient energy to react.
>
> I will give you the detailed account on your reply to this, which I require for publication, in order to put at rest the growing impression that your account is merely a *splendid creation* of your own brain, not having any truth in fact. My dear sir, I have battled the storm of public derision too long on the subject of Mesmerism, to be now found in the rear ranks—though I have not publicly lectured for more than two years, I have steadily made it a subject of deep investigation.
>
> I sent the account to my friend Dr. Elliotson of London; also to the "Zoist,"—to which journal I have regularly contributed.
>
> Your early reply will oblige, which I will publish, with your consent, in connection with the case I have referred to. Believe me yours, most respectfully.

Poe, carrying the farce to its limits, sneered over his victim:

> We have no doubt that Mr. Collyer is perfectly correct in all that he says—and all that he desires us to say—but the truth is, there was a very small modicum of truth in the case of M. Valdemar—which, in consequence, may be called a hard case—*very* hard for M. Valdemar, for Mr. Collyer, and ourselves. If the story was not true, however, it should have been—and perhaps "The Zoist" may discover that it *is* true, after all.[3]

To which there was little for Collyer to reply.

Perhaps Poe was hard on Collyer because he had caught such a big fish. As will soon be apparent, Collyer's own career was so full of malarkey that one might almost suspect him of having invented *his* revivification just to cash in on Poe's. But the truth was that Collyer actually had the adventure he reported, though the facts were not quite what his letter implied. In the spring of 1841, Collyer had "revived" a sailor who had drunk himself into a stupor ("No perceptible respiration, no pulse, surface cold and clammy")—but his technique had not been mesmerism at all, rather "a *hot bath,* and constant friction of the whole body, which was continued for over three hours."[4] Collyer fails to mention the hot bath and chafing in his letter to Poe simply because in 1845 he was still selling himself as a mesmerist. Another year and the anecdote would have had a different twist and proclaimed another "first." In his time Collyer proposed himself for many such honors: he claimed credit for the phrenological organ of Tune, then phrenomagnetism, psychography, and anesthesia.[5] Collyer's career is so fabulous as to be worth recounting briefly here, as an (admittedly extreme) example of the sort of man who became a mesmerist in the 1840s.

The account is of particular interest because Hawthorne may have seen Collyer perform his magnetic feats in Boston or Salem, and may have used him as a model for Professor Westervelt in *The Blithedale Romance.* Collyer lectured on phrenology, mesmerism, phrenomagnetism, and psychography throughout New England from about 1839 to 1843, with a long and successful engagement in Boston from May through July 1841, moving on to Salem in August. Hawthorne was at Brook Farm during this period, and might have seen Collyer, just as Coverdale saw Westervelt, on one of his visits to the city. In any event he had heard of Collyer, for he referred to him in "The Hall of Fantasy," published in *The Pioneer,* February 1843. As the narrator and his guide pass out of the "hall" at the end of the sketch, they meet "the spirits of several persons, whom Dr. Collyer had sent thither in the magnetic sleep."[6]

Collyer's chameleon activities have led one scholar to suppose there must have been *two* Robert H. Collyers, M.D.—one a more or less respectable phrenologist, an English disciple and friend of Spurzheim, whose visit to the States left a bad taste in his mouth; the second Collyer an imposter who capitalized on the first's name and reputation to perpetrate various frauds and immoralities.[7] The impersonation was not so unlikely—LaRoy Sunderland, for example, complained that someone "stole the entire name, advertisement, hand-bills, and testimonials" of his own professional identity, "for a course of lectures on Pathetism," Sunderland's version of the mesmeric science in 1843.[8] However, all the evidence points to the existence of only one Collyer, a follower of Spurzheim (he claims to have met him in Paris in 1831) who came to the States in 1836 and lectured in New York on the "Wonders of the Microscopic World." He toured the South and West for a year or so, lecturing on phrenology and learning his trade.

In 1839 Collyer turned up in Pittsfield, Massachusetts, where he graduated from the Berkshire Medical College. About that time he was converted to mesmerism. He almost immediately discovered, he claimed—but so did LaRoy Sunderland and others—the hybrid science of phrenomagnetism, which was essentially a technological innovation, the excitation of the phrenological organs by the magnetic action of the fingers. A few years later he was similarly insisting on his priority over Wells, Morton, and Jackson in the discovery of the inhalation of "narcotic fumes" as an anesthetic.

Between 1841 and 1843 Collyer says he addressed crowds of one thousand to fifteen-hundred all over New England. In addition to his own works he brought out a new edition of Chauncy Townshend's *Facts in Mesmerism,* with a long appendix devoted to his own experiments. (Ironically, it was probably this edition of Townshend that Poe used for *his* "facts" in "M. Valdemar."[9]) In July 1842 he started the *Mesmeric Magazine* in Boston, and managed to get out one issue.

By this time his activities were beginning to prove a thorn in the side of proper and not-so-proper pseudoscientists. The dignified George Combe, touring the United States under the most respectable of auspices, was "much grieved" when Collyer's "mountebankism" outdrew him in simultaneous lectures in Hartford. The more rough-and-tumble Orson S. Fowler advertised in 1843 for witnesses "who know of Collyer's having committed immoralities or crimes, great or small, or who know of any who do know of his having done dirty deeds, or having committed seductions, or adultery, or having even gone off without paying his debts, or of his having violated either morality or law. . . ."[10] Fowler had made the mistake of printing some nasty remarks about Collyer, and was being sued for libel.

In May Collyer was in Philadelphia, seeing his *Psychography* through the press, and attending a Millerite rally with—Edgar Allan Poe. But by the autumn of 1843 he had left for Liverpool (unwilling to confront Fowler in court?), and wrote back angrily to the States, announcing the imminent publication of a new book, *Lights and Shadows of American Life,* which would be "a double-edged sword" for his "enemies and traducers."[11]

By December of 1845 he was back in Boston, in time to read his "friend" Poe's "Case of M. Valdemar," with what results we have already seen. The next year he was back in Europe, and the following year he reports running into Horace Wells, one of the contenders for the ether prize, in an oyster saloon in New York City. (Perhaps it was then that he decided to enter the competition.) In 1849 he was robbed by twenty-three bandits in the Sierra

Madre Mountains of Mexico, and spent the next few years in California with the Gold Rush, where he invented a new method for crushing quartz and a new "amalgamating process." He returned to Europe in the mid-1850s and continued to follow developments in his many specialties. In 1863 he exhibited a fossilized human jaw before the Ethnological Society in London, and in 1876 he was peripherally involved in the notorious Slade prosecution, in which an American "slate-writing medium" was sentenced to three months' hard labor in an English prison for fraud. In the 1860s and 1870s he was still discovering new sciences much like the old ones—"phrenography, or mind writing," and "vital photography."

Collyer's poltergeist career might have provided coloring for a composite picture of the pseudoscientists, a footloose brotherhood whose chief virtues, like his, were ingenuity and brass. Along with a merciless cynicism, these are the salient traits of Westervelt's character in *The Blithedale Romance.* Whether Hawthorne got them from Collyer or from some similar performer is unimportant, though Collyer is the single most likely source. As it happens, other developments in the history of mesmerism in America were still more significant influences on *The House of the Seven Gables* and *The Blithedale Romance*.

Collyer was a name dropper; his "friends" included not only Poe and Spurzheim, Elliotson and Slade, but also François Gouraud (also known as Francis Fauvel-Gouraud), the first exhibitor of daguerreotypes in the United States, Thomas Henry Huxley, and even Richard F. Burton. It is remarkable therefore that he never claimed the acquaintance of Charles Poyen, a young compatriot of Gouraud, who in 1836 did for Mesmer what Gouraud did for Daguerre and what Spurzheim did for Gall, so far as America was concerned.

On March 23, 1836, Dr. Poyen advertised in the Boston papers to the effect that "persons who feel an interest in [animal magnetism] . . . may call upon me at my lodgings . . . [and] will find me ready to give them as ample an instruction as they desire, without any other compensation than the pleasure of fulfilling a duty—that of spreading more widely a truth I have undertaken to make known in this country, as being equally interesting to science, and useful to health."[12] Apparently encouraged by the public response to his advertisement, Dr. Poyen was touring New England before long, bringing the magnetic light to the villages. Hawthorne may possibly have heard him lecture in Boston while he was working there as editor of the *American Magazine of Useful and Entertaining Knowledge*; he knew of him by July 1837, for his name appears in Hawthorne's journal description of the exuberant young Frenchman M. Schaeffer, whom he met during his summer in Maine: "Once he offered to magnetize me, in the manner of Monsieur Poyen" (*AN* 58).

Even if Hawthorne did not witness the new miracles, Elizabeth Peabody, soon to play an important role in his life by introducing him to her sister Sophia, did see Dr. Poyen perform in Boston and even met and talked with him. She was particularly interested in mesmerism because she thought its curative powers might benefit Sophia, whose chronic headaches had made her an invalid for years. Elizabeth wrote Mary, the third sister, all about it:

> Mr. Poyen said there was some experiments of the Animal Magnetists that went to form the theory—that persons differed from each other as bodies do—in being *positive* & negative—& had attractions and repulsions thereby.—He said that I was a highly magnetised body—he thought I might *magnetise* if I could concentrate my power in a strong act of will—& I do not know but I shall try to cure Sophia.—I asked him to tell me how I should go to work & he did—so—tell Sophia to be prepared—but you need not tell any body else.[13]

Elizabeth's success with her sister is unrecorded, but that was not the end of Sophia's encounters with magnetizers. In September of 1837, only a few months before Hawthorne's first meeting with Sophia, Dr. Poyen lectured in Salem. His visit was so profitable that he returned in October, when the *Salem Observer* grudingly reported that mesmerism was "making considerable noise in the community" (October 14). Even if Hawthorne saw him, he would not have been among the converts; but at least one new magnetic enthusiast was inspired by Poyen's visit, and—though Hawthorne may never have known it—their lives were soon entangled. The man was Dr. Joseph Emerson Fiske (1811-1882), at that time a young dental assistant to Dr. Nathaniel Peabody of Charter Street, father of the "Peabody sisters of Salem."

Joseph Fiske had lived a varied life—not unlike that of Robert Collyer, or of Holgrave in *The House of the Seven Gables*—up to his final settling in Salem. He graduated from a medical college in Philadelphia but never established a practice. He wandered about New England instead, working here as a dentist, there as a schoolteacher. An inventive and enterprising young man, during his years in Salem he took out several patents—on an improved gas meter and a new conduction system for airtight stoves.[14] By the time he was forty he had built a dental practice lucrative enough to allow him to invest in property in the surrounding area.[15]

Although there is nothing to prove that Hawthorne ever knew Dr. Fiske, they probably met at the Peabody house, where Dr. Fiske assisted Dr. Peabody with extractions and where after November 11, 1837 Hawthorne more and more frequently called. The young dentist was a charming man, and Sophia declared, "He deserves to be happy, he is so good"; but Hawthorne had no occasion to worry about a rival for Sophia's affections, for Dr. Fiske had married in March of 1837.[16] Still, if Hawthorne had any inkling of what was going on at the Peabody house not long after Dr. Poyen's lectures in Salem and all through the following year, he must have felt a strong dislike for the "good" doctor. Exactly like Elizabeth Peabody, Dr. Fiske listened to Dr. Poyen, made the discovery that he himself had magnetic powers, and offered to do what he could with Sophia's headaches.

In October 1837 Dr. Fiske told Dr. Poyen of his enthusiasm for mesmerism and agreed to write a testimonial letter for the book on *Animal Magnetism in New England* which the Frenchman was planning. Before the year was out, Dr. Fiske's letter was in print:

Salem, Oct. 22d, 1837.

Dr. CH. POYEN,—

My Dear Sir,—You wish me to state in a few lines, the result of my experiments in Animal Magnetism, to appear in a volume which you are preparing on the subject.

I am induced to comply with your request, only as I think it the duty of those who have had an opportunity of satisfying themselves about a matter so generally ridiculed and opposed, to help, as far as they can, in enlightening the public mind concerning it. Such is the motive which prompts me to give you my name. I must state, in the first place, and you are aware that I have as yet but little experience in the practice of Animal Magnetism. I began to occupy myself with it, only since you have come among us, and my professional occupations taking most of my time, I have experimented upon but few individuals. I have, however, obtained some results which have confirmed me in the opinion that the subject is not all a delusion, as a great many pretend it to be, but is one which is well worthy of a thorough investigation by scientific men. I have succeeded in producing well-marked effects on three persons, one of whom has become a somnambulist, (so called.) My experiments have been so far made with the view of ascertaining whether the *will* of the magnetizer could be communicated to the somnambulist without the aid of language or signs. I can say the results obtained were in the affirmative, and were of a positive character, and as truly astonishing to myself as to those who witnessed them. There could have been no deception on the part of the somnambulist, as my experiments were made through the operation of the *will*, without language or motion, and every precaution was made to guard against the deception;—besides, she could have no interest whatever in feigning such a state; and if she had, she could not have done it. No person, in their natural state, could *know* when another *wills,* and what particular *thing* he wills, provided there is no language or sign to express it.

At your request, I will certify that I have not yet seen any ill effects, either moral or physical, follow any of my experiments. I am very truly yours,

JAS. E. FISK. [sic][17]

It is possible that Sophia Peabody was one of these first three subjects on whom Dr. Fiske attempted to impose his will; in any case, during the next year he was regularly using his magnetic powers to ease Sophia's headaches. On May 2 of 1838 she writes Elizabeth about a particularly bad attack after a round of visiting with her neighbors (including Mrs. Fiske):

I came home quite used up—& was more excruciatingly tortured than for twelve months. I could in no way touch the bed. When I laid down upon it, it seemed to recede from under me. I needed a millstone to crush me down. I tried George's hydrostatic, but that would not do. It is the most *desperate* sensation to which I am subject & as I told Sarah, the vision of a bare bodkin passed before my mind. But Dr. F. came after tea—& now will you not kneel to him in gratitude when I tell you that he entirely relieved me! As much as

> you love me, so much must you feel indebted to him. Nothing else in the whole world could have done me any good—may GOD bless him![18]

So convinced was Sophia of Dr. Fiske's powers, she felt his influence might even protect her from taking cold, and after describing how she foolishly exposed herself to a chilly wind a few days after this last incident, she tells Elizabeth, "But I believe I am safe, with the aid of Dr. F. last evening."[19] The implication that he was treating her almost daily is hard to avoid.

Meanwhile Hawthorne's visits to the house on Charter Street were growing more frequent. He had been expected on the very evening of Sophia's bad attack, but for some reason had not come. Their acquaintance was settling into courtship. By early 1839, when Hawthorne was again away from Salem, working as weigher and gauger in the Boston Customs House, his letters had become love letters, and he referred to her as his "Dove" and even his "Wife," though they were not married until 1842. Their courtship was prolonged for two reasons: Hawthorne refused to marry unless he could support Sophia comfortably (it seems possible that she never cooked a meal during their married life, although sometimes *he* did, when they were between cooks), and Sophia refused to marry so long as her headaches continued to invalid her. During their long engagement each worked at clearing away these obstacles.

On Sophia's side, Dr. Fiske was playing his part, but in 1840 the Peabodys moved to Boston, where Elizabeth had opened her West Street Bookshop and where she set Dr. Peabody up in a dental office, adding for her brother Nathaniel a small corner for the sale of homoeopathic medicines, another pseudoscientific fad to which the Peabodys were drawn. Sophia had to find a new magnetizer. Elizabeth no doubt offered her services, but her tactless if good-natured egocentricity could hardly replace Dr. Fiske's firm but gentle "operation of the *will.*" Still, in Boston in 1840 there were plenty of mesmerists to go around, and the shop on West Street, a gathering place for intellectuals and reformers of all sorts, must have provided a full selection. By 1841 Sophia had found a replacement for Dr. Fiske in an old friend, Mrs. Thomas Park (Cornelia), with whom Sophia had stayed in Roxbury during the cholera scare of 1832.[20] Mrs. Park was a good friend—one of the few Sophia invited to her wedding—and thus someone she could trust. Moreover, since her new magnetizer was female, it became somewhat easier to explain the situation to Hawthorne, who did not know about Dr. Fiske's professional relations with Sophia.

She wrote Hawthorne at Brook Farm, rather cautiously at first, mentioning Mrs. Park's experiments with a somnambulist Miss Larned—visions of other worlds, the usual clairvoyant stock-in-trade of the mesmerists. Hawthorne had his hands full of visions already, for he had joined the transcendentalist Brook Farmers out of mixed motives and with mixed feelings. However much he might have fancied utopia, that conception always paled beside his dream of wedded bliss with Sophia in a cottage he had hoped to build at the West Roxbury community. Now, having discovered that hoeing weeds and shoveling manure were not practical complements to writing, he was reckoning up his loss of time and money, and casting about for other grounds on which to build his dream home. Their marriage only months away, he was shocked by Sophia's interest in animal magnetism, and seems to have sensed the buildup to further explorations—though not, apparently, to the revelations that Sophia actually had in mind. His reply is worth quoting at some length:

> But, belovedest, my spirit is moved to talk with thee to-day about these magnetic miracles, and to beseech thee to take no part in them. I am unwilling that a power should be exercised on thee, of which we know neither the origin nor consequence, and the phenomena of which seem rather calculated to bewilder us, than to teach us any truths about the present or future state of being. If I possessed such a power over thee, I should not dare to exercise it; nor can I consent to its being exercised by another. Supposing that this power arises from the transfusion of one spirit into another, it seems to me that the sacredness of an individual is violated by it; there would be an intrusion into thy holy of holies—and the intruder would not be thy husband! Canst thou think, without a shrinking of thy soul, of any human being coming into closer communion with thee than I may?—than either nature or my own sense of right would permit me? *I* cannot. And, dearest, thou must remember, too, that thou art now a part of me, and that by surrendering thyself to the influence of this magnetic lady, thou surrenderest more than thine own moral and spiritual being—allowing that the influence *is* a moral and spiritual

one. And, sweetest, I really do not like the idea of being brought, through thy medium, into such an intimate relation with Mrs. Park!

Now, ownest wife, I have no faith whatever that people are raised to the seventh heaven, or to any heaven at all, or that they gain any insight into the mysteries of life beyond death, by means of this strange science. Without distrusting that the phenomena which thou tellest me of, and others as remarkable, have really occurred, I think that they are to be accounted for as the result of a physical and material, not of a spiritual, influence, *Opium* has produced many a brighter vision of heaven (and just as susceptible of proof) than those which thou recountest. They are dreams, my love—and such dreams as thy sweetest fancy, either waking or sleeping, could vastly improve upon. And what delusion can be more lamentable and mischievous, than to mistake the physical and material for the spiritual? What so miserable as to lose the soul's true, though hidden, knowledge and consciousness of heaven, in the mist of an earth-born vision? Thou shalt not do this. If thou wouldst know what heaven is, before thou comest thither hand in hand with thy husband, then retire into the depths of thine own spirit, and thou wilt find it there among holy thoughts and feelings; but do not degrade high Heaven and its inhabitants into any such symbols and forms as those which Miss Larned describes—do not let an earthly effluence from Mrs. Park's corporeal system bewilder thee, and perhaps contaminate something spiritual and sacred. I should as soon think of seeking revelations of the future state in the rottenness of the grave—where so many do seek it.

Belovedest wife, I am sensible that these arguments of mine may appear to have little real weight; indeed, what I write does no sort of justice to what I think. But I care the less for this, because I know that my deep and earnest feeling upon the subject will weigh more with thee than all the arguments in the world. And thou wilt know that the view which I take of this matter is caused by no want of faith in mysteries, but from a deep reverence of the soul, and of the mysteries which it knows within itself, but never transmits to the earthly eye or ear. Keep the imagination sane—that is one of the truest conditions of communion with Heaven.

Dearest, after these grave considerations, it seems hardly worth while to submit a merely external one; but as it occurs to me, I will write it. I cannot think, without invincible repugnance, of thy holy name being bruited abroad in connection with these magnetic phenomena. Some (horrible thought!) would pronounce my Dove an impostor; the great majority would deem thee crazed; and even the few believers would feel a sort of interest in thee, which it would be anything but pleasant to excite. And what adequate motive can there be for exposing thyself to all this misconception? Thou wilt say, perhaps, that thy visions and experiences would never be known. But Miss Larned's are known to all who choose to listen. [Thy sister Elizabeth would like nothing so much as to proclaim thy spiritual experiences, by sound of trumpet.]

October 19th. Monday.—Most beloved, what a preachment have I made to thee! I love thee, I love thee, I love thee, most infinitely. Love is the true magnetism. What carest thou for any other?[21]

The reader familiar with *The Blithedale Romance* will recognize here the opinions, even the anxious rhetoric, of chapter xxiii, "A Village Hall." These connections and other impressions to be gathered from Hawthorne's letter will engage us further; for the moment, however, it is more to the point to notice the wavering posture Hawthorne falls into here, arguing, demanding, cajoling, pleading. His reference to Elizabeth shows that he was aware of her interest in mesmerism, and his knowledge of the Peabody family's eccentricities made Sophia's susceptibility seem a present danger. At the same time, he apparently suspected nothing of Sophia's deeper purposes in sounding him out on the magnetic question: "what adequate motive can there be for exposing thyself to all this misconception?"

Before long Sophia must have replied truthfully, for the treatments continued, and on June 30, 1842, just nine days before their marriage, Hawthorne wrote her a note, from the boarding house in Boston where he was staying until the wedding, that reveals the reluctant compromise he had made with her:

Belovedest, didst thou sleep well, last night? My pillow was haunted with ghastly dreams, the details whereof have flitted away like vapors, but a strong impression remains about thy being magnetized. God save me from any more such! I awoke in an absolute quake. Dearest, I cannot oppose thy submitting to so much of this influence as will relieve thy headache; but, as thou lovest me, do not suffer thyself to be put to sleep. My feeling on this point is so strong, that it would be wronging us both to conceal it from thee.[22]

Hawthorne's feeling was so strong, in fact, that after the wedding Sophia acquiesced; so far as we know there were no more magnetic treatments. Nor was there longer any need of them, since her headaches seem to have vanished after she became a bride. There were recurrences now and then, but nothing like the "desperate sensation" of her former attacks. In a courtship letter of 1839 Hawthorne had written Sophia, with remarkable clairvoyance of his own: "I invite your spirit to be with me. . . . Come—and let me renew my spell against head-ache and other direful effects of the east-wind."[23] Apparently he had been right: "Love is the true magnetism." Marriage and children were better cures than visits to Cuba or the mesmerist's chambers.

One can only guess at the final disposition of Sophia's secret; if she told Hawthorne of Dr. Fiske's treatments, this would dovetail neatly with the fact that Holgrave had practiced dentistry before taking up mesmerism, and that Westervelt's sinister countenance is embellished with a set of perfect, but false, teeth. Unless Sophia and her sisters were more circumspect than I can imagine, Hawthorne must have known that Dr. Fiske dabbled in magnetism, so that the connection with dentistry can be made out by appeal to his local reputation if not to Hawthorne's full knowledge of Sophia's secret. Or, just as easily, the connection might be put down to the relatively common association of the two practices in the public mind, because of the use of mesmerism as an anesthetic, which continued from the late 1830s until well after the discovery of ether in 1846 (also by a dentist, whether one accepts the claims of Morton or of Wells[24]).

It is perhaps indicative of a certain maiden reticence on Sophia's part that Hawthorne had resorted in his argument to a comparison of the magnetic visions to opium dreams; Sophia had told him very little about the history of her headaches if he did not know that her earlier physicians had prescribed morphine (before mesmerism the only sure anodyne for pain) and that she had become addicted for a time.[25]

Fascinating as Sophia's case history might be, our concern here is chiefly with Hawthorne's reaction to the magnetic peril. In his October letter Hawthorne's arguments against mesmerism fall into two categories: first, if the claims of the pseudoscientists are true, we are then dealing with spiritual phenomena which we do not understand and which are better left unexplored, for it is immoral and sacrilegious to pry into another's soul or to let someone pry into yours; second, whether or not the phenomena are genuine, association with the unsavory class of people who perform magnetic feats is degrading, and one must expect ridicule, or, what is just as bad, notoriety.

A third consideration ought to be kept in mind, if in the background; namely, that evident medical successes were the source of Sophia's interest in mesmerism and thus, whether or not he knew it, necessarily influenced Hawthorne's views and reactions. Harriet Martineau was not the only famous lady to be healed by magnetic passes. When Miss Martineau met her American counterpart Margaret Fuller in 1845, they must have had many lively impressions to exchange, for Margaret also had been successfully treated the previous year, for headache and spinal curvature.[26] Given Margaret Fuller's propensities, it is hard to believe that she had not also traded notes with Sophia Hawthorne before she left the States, on a subject so close to both their interests. If Sophia no longer required such ministrations herself, nonetheless she contined attentive to the experiences of her friends. As late as the last year of Hawthorne's life, she was reporting to her friend Annie Fields the miraculous cure of Louisa May Alcott's "typhus fever":

> . . . A certain Mrs. Bliss, housekeeper and companion of Mrs. Horace Greel[e]y came to Concord the other day to Mrs. Greel[e]y (who is living here now) and Mrs. Greel[e]y said she was one of those persons who can discover the ailments of any one by a magnetic power. So she came to Louisa, and did actually find out what was now the difficulty, not by questions, but by holding her hands and reading her with closed eyes. I will tell you all about it sometime, but now only the result, which was, that after she went away, Louisa rose out of bed and walked across the room alone, and even stood up a while for Annie to fit a wrapper which she was making for her! Hitherto she could not stand one moment, and had to be lifted to her easy chair, when she was inclined to sit up. She had also suffered with excruciating backach[e] and limbsach[e]. But Mrs. Bliss took all pain from her back, and yesterday she came down stairs alone! and stayed an hour. She says she intends to hold levees next week. As Mrs. Bliss has discovered her internal maladies, I can see now that she may get well,

> and I am truly rejoiced for them all, and a millstone weight is lifted off my heart. . . . [27]

Hawthorne's fears about notoriety were, of course, fully justified; Sophia's own gossiping proved the point, had there been any doubt. If one consented to be a subject of mesmeric experiment, he (or more likely she) ran the risk of publicity; no matter how strong one's wish to remain anonymous, the average private citizen could hardly exert the kind of pressure necessary to seal the lips of either unscrupulous charlatans or dedicated scientists, whose different goals could be realized only by education or advertising. The names of dozens of young ladies were thus commonly associated with animal magnetism—the Misses Bracket, Ayres, and Gleason and Mrs. Andros, among the most famous. Dr. Reese, in his *Humbugs of New-York,* had declared that all the so-called "sleeping beauties" were either dupes or cheats. Even if one believed in the trances and their revelations, there was a powerful temptation to hold demonstrators of the art in the same estimation as "show-girls" have generally been held—that is, with a mixture of contempt, fear, and envy.

Accusations of sexual immorality were often leveled at the mesmerists themselves, even by "reformed" mesmerists: "I cannot here refrain from warning young females, and even married ladies, not to trust themselves alone with practical magnetisers."[28] Of course the dirt rubbed off on the ladies. Dr. Poyen, in his *Progress of Animal Magnetism in New England,* attempted to forestall such charges against himself and his somnambulist by printing the following testimony:

> Pawtucket, Jan. 2, 1837
>
> This will certify, that Miss Cynthia Ann Gleason has lived, these last fourteen months, in our family; that she has invariably behaved as a prudent, industrious, and faithful person, and that we have the fullest confidence in her moral character.
>
> JOHN FALES
> CAROLINE FALES[29]

It is hard to say which sort of notoriety does more damage to the reputation—being attacked in print or being defended there. To be sure, most newspapers were too chivalrous to raise the moral issue except in the most general terms, but the mesmerists and their subjects were fair game for satire, and names might be named in the spirit of fun. Thus the *Salem Observer* needled Poyen and his assistant in a bogus advertisement for January 27, 1838, announcing the discovery by a veterinarian of a mare "with all the powers of Miss Gleason or any other somnambule" in diagnosing and prescribing for equine disorders.[30]

The sort of fame likely to favor the somnambule was ill fame, with all the sexual associations that term calls up. If this is not explicit in Hawthorne's letter to Sophia, it becomes so in the parallel passages from *The Blithedale Romance,* where, although still characteristically disguised, Hawthorne's uneasy fascination with the sexual implications of magnetic power is the first thing one notices:

> At the bidding of one of these wizards, the maiden, with her lover's kiss still burning on her lips, would turn from him with icy indifference; the newly made widow would dig up her buried heart out of her young husband's grave, before the sods had taken root upon it. (*BR* 198)

As usual when dealing with controversial material, Hawthorne inverts everything, but the hint is strong enough that the mesmerist who can turn hot lips to cold can also turn cold lips to hot.

Magnetism and sexuality were frequently linked together, and not merely in the public imagination. The anonymous author of *The Confessions of a Magnetiser* offered detailed testimony to these sexual hazards. This operator, before his reform, "was called on by a young gentleman to aid him in calling back the alienated affections of a young lady to whom he had been engaged. . . . [S]he was completely reclaimed to the young man, and alienated from her other suitor, who, without this process, was likely to marry her." The rest of the story runs like a comic opera based on such passages from *The Blithedale Romance:*

> Then he tells how, himself a previously married man, and this now married lady, were both well nigh ruined soon after, by their unlawful attachment to each other, which originated during the above magnetic process; and how he was relieved from that wretched condition, by his own wife's learning magnetism from his

> books, &c., and then drawing his affections back to herself in the same way; and how the other young married lady, half ruined by her thus divided affections, was again won back to her husband by *his* magnetising her again and willing her affections back to himself, keeping the whole process still a secret from her.[31]

Perhaps Henry Jones has his tongue in his cheek as he condenses and summarizes these anonymous confessions, but frankly I do not think so, any more than I believe Hawthorne is smirking as he heightens his rhetoric in the passage quoted from *Blithedale.* If mesmerism was sometimes a joke during this period, seduction was rarely a laughing matter.

One reason for believing Jones in earnest is that he, like Hawthorne, suspected that the magnetizer might be more than a lascivious humbug; he regarded mesmerism "not as among the Sciences at all, nor as a mere human imposition, but as SORCERY, or the mysterious works of *'unclean spirits,'* or the spirit of Satan the false prophet."[32] Hawthorne's mesmerists, like almost all his pseudoscientists, are men of strong intellect, ambitious after the fruits of the Tree of Knowledge more than the favors of unwilling clairvoyants. In this they are not Adamic so much as Faustian, and their mysterious power, at least in the cases of Maule and Westervelt, seems to derive from a compact with the devil. Westervelt in particular is said to have "bartered his own soul for seven years' possession of a familiar fiend" (*BR* 110). Such hints of the satanic nature of the magnetic art may seem unnecessarily literal to the modern reader. Hawthorne himself seems to have felt this, for he puts the least ambiguous of them in the doubly fancied tales within tales—Holgrave's story of Alice Pyncheon and Zenobia's legend of the Veiled Lady, where a certain special license was presumably in force. But he had ample precedent in his time for a more straightforward attribution of mesmeric powers to the devil. In a novel by T. S. Arthur published in 1848, the heroine is subject to headaches much like those which afflicted Sophia—"the pain often became so intense as almost to deprive her of reason"—and she similarly submits to mesmerism for relief. Her lover applies to a friend for advice about the unusual cure his sweetheart undergoes:

> "By what strange power do these men work?" said Ralph. "It cannot be by a Divine power."

> "They work by the power of evil spirits. No power in heaven would lend itself to such disturbing action upon the human mind."[33]

An anonymous writer for the *Southern Literary Messenger* reasoned his way to identical opinions with a similar show of cool-headed logic:

> If these effects are, as we concluded, throughout prejudicial,—if the magnetic gift or power, not only is and may be abused, but can never be anything else but pernicious in its consequences,—if it is a gross and serious evil *per se,* and cannot be so ordered or modified as to result in any good, we have been, and we think that others, taking what has been said into consideration, must be struck with the probable correctness of the notion, that the whole *originates from Satanic agency.*[34]

By such a line of reasoning, an opponent of the magnetizers might allow the very common identification, which Hawthorne himself makes in *The Seven Gables,* of modern mesmerism with the witchcraft of colonial times, without necessarily opening up the vein of defense the mesmerists found easiest to work, namely, that just as the witches had been persecuted by ignorance and superstition, so too were the modern wizards unfairly accused of black magic. Once a satanic power was posited behind the magnetic phenomena, the argument might be turned on the mesmerists; it could be maintained that the authorities of witchcraft days had been perfectly justified. For many people it was still easier to believe that witches had supernatural power than it was to accept the pseudoscientific contention, as Poyen phrased it, "that the phenomena once attributed to the action of the devil, are the results of a peculiar modification of which the nervous organization of man is susceptible, when placed in certain circumstances."[35]

Hawthorne seems to waver in his opinion on these identifications. Just as he avoids directly attributing magnetic power to satanic agency, so he hesitates to pass judgment on the supposed witches, whom his ancestor John Hathorne had helped to condemn. On the one hand, in "Alice Doane's Appeal" (*SI* 279), he regards the witches as innocent victims of "a guilty and miserable band; villains . . . , lunatics . . . , and children, who had played a game that the imps of darkness might have envied them. . . . "[36]

On the other hand, Hawthorne's son Julian records that his father often spoke, "half fancifully and half in earnest, of the curse invoked by one of the witches upon Colonel John Hathorne and all his posterity, and of the strange manner in which it had taken effect."[37] Such seems precisely his attitude, "half fanciful, half in earnest," toward the whole realm of the supernatural, including both witches and their modern counterparts, the mesmerists. In *The Blithedale Romance* Coverdale avows—and here he surely speaks for Hawthorne—his disbelief in these powers:

> It is unutterable, the horror and disgust with which I listened, and saw, that, if these things were to be believed, the individual soul was virtually annihilated, and all that is sweet and pure, in our present life, debased, and that the idea of man's eternal responsibility was made ridiculous, and immortality rendered, at once, impossible, and not worth acceptance. But I would have perished on the spot, sooner than believe it.

Immediately, however, doubts arise, and just as in Hawthorne's letter to Sophia, he cannot resist wondering what sort of spirits those must be whose agency the mesmerist can call upon:

> Alas, my countrymen, methinks we have fallen on an evil age! If these phenomena have not humbug at the bottom, so much the worse for us. What can they indicate, in a spiritual way, except that the soul of man is descending to a lower point than it has ever before reached, while incarnate? We are pursuing a downward course, in the eternal march, and thus bring ourselves into the same range with beings whom death, in requital of their gross and evil lives, has degraded below humanity. To hold intercourse with spirits of this order, we must stoop, and grovel in some element more vile than earthly dust. (*BR* 198–99)

Unwilling or unable to make up his mind whether the mesmeric phenomena are genuine or fraudulent, Hawthorne leaves the question unanswered and contents himself with condemning the entire practice, whichever view of it may be correct.

His position in his letters and journals is exactly the same. In his own life, as in his fiction, Hawthorne both believed and disbelieved in this sort of magic. Like Harriet Martineau's skeptical friend, "if he saw the incidents himself, he would not believe them." Hawthorne had precisely the same reaction to the "spiritualist" manifestations of mesmerism: "Do I believe in these wonders? . . . Of course. . . . But, again, do I really believe it? . . . I would not believe my own sight or touch of the spiritual hands" (*EN* 617). This ambivalence was probably one of the reasons why he introduced mesmerism so prominently into his works. It suited his sense of what romance ought to be—a fantasy spun out of possibilities that were not quite actualities, though, given the right atmosphere, they might be presented as such.

ii

Sometime between Hawthorne's first and second letters of admonition to Sophia, he entered in his notebook an idea for a sketch: "Questions as to unsettled points of History, and Mysteries of Nature, to be asked of a mesmerized person" (*AN* 228). Although Hawthorne mentions magnetism, mesmerism, and spiritualism in other entries in his journals, this one brief memorandum, jotted down at a time when the subject was impinging on his personal life, seems to be the only evidence of his explicitly weighing the possibilities of mesmerism for literary use.[38] There is no way of knowing whether he actually returned to this entry or had it in mind at all when he wrote Chapter xiii of *The House of the Seven Gables* a decade later. If Hawthorne sensed in 1842 that mesmerism would furnish him the materials for two novels, he gives us no inkling of it. Rather we are struck by the relative sterility of the notebook idea, which would at best have provided a framework for another of Hawthorne's many "newspaper sketches," like "The Toll-Gatherer" or "A Rill from the Town Pump"—a use of the subject that would exploit its current popularity in the most limited and schematic way. Much of Hawthorne's early work is marred by quaint contrivances of this sort, rather in the manner of Poe's tales of the grotesque, thin and brittle elaborations of puns and "sight gags" like "The Bosom Serpent" or "The Man of Adamant." But if mesmerism, in some of its bizarre aspects, might cater to this kind of cuteness, it could also provide a complex and suggestive emblem at the center of a larger work. In such a case nothing so pat as the 1842 idea would be allowed to dominate, for its neat closure would not lead anywhere; there could be no plot, only a string of examples. *The House of the Seven Gables* and *The Blithedale Romance* take the mesmeric phenomenon much more seriously, as something problematic rather than settled, more than merely another conceit on which to drape a plot. The subject afforded Hawthorne the resonating center that always made the difference between success and failure in his fiction. It resounded in his own life and times as a symbol and a fact on the most distant fringes of man's knowledge about himself, however much nonsense and humbug might echo tinnily along with the truth.

Of all the pseudosciences, mesmerism was most open to literary exploitation, since it touched so many sensitive points of human experience. Phrenology might be worth a joking reference in *Fanshawe* (*F* 395), and homoeopathic ideas might turn up quite elaborately in the alchemical lore of Drs. Heidegger, Rappaccini, Aylmer, Grimshawe, and Dolliver, but these were not enough to generate a whole novel, as the aborted condition of the late romances goes to show. Physiognomy had important uses, but as a means of presentation rather than a subject. Mesmerism, with its showy pseudoscientific trappings and extravagant supernatural claims, and the well-attested authenticity of its phenomena, was a subject of greater potential, as most novelists were quick to realize.

Reduced to their barest essentials, the plots of *The House of the Seven Gables* and *The Blithedale Romance* may be formulated in such a way as to seem identical: A crime against society and the social fabric has been committed (by Colonel Pyncheon; by Fauntleroy), which has resulted indirectly in the rise to power of a witch or wizard (the Maules; Westervelt) with mesmeric control over the actions of a daughter or granddaughter of the original sinner (Alice and Phoebe; Priscilla and Zenobia). The daughter exhibits clairvoyant and spiritualist powers under the influence of the mesmerist, but suffers correspondingly in his bondage, especially in reputation, since a sexual threat is pervasively if vaguely attendant on this subjugation. Release comes only as a result of love, which is a matter of the lover (Holgrave; Hollingsworth) proving his faith in the girl by renouncing his earlier reforming ambitions and attitudes in order to be himself reformed by her. Concurrent with the rescue of the girl is the death of some character who has betrayed either the girl herself or some figure who represents her

(Jaffrey has betrayed Clifford, who is the reincarnation of Alice; Zenobia has betrayed Priscilla).

The central motif—the subjugation and rescue of the mesmerist's clairvoyant—is classic. Orestes Brownson's *The Spirit-Rapper,* George Lippard's *The Quaker City,* and T.S. Arthur's *Agnes* all have the same pattern in their mesmeric plots, and later novels such as James's *The Bostonians,* Howells's *The Undiscovered Country,* and Du Maurier's *Trilby* exemplify the variations that could be rung on this theme even after people had stopped taking it very seriously. As popularly understood, the phenomena of mesmerism naturally led to such an archetypical story. The mesmerist's power over the will of his somnambulist shocked and intrigued the public more than any of the mysterious feats of clairvoyance, telepathy, and psychokinesis. One favorite debate between the advocates and the opponents of mesmerism was the question of whether a magnetist could force his subject to do anything immoral. Defenders of animal magnetism often denied, as did John Bovee Dods, "that any person can be thrown into the state against his will." But Dods himself hastened to add "if he will at the same time use physical resistance," and he further advised his readers "never [to] allow anyone to magnetize you unless it be in the presence of a third person."[39] Others claimed that the mesmerist could induce a trance simply by willing it, without the subject being aware of any danger. Dr. Fiske, it will be remembered, reported success in imposing his "*will,* without language or motion." In *The Spirit-Rapper,* Brownson's narrator describes an experiment which involved a magnetic bouquet of flowers:

> I passed one day by a boarding school, and threw over the wall, unseen myself, a bunch of flowers I had mesmerized. One of the young ladies saw it, picked it up, smelled it, and placed it in her bosom. Almost instantly she became strangely affected, seemed bewitched, acted as one possessed. . . . [T]he poor girl herself complained of feeling herself under a foreign power, and one which made her say and do things to which she felt, even at the moment, the greatest repugnance.[40]

This account is fictional, but many actual practitioners claimed they used mesmerized glasses of water, rings, and the like to induce trances without the subject's acquiescence or knowledge.

The most common means of subjugating the will of the somnambulist was, of course, the eye of the mesmerist, which when fastened on the eye of his victim, engaged them in a test of mental and spiritual power, the outcome of which was usually as certain and beyond the control of the helpless female as in Brownson's story of the magnetized flowers. Lippard's description in *The Quaker City* is typical:

> "Look upon me, fair girl, gaze in mine eyes, and mark my words. In this great world where thou art friendless and alone, *I* will be thy friend."
>
> "You!" murmured Mabel. "And will you not too, deceive and betray?"
>
> "Deceive a soul like thine?" exclaimed Ravoni, with a bitter smile, "Leave that to priests and worldlings! Could *I* deceive *thee*?"
>
> He leaned gently forward, and his dark eyes shone into her soul. With parted lips and gasping breath, Mabel gazed upon him, and murmured "Never! Never!" There was an irresistible power in his look, his tone, and speaking brow. She felt drawn to him, and yet it was not with passion! It seemed to her, that she could lay forever at his feet, and listen to the wild music of his tone, without a word or motion in reply.
>
> Was the Sorcerer subduing her *Will,* with the wierd Magnetism of his spirit? In other words, was the Man of deep and powerful intellect silently overshadowing her Soul, with his irresistible Will?[41]

Lippard's question is merely rhetorical; there is no doubt as to the power of Ravoni's will, manifested in his eye, the ancient symbol of power, will, and sexuality, as well as the "window of the soul." The tradition of its hypnotic function goes back much earlier than Mesmer (who, by the way, did not localize his powers in the eye) to a rich folklore of the "evil eye." In his *Italian Notebooks* Hawthorne points out that "The evil eye may be classified with the phenomena of mesmerism." It struck him as odd that in traditional belief "The evil influence is supposed not to be dependent on the will of the possessor of the evil eye; on the contrary, the persons to whom he wishes well are the very ones to suffer by it" (X 383-84). In his own use of mesmeric materials, for instance the attribution of Holgrave's power to the "Maule eye," he made the will of the mesmerist the crucial factor in the spiritual mechanics of the act and also in the moral that was to be drawn: the guilt of the mesmerist as well as the jeopardy of the somnambulist.

During the 1840s Hawthorne returned again and again, in his stories and his notebooks, to this idea of one soul immorally dominating another, by means of some mysterious exercise of the will—a theme that was finally to eventuate in the relationship of Chillingworth and Dimmesdale in *The Scarlet Letter.* "Supposing that this power arises from the transfusion of one spirit into another," he had written Sophia in 1841, "it seems to me that the sacredness of an individual is violated by it; there would be an intrusion into thy holy of holies." Such a violation constituted an important condition of the unpardonable sin, as described in the *American Notebooks:*

> The Unpardonable Sin might consist in a want of love and reverence for the Human Soul; in consequence of which, the investigator pried into its dark depths, not with a hope or purpose of making it better, but from a cold philosophical curiosity,—content that it should be wicked in whatever kind or degree, and only desiring to study it out. (*AN* 251)

This entry of 1844 is related to an earlier one in 1842, the year Hawthorne was so concerned with mesmerism in his personal life:

> A moral philosopher to buy a slave, or otherwise get possession of a human being, and to use him for the sake of experiment, by trying the operation of a certain vice on him. (*AN* 237)

In both entries mesmerism is certainly in the background, though not explicitly mentioned. Compare another passage from *The Quaker City:* "He was about to make a dread and awful experiment, not with machinery of wood or iron, or with the air or the lightning in its bosom, or with the earth or the secrets of its depths, but with something more terrible than all, the Soul of Man."[42] This is Lippard's mesmerist Ravoni about to bring a dead girl back to life to join his harem of hypnotized slaves. In Hawthorne too the philosopher-slave relation was a version of that between the mesmerist and the somnambulist, and the "psychological experiments" (*SI* 94) that Ethan Brand performed on the daughter of old Humphrey were of the same sort that Matthew Maule later inflicted on the daughter of another foolish father, and Westervelt on the daughter of still another. (In *The Quaker City,* by the way, all the girls of Ravoni's harem have been stolen away from their fathers, and his high priestess, Mabel, has been stolen away from *two* fathers, one false and one true!)

All these magnetic relations have heavy sexual overtones: Ethan Brand's Esther is apparently "ruined"; Alice Pyncheon cannot marry because she is "so lost from self-control" (and she is released from the spell, only to die, on Matthew Maule's wedding night); Holgrave's decision not to exercise his hereditary powers is made out of his respect for "Phoebe's yet free and virgin spirit"; and Priscilla is similarly threatened by Westervelt's designs on her, so that after her rescue Coverdale hastens to state that "she had kept, as I religiously believe, her virgin reserve and sanctity of soul, throughout it all" (*HSG* 209, 212; *BR* 203).

At the critical moment in *Blithedale* the power of love *does* prove stronger than that of mesmerism, when Hollingsworth defies Westervelt and calls Priscilla out of her trance and into his arms. One wonders just how Hawthorne meant this scene—as a statement of fact, or as a hopeful fantasy of good winning out over evil. There is a very similar scene in *The Quaker City,* but when the rescuer calls to Mabel, "Come with me. There is danger for you in this place, danger worse than death," she first replies, "I will go with you . . . Lead me to my father," and then one glance from Ravoni's mystic eyes melts her back into submission.[43] Although Priscilla is allowed to escape from her bondage, it is in unexplained contradiction to all the evidence already presented, both in *Blithedale* and in Hawthorne's earlier works, regarding the fatal hold exerted by the mesmerist on his subject. There is wishful thinking in Hollingsworth's victory over Westervelt, and the final effect is scarcely one of pure affirmation of the strength of true love.

However often the theme of sexual bondage recurs in these fictions, it is part of a larger structure also repeated, even in those works that do not explicitly treat the mesmeric relation. What, for example, is the significance of the fact that the somnambulist is almost invariably subdued, if not in the very presence of her father, then at least in relatively explicit defiance of him? The emphasis seems to be not so much on the sexual (in these contexts Oedipal) aspect of the scene as on the nature of the bond between the mesmerist and his victim—namely a dominance which competes with absolute parental authority. The mesmerist's will is more powerful even than the natural ties of affection and duties of filial obedience. I do not mean to belittle the sexual investment in these patterns, but only to draw attention to a special emphasis Hawthorne gives to what, after all, are the commonplaces of romantic fiction.

In "Ethan Brand," *The Seven Gables,* and *The Blithedale Romance,* the unpardonable sin is not just any form of moral slavery. The popularly conceived power of the mesmerist to exert his will precisely against the better instincts of his somnambulist is reflected not only in his defiance of the natural relations of parent and child, but also in his unpardonable intrusion into sacred spiritual realms—the "holy of holies" of the victim's soul. It is not the unpardonable sinner's intention to debauch his slave for his own gratification, but rather to experiment upon her, to investigate her soul, by willing her participation in some activity which, although it may be a "vice," he himself is not a direct party to. A glance at Matthew Maule's practice on Alice Pyncheon, Holgrave's on Phoebe, or Westervelt's on Priscilla, confirms this analysis. "Self-control," "virgin reserve," and "sanctity of soul" are the key phrases, implying a compartment of the individual soul that ought to be preserved from the gaze or influence of all but the most intimate fellowbeings. The exercise of the mesmerist's will in prying into this realm is not described as a matter of hot-blooded lust but of "cold philosophical curiosity," a kind of spiritual voyeurism.

Emerson, it will be remembered, saw something in mesmerism for the philosopher as well as the physician to "profit by." Hawthorne's use of the phrase "cold philosophical curiosity" indicates that he disapproved of the philosopher's meddling in these sacred areas, especially as this meddling might corrupt the souls of its unwilling or naive victims. But Emerson had in mind quite a different sort of philosopher—an observer and interpreter of historic public enthusiasms, not a pseudoscientist caught up in fads of the moment. Indeed, he conceived the lesson to be gained so differently from Hawthorne that it is worth drawing attention again to Emerson's speculation. When Hawthorne had expressed admiration for "the struggle of the race after a better and purer life than had yet been realized on earth," mesmerism had been one of the many "reforms" on view in "The Hall of Fantasy" that seemed to offer an affirmative lesson to a philosophic mind. Such was approximately Emerson's point when he wrote on the subject many years later. But Hawthorne's temperament never sustained such bland optimism very long. Let the philosopher renounce his inquiry, he finally came to advise, let him learn a deeper "reverence of the soul, and of the mysteries which it knows within itself, but never transmits to the earthly eye or ear."

The physician, on the other hand, might have better motives and thus more justification in his use of the new pseudoscience. The power of "mind over matter," of the will over the body, is as frequently affirmed in Hawthorne's fiction as in Emerson's essays, and Hawthorne seems to go even further in recognizing the existence of psychosomatic ailments such as Sophia's headaches and Dimmesdale's stigma. But in Hawthorne's imagination the physician no less than the philosopher is liable to disrupt both the bodily and the spiritual health of his patient—even if his aim in exerting his will on her is therapy (Aylmer in "The Birthmark"), and all the more if his motive is sinister (Chillingworth in *The Scarlet Letter*). In 1842, when he seems to have been thinking about these matters continually, Hawthorne noted the possibility of "A physician for the cure of moral diseases" (*AN* 235), but the risks outweighed the virtues of mesmeric treatment: if moral diseases might be cured by the influence of one mind over another, they might just as easily be caused by the same power. Reports of insanity induced by magnetic and spiritualist experiments were relatively common, especially after 1850, so Hawthorne was not without evidence for his apprehensions.[44] Mesmerism might be viewed as a dangerous addition to the *materia medica,* much in the way that shock therapy is regarded today. And whatever the practical consequences, Hawthorne believed that certain recesses of the spirit ought to be out of bounds to both philosopher and physician. The job of the "modern psychology" mentioned in *The House of the Seven Gables* was to "reduce" the phenomena of mesmerism to some "system," but not, apparently, to investigate or experiment with its mysterious effects.

Strong as Hawthorne's feelings were on these psychological and spiritual considerations, they do not totally explain the anxieties about mesmerism that take shape in his fiction. The figures of intellectual and sexual power that other novelists imagined as their villains Hawthorne found equally conceivable as heroes, and the ambivalence implied in the Holgrave-Westervelt alternatives locates for us the area of his deepest concerns. To choose a mesmerist as hero was to identify certain magnetic powers in himself, and to cast the mesmerist as the villain was to express misgivings about those same powers. Holgrave is the clearest example of this ambivalence, since he wavers between hero and villain. He is an artist—not merely a daguerreotypist who magically (pseudoscientifically) reads character in faces, but also a compelling writer, whose stories of real people mysteriously enslave their hearers to lives that reenact those of his characters.

The method of the animal magnetist in imposing his will upon his somnambulist is very much like that of the writer of realistic fiction. Hallucinatory visions are induced by suggestions from the hypnotist, so that the subject is affected by imaginary events as if they were realities. Holgrave's abortive hypnosis of Phoebe is partly brought about by "literary" means, his reciting the tale of Alice Pyncheon. Phoebe falls under the spell of his words: "a certain remarkable drowsiness . . . had been flung over the senses of his auditress. It was the effect, unquestionably, of the mystic gesticulations, by which he had sought to bring bodily before Phoebe's perception the figure of the mesmerizing carpenter. . . . A veil was beginning to be muffled about her, in which she could behold only him, and live only in his thoughts and emotions" (*HSG* 211). This might be a description of a reader or a listener getting involved in a story, or of a hypnotic subject going under. The one blends into the other almost imperceptibly; if the "mystic gesticulations" are necessary as mesmeric "passes," Holgrave's entrancing story is equally essential, since it constitutes not only the means of suggestion, but also the potential result of the hypnosis, namely Phoebe's imprisonment in the world of Alice Pyncheon, where she would relive her life and share her fate. Moreover, since Holgrave also has his counterpart in the story of Alice Pyncheon and Matthew Maule, the outcome of the plot, had he persisted in his tale, would have entrapped him too. Hawthorne had envisioned such a situation long before Poyen had begun to introduce mesmerism to the United States:

> A person to be writing a tale, and to find that it shapes itself against his intentions; that the characters act otherwise than he thought; that unforeseen events occur; and a catastrophe comes which he strives in vain to avert. It might shadow forth his own fate,—he having made himself one of the personages. (*AN* 16)

According to the special relations of will, imagination, and reality, as Hawthorne conceives them, the temptation of the mesmerist is to behave like this storyteller whose fancies immediately take shape as realities.

To suggest or will an event which is then mysteriously carried out is a familiar motif even in Hawthorne's nonmesmeric stories—for example, the murder scene in *The Marble Faun,* or the "coming-true" of "The Prophetic Pictures"—both cases in which an artist assumes the role of mesmerist. Accordingly, the unpardonable sin is to be a kind of artist, something more than merely a philosopher or physician dabbling in animal magnetism.

The magical power of imagination was Hawthorne's chief theme in all his writings, and the usefulness of the new pseudo-science lay in its adaptability to this theme. His art could be taken as a variety of mesmerism, a spell he wove over his readers, which might change their lives, and for which he might be responsible. He too might find his own life changed as his imagination raised unsuspected and even forbidden thoughts from the hidden corners of his mind. He was like the "writing mediums" that began to spring up in the 1840s, mesmerist and somnambulist in one, whose magnetic trances could be self-induced, and who, upon awakening, might be startled by reading the products of his own unconscious imagination. A relatively optimistic interpretation of such possibilities was this notebook entry of 1838:

> A person to look back on a long life ill-spent, and to picture forth a beautiful life which he would live if he could be permitted to begin his life over again. Finally to discover that he had only been dreaming of old age,—that he was really young, and could live such a life as he had pictured. (*AN* 182)

Just as the previously quoted entry of 1835 describes the danger that awaits Holgrave as mesmerist finding himself caught in his own plot, so this later entry foreshadows his means of avoiding it, by dispelling the vision and awakening to reality. But "reality" is an illusive matter in fiction. What counts as reality is whatever the author tells us to trust as real. For Hawthorne a man's experience of reality depends very much on his attitude toward it, as stories like "Young Goodman Brown," "The Minister's Black Veil," and "Rappaccini's Daughter" go to show. Perhaps the protagonist's failure to distinguish dream from reality in these tales is more obviously a problem for a somnambulist than a mesmerist, but it has its bearings on Hawthorne's larger consideration of the authenticity of imaginative experience.The lesson of Young Goodman Brown is that faith and doubt are more likely causes than effects of the experiences that accompany them. Rev. Hooper and Giovanni are similarly men "of little faith," whose attitudes tend to create the "realities" that confirm their intuitions of man's evil nature.

It follows for the artist—who, like the mesmerist, would seem in a position to control his fantasies—that the good side of life might be supposed to outweigh the evil, and that it is even the writer's duty to see that it does. "Keep the imagination sane," Hawthorne wrote to Sophia in 1841. But it is also the writer's business, and the novelist's chief resource, to investigate human acts and motives. What if such investigations, even into one's own mind, should uncover evil instead of good? Might such discoveries not reflect back on the discoverer? How could the writer "keep the imagination sane" without restricting it to those good-natured platitudes that float on the surface of most minds? Just beneath those platitudes, perhaps, lay depths of evil that might remain inactive and innocuous so long as they were undisturbed, but would break into vicious and contagious life once their existence were so much as admitted.

Hawthorne never solved this dilemma, so that beyond this point in the analysis there is nowhere to go. He used mesmerism as a metaphor for the writer's art, and explored the question of his own guilt or innocence through it. In *The Blithedale Romance* he even tested the possibility of distinguishing the imaginative functions of the writer (Coverdale) and the mesmerist (Westervelt) that he had seen as a single function in Holgrave, but without success in absolving the writer from the unpardonable sin. As his career neared its disappointing end, his novels grew more and more fragmented—that is, analytical—and the figure of the artist-mesmerist disintegrated into a chaos of artists, alchemists, and related characters, from which he could no longer synthesize a plot. One virtue of the mesmerist was that he "held still" for an author, since the culture itself had given rise to the figure and mythologized him. Hawthorne recognized the ways that mesmerism expressed his own ambivalent position on questions of will, imagination, and reality, and he made what use he could of it to bring his problems as a writer into the center of *The House of the Seven Gables* and *The Blithedale Romance,* where if he could not solve them (no more could his characters) he could at least continue, tentatively and equivocally, to practice the art he mistrusted. These novels were themselves acts of the imagination, and so each of them was a test as well as a treatment of the problems of the artist. Though it is probably too much to say that they succeeded completely in either, there were no more serious or instructive attempts at the subject than his.

Three

Physiognomy and Phrenology

ON July 29, 1838, HAWTHORNE entered in his journal an account of his meeting at North Adams, Massachusetts, with a "disagreeable figure" named Haynes, a former lawyer whom drink had reduced to soap making for a living, but whose manner and speech intrigued Hawthorne, so that he sat talking with him "long after everybody else had left the stoop, giving vent to much practical philosophy and just observation on the ways of men":

> . . . he talked to me about phrenology, of which he seems a firm believer and skilful practitioner, telling how he had hit upon the true characters of many people. There was a great deal of sense and acuteness in his talk, and something of elevation in his expression; perhaps a studied elevation—and a sort of courtesy in his manner; but his sense had something out-of-the way in it; something wild, and ruined, and desperate, in his talk, though I can hardly say what it was. There was something of the gentleman and man of intellect in his deep degradation; and a pleasure in intellectual pursuits, and an acuteness and trained judgment, which bespoke a mind once strong and cultivated. "My study is man," said he. And looking at me "I do not know your name," said he, "but there is something of the hawk-eye about you too." (*AN* 91-92)[1]

From Hawthorne's point of view, the connection between phrenology and lawyer Haynes's "acuteness and trained judgment" was merely fortuitous. He had long since inspected the pretensions of phrenology, and although the phrase "skilful practitioner" seems to imply that the science *could* be skillfully practiced, Hawthorne never said or wrote anything to suggest that his opinions on the subject went much beyond amused skepticism. Nevertheless, there are some interesting connections to be made out between phrenology and the soap maker's success in identifying Hawthorne as a fellow student of man, with "something of the hawk-eye" about him.

Lawyer Haynes seemed to locate Hawthorne's powers in the eye—a mistake so far as phrenological diagnosis was concerned, however well it might have served as the symbol of mesmeric endowment. There *was* a specific phrenological bump for the study of human character, the organ of Human Nature or Physiognomy, but it was situated in the middle of the forehead at the hairline rather than in the eye. A person whose Human Nature was "large," as the phrase went, had "excellent judgment in matters of character; read men and women intuitively; love[d] to study the 'Signs of Character' in the features, voice, walk, manners, etc., and could become a good practical delineator of character."[2] Hawthorne's own organ of Human Nature, as it appears in photographs, is "large" (between "full" and "very large"), so that one phrenologist was led to "predict" of him, posthumously, that "His large Human Nature would aid him in the faithful portraiture of character, whether in domestic or public life. . . ."[3] Lawyer Haynes had apparently read his man accurately, though he took the wrong feature for his text. This was not entirely his fault, however, since the physiognomic organ had not yet been discovered when Haynes made his evaluation; it was not until 1842 that Human Nature was squeezed in between Benevolence and Comparison—a logical place for it in the phrenological system.[4]

When Lawyer Haynes complimented Hawthorne on his "hawk-eye," he not only betrayed a certain phrenological naiveté, but also showed that his own (and by implication Hawthorne's) inclination was more physiognomical than phrenological, a practical interest in the human face rather than the more fashionable skull. Even though from the phrenologist's point of view the eye was not the seat of physiognomical sensitivity, it was nonetheless obvious that the skill needed to read character, in the face at least, depended on seeing its features. Phrenologists sometimes liked to put their abilities to the test by conducting cranial examinations blindfolded, but no physiognomist attempted an analysis by feeling his subject's nose. It is perhaps on this point—of visual orientation—that phrenology and physiognomy most clearly divide. Easy as it might be to distinguish between a man's face and his skull, it was the manner of taking readings, not the areas explored, that developed as the significant difference between the sister sciences. In its desperate need to be scientific, phrenology pulled back from the more intuitive and synthetic approach of physiognomy, based on interpretation of the "look" of a face more than on any clearly established principles. "Phrenology has furnished the philosophy of physiognomy," said its most famous living theorist in 1840. Without it, the "reading of character is guess work."[5]

Of course phrenological theory also depended on ocular demonstration in the early days. There were ways of translating the anatomical evidence piled up by Gall and Spurzheim into nonvisual terms, but as the many illustrations in their books testify, seeing came first. In 1841 the practice of manual examination of the skull led, through accidental combination with mesmerism, to a new method of discovery and verification of organs—phrenomagnetism. The phrenomagnetist's fingers could excite the various faculties into activity much as the twentieth-century investigator's electrodes stimulate cortical responses. With this methodological advance, pseudoscience at once opened its newly impartial eye to dozens of previously unlocated human traits. In America many phrenologists soon abandoned visual investigation in favor of these more sophisticated methods, and the shift was marked in the textbooks by the supplanting of anatomical drawings with schematic representations of the cranium that were little more than charts—or later, as the skull grew even more crowded with newly discovered faculties, by the eschewing of illustration altogether in favor of lists of the phrenological organs.

Physiognomists, on the other hand, defended their old-fashioned methods as sanctioned by tradition, science, and common sense: "Altogether, independently of phrenology, it has of old time been acknowledged, that fulness of the forehead, combined with those forms which have been noticed, is an indication of intellectual capacity; and, as we have shown, of human character and beauty. All physiologists have agreed in this view; whilst they are equally confident in affirming that anatomy affords no foundation for mapping the cranium into minute sub-divisions or regions. As nature, by covering the head, has intimated her intention that we shall not there scan our neighbours' capacities, she has given us the universal language of *expression.*"[6] This was the opinion of the famous anatomist Sir Charles Bell. Bell was not strictly a physiognomist because he, like Darwin after him, was more concerned with the expression of emotion than with the permanent signs of character in the face; but his book on the philosophy of expression, first published in 1829, was read by scientists and pseudoscientists alike for several decades. Also complicating the picture are the "practical" phrenologists, found chiefly in America. "Practicality" meant application of character-reading principles to individual customers' heads. American vanity being what it was, there was a fine market for cranial technology. The more obviously a phrenologist devoted himself to such ends, the more likely he was to mix his phrenology with physiognomy. For instance, the Fowler brothers, most successful of all the American phrenologists, developed two main lines of approach, depending on audience and circumstances. When they delivered lectures and wrote books, their appeal was chiefly theoretical and they stayed fairly clear of physiognomy. After the lecture or at the end of the book (in a checklist designed for quick "autograph" readings by the author) they brought physiognomy more prominently into the picture again. Orson Fowler's own advice on "Practical Phrenology" was to "make your *first* observation upon the *Physiology,* which involves also the Temperaments," areas that came under physiognomical jurisdiction in the usual division.[7] Physiognomy always had more practical appeal than phrenology, since every man fancied himself a good judge of faces and so believed others might be as well. But physiognomy was less suitable for lecturing purposes, since codification of the thousands of facial nuances was impossible, as Lavater's massive *Physiognomische Fragmente* (4 vols., 1775-1778) had chiefly gone to show—whereas phrenology's limited and discrete set of organs lent itself to the "social science" approach of contemporary faculty psychology.

Hawthorne's first contact with phrenology was probably with this more academic brand, during his undergraduate years at Bowdoin College. A medical department had been added to the college in 1820, the year before he entered, and Hawthorne is known to have had several friends among the medical students; he was willing to recommend one of them, a Dr. Ward, to a practice in Salem.[8] Hawthorne's introduction to phrenology probably came through these friends.

In 1824 Dr. Charles Caldwell brought out his *Elements of Phrenology,* the first American book to stir widespread interest in the subject. Other physicians had also begun to explore phrenology, including a member of the Bowdoin medical faculty, Dr. John Doane Wells, who in 1823 returned from a year's study in Europe (financed by the college), where he had heard Gall lecture and had become a convert to the new doctrines. Thus students of medicine at Bowdoin during Hawthorne's undergraduate years—men like Isaac Ray and Luther V. Bell, later known as phrenologically oriented psychiatrists—could study phrenology in classes conducted on their own campus.[9] At this stage phrenology was still very much concerned with the physiology of the brain, a subject that Dr. Wells taught. Even if we cannot be sure that Hawthorne read phrenology or talked about it with his friends, we do know that in 1825 he registered for Dr. Wells's special series of lectures in anatomy and physiology, open to all seniors in the college upon payment of a fifteen-dollar fee.[10] That phrenology would go unmentioned in such a course is inconceivable, and it is even possible that Hawthorne was attracted to these expensive lectures because he could hear phrenology expounded there by a disciple of Gall himself.

Whatever the means, during his college years Hawthorne became well enough acquainted with phrenological doctrine to jest at it briefly in his undergraduate novel *Fanshawe:* "A phrenologist would probably have found the organ of destructiveness in strong development, just then, upon Edward's cranium; for he certainly manifested an impulse to break and destroy whatever chanced to be within his reach" (*F* 395). The passage is an insignificant one, but its tone suggests that Hawthorne had fallen in line with the typical American response to phrenology in the 1820s, which, one phrenologist fretted, made the new science a butt of "playful allusion—at times of pointed satire or coarse invective."[11]

If by the date of *Fanshawe* Hawthorne had found a stance to take towards phrenology, he was still investigating its sister science physiognomy after his graduation from Bowdoin. The charge books of the Salem Athenaeum show him reading Jacques Pernetti's *Philosophical Letters upon Physiognomies* (London, 1751) in June of

1828, and Lavater's *Essays on Physiognomy* in Moore's translation (4 vols., London, 1797) during October and November.[12] That he consulted these two works within the year suggests more than a casual interest in the subject, though no further indications of his attitudes emerge until 1836, when he became editor of the *American Magazine of Useful and Entertaining Knowledge.*

During his editorship, from March to September, Hawthorne's job was to fill this magazine with edifying pap, much of it determined by the engravings that the publishers could borrow from other sources.[13] Hawthorne put in long days at the Boston Athenaeum scouring the papers and magazines for filler. There he saw what other editors considered good copy. By 1836 phrenology was in full bloom in American, and the journals were taking advantage of the craze. Just to give a few examples from Hawthorne's own reading list, we may note enthusiastic articles on phrenology appearing in the *American Journal of Science and Art* ("Silliman's *Journal*") for 1833, in the *New England Magazine* (to which Hawthorne was himself a heavy contributor) for 1834, and in the *American Quarterly Review* for 1836.[14] Like Hawthorne, Edgar Allan Poe was a magazine editor at this time and had written an article on phrenology for the March 1836 number of the *Southern Literary Messenger.* It began:

> Phrenology is no longer to be laughed at. It is no longer laughed at by men of common understanding. It has assumed the majesty of a science, and, as a science ranks among the most important which can engage the attention of thinking beings. . . .[15]

The newspapers were also filled with phrenology after the celebrated Spurzheim died in Boston, in the middle of his American tour in 1833. The *Salem Observer,* for instance, reported visits of phrenologists to Salem and the surrounding area in 1834, 1835, and 1836, while phrenological books and casts as well as lectures and private readings were advertised regularly in its columns.[16]

For the April issue of their magazine, Hawthorne's publishers apparently acquired engravings, front and back views, of a phrenologically charted head, and Hawthorne produced a "brief article, with which we intend to illustrate the above Phrenological Cuts, . . . comprehend[ing] all that it is now worth while to read about the matter."[17] This article is little more than an annotated list of the phrenological organs, with comments that are either slightly tongue-in-cheek—

> *Combativeness.* This is the organ of quarrelling and fighting—propensities which seem more likely to produce bumps on the head, than to be caused by them.

—or merely perfunctory—

> *Inhabitiveness.* The size of this organ determines the de[g]ree of attachment to home. It is situated immediately over Philoprogenitiveness.[18]

There is, however, an interesting distinction made in the preface to this catalogue, between phrenology and physiognomy:

> Phrenology, therefore, in reference to the opinion of the wise, must still be ranked among the doubtful sciences. For ought we know, it may hereafter be as irrefragably confirmed as any other doctrine, in physics or metaphysics. On the other hand, the next generation may see cause to reject it, as utterly as we do judicial astrology or the physiognomy of Lavater.[19]

There is little doubt that Hawthorne was himself responsible for these sentences, which register a degree of editorial caution that would have seemed stodgy to Poe and other editors. According to Hawthorne, phrenology had not yet achieved "the majesty of a science," nor could it be used as "philosophical" underpinning for physiognomy; on the contrary, it remained contaminated with the already exploded theories of the physiognomists and was perhaps to meet the same final rejection by scientists.

His gratuitous slap at Lavater probably reflects Hawthorne's desire to disassociate himself from the opinions of the previous editor, who in January 1836 had printed an article on physiognomy in which Lavater was praised for having "elevated it to the rank of a science"—a science that, if "not exactly the doctrine of Gall, . . . nevertheless [offered] an analogy which deserves to be remarked."[20] In the March issue Hawthorne had already begun the debunking operation when he printed—from an "old volume," the existence of which is dubious—a column of humorous physiognomical notes on "The Science of Noses," an "ancient and forgotten science . . . far preferable to the phrenological inventions of later times."[21] This and his volley in the April issue establish two facts about Hawthorne's view of physiognomy: first, that as a science (note how often the word appears in these extracts) its pretensions are "utterly" false; second, that as a humorous subject it may serve literary or semiliterary ends.

The same attitudes dominate Hawthorne's treatment of phrenology in the columns of his magazine. Whereas it must be classified as a "doubtful science," its lore provides an editor occasions for amusing remarks. In the same issue that "Combativeness" was defined as "the organ of quarrelling and fighting," Hawthorne slipped into the magazine an additional squib:

> A phrenological gentleman says, that the organ of Combativeness is so strongly developed in the heads of Frenchmen and Americans, as to be a very decided national characteristic. He hence infers, that these two nations ought most carefully to avoid going to war, and to choose any antagonists rather than each other. This precaution, he avers, is the more indispensable, because the combative organs, on both sides, will increase with indulgence, and finally become quite uncontrollable.[22]

Hawthorne probably invented this anecdote of national propensities, as well as "The Science of Noses," out of amused reaction to current phrenological pontifications such as the following serious analysis of the national motives of the American Revolution:

> In the American war England desired to gratify her Acquisitiveness and Self-esteem, in opposition to Benevolence and Justice, at the expense of the transatlantic colonies. This aroused the animal resentment of the latter, and the lower faculties of the two nations came into collision; that is to say, they made war on each other. . . .

These are the words of George Combe, and it is perhaps more than coincidence that in the same March and April issues which satirized physiognomy and phrenology Hawthorne also printed several long extracts (though not this one) from the Scottish phrenologist's best-selling *Constitution of Man,* in its seventh edition that year.[23] While introducing his diffident synopsis of phrenology with the warning that "till Phrenology shall have proved itself a branch of Useful Knowledge, we had rather fill our pages with certain and admitted truths, than with controverted theories," he was at the same time reprinting, without comment, some ten pages from the most famous phrenological work of the day.[24]

Combe, who later became a close friend of Hawthorne's philanthropic brother-in-law Horace Mann, had interests that ranged widely through the realms of social and moral uplift, with phrenology providing a scientific basis for the do-good speculations he published in books like *Lectures on Popular Education* (1834), *Lectures on Moral Philosophy* (1840), *Notes on the United States* (1841), *Remarks on the Principles of Criminal Legislation* (1854), *Phrenology Applied to Painting and Sculpture* (1855), and others. American moralists such as Channing and Emerson admired *The Constitution of Man* "in spite of its phrenology," and perhaps Hawthorne also found that its sentiments atoned for its science.[25] It seems relevant that the word "phrenology" occurs only once in the six columns from Combe reprinted in *The American Magazine of Useful and Entertaining Knowledge.*

The first extract, published in the March issue, was entitled "Exercise of the Brain," and addressed a problem of growing interest to the intellectual community in the 1830s—the "influence of mental cultivation and mental excitement upon health," as another contemporary phrenologist put it.[26] It was widely believed, for instance, that excessive mental activity—especially the exercise of the imagination—was both morally and physically harmful. Older categories of mental disease—melancholy, hypochondriasis, and the like—were modernized to cover a wide spectrum of ailments, many of which are still considered psychosomatic.

These Victorian theories, although not explicitly psycho-sexual, were certainly influenced by the nineteenth century's unique horror of masturbation, so that all kinds of "idle" or "solitary" activities of the psyche became suspect, especially as they might facilitate daydreams or fantasies. Artists and writers were thought to be particularly susceptible to the temptations of the imagination, and the horrible example of Rousseau was cited again and again. "The disorders of literary men" were the subject of a book Hawthorne read in 1828, enumerating the dangers of mental activity to the "organic system"—on which, "if the influence of the passions is more immediate, that of the mind is not less sure, nor certainly less to be dreaded."[27] The more talented the writer, the greater risk of physical or mental disintegration. Thomas C. Upham, who taught intellectual and moral philosophy at Bowdoin (after Hawthorne's day), summarized the testimony of the experts: "It is well known that men of marked imaginative genius, combined with deep sensibility, often become mentally disordered."[28]

There is no sure way of knowing what Hawthorne thought of these warnings. If—as seems likely—he himself was the Oberon of "Fragments from the Journal of a Solitary Man," there is some presumption that the "morbid fancies" (*SI* 317) reported there were Hawthorne's own imaginings at the age of 24—so that the special interest he took in the pathology of literary minds in the year 1828 would be partially accounted for. By 1837, the year he published the "Fragments," he had no reason to alter the diagnosis of his case; in a letter to Longfellow he described himself as an owlish recluse who, in the dozen years since his graduation from college, had grown more and more out of touch with reality.[29] However much an exaggeration this avowal might be, Hawthorne's personal experience must have contributed to the development of the solitary, self-indulgent, Faustian scientists, deluded by their own imaginings, who appear so often in his works.

One of these "mad scientist" tales, "The Birthmark," owes something to Hawthorne's reading in still another phrenological work, *The Principles of Physiology* (New York, 1842), by George Combe's medical brother Andrew. The passage that caught Hawthorne's eye (p. 240) has nothing to do with phrenology directly, but involves a case study of self-induced insanity reported by Scipion Pinel in his *Physiologie de L'Homme Aliènè.* As Hawthorne describes it in his *American Notebooks,* the case concerned "a young man of great talents and profound knowledge of chemistry, who had in view some new discovery of importance. In order to put his mind into the highest possible activity, he shut himself up, for several successive days, and used various methods of excitement . . . , [as a result of which] he was seized with a fit of frenzy, which terminated in mania" (*AN* 235-36).

Andrew Combe had recited the case in connection with his discussion of "excessive mental activity," the same subject that drew Hawthorne to Robbins's *Remarks on the Disorders of Literary Men* in 1828 and to George Combe's *Constitution of Man* in 1836. Combe quotes Pinel to this effect: "Men of exalted intellect perish by their brains, and such is the noble end of those whose genius procures for them that immortality which so many ardently desire."[30] In drawing his moral for the career of Aylmer in "The Birthmark," Hawthorne gave this same irony another twist: the solitary researches of genius unfit the scientist for human companionship, so that he is doomed to destroy the very persons whom he intends his work to benefit. This is the ultimate alienation of the "mad scientist."

Other contemporary works on the nature of the mind differ considerably in outlook—some pessimistically threatening disaster for every active imagination, others adhering to the more soothing phrenological doctrine, enunciated in Hawthorne's extract from George Combe, that "moderate" intellectual exercise might even be beneficial, so long as the laws of nervous economy were not infringed. Whatever his perspective, every expert had in view the comprehension of all mental phenomena within a single system, a "modern psychology." It is significant therefore that Hawthorne gave the title "Advantages of Moral Science" to his second borrowing from *The Constitution of Man*. Since this extract was actually a combination of two passages, separated in the original by 200 pages, Hawthorne (or his sister "Ebe," who helped with the editing) must have taken some pains dissecting out the argument on the proper uses of the intellect and the possibility of systematizing them.

In the first portion quoted, Combe offers a mild argument for the propriety of his investigation: "it appears probable that, in this world, we shall never know the essence, beginning, or end of things; because these are points which we have no faculties calculated to reach: But . . . we can be happy here only by becoming acquainted with the qualities and modes of action of our own minds and bodies, with the qualities and modes of action of external objects, and with the relations established between them; in short . . . our mental capacities are wisely adapted to the attainment of these objects. . . ." Combe's intention is to call for support of phrenology as a means of advancing such knowledge. The next 200 pages of *The Constitution of Man* are largely devoted to the necessity for "a true system of human nature and its relations," to combat the present confusion of theories and dogmatisms which "operate simply as instincts, exhibiting all the confliction and uncertainty of mere feeling. . . ." Hawthorne leaps all these phrenological discussions to the culminating arguments, and then cuts Combe off just before a crucial sentence, which read: "If, then, phrenology be true, it will, when matured, supply the deficiencies now pointed out." The effect was to leave much more doubt whether phrenology was the moral science called for.

What interested Hawthorne in these extracts from *The Constitution of Man* was Combe's statement of the problem, not his phrenological solution. What are the capacities of the intellect? Is it possible to abuse the imagination by excessive indulgence? Are there forbidden areas of knowledge? Can men achieve a science of human nature and its relations? Hawthorne was not so impressed as Emerson or Channing with Combe's answers, but he must have recognized how similar the questions were to those he was posing himself in his fiction of the 1830s. Even the connection between such questions and the pseudoscientific study of the human countenance was appropriate, however odd that might seem at first.

ii

Hawthorne's use of physiognomical symbolism may be observed in his earliest tales—such as "Alice Doane's Appeal," "Roger Malvin's Burial," and "My Kinsman, Major Molineux"—each of which is built around the theme of self-recognition and utilizes images of the human countenance. Patterns of uncanny resemblance and déjà vu provide the metaphorical events of these gothic plots. Between "My Kinsman, Major Molineux" and "The Birthmark," say 1830 to 1843, the period of his best tales, Hawthorne returned many times to similar motifs. For example, the two years immediately following his editorship he published "The Minister's Black Veil" (written earlier but published in 1836), "The Prophetic Pictures" and "Monsieur du Miroir" (1837), and "Edward Randolph's Portrait" (1838). His notebooks during the period reveal him contemplating more stories of the same kind. Some of these ideas, like "The Great Stone Face" (*AN* 184), were not used until much later; others echoed images already incorporated in tales. A notation of 1836 on "the misery of being always under a mask" (*AN* 23) postdated "The Minister's Black Veil," and a still later entry returned to the grotesque notion, already exploited in "My Kinsman, Major Molineux" (*SI* 227), of a face in which "half of the visage shall express one mood, and the other half another (*AN* 29). A dozen others show him pondering further uses of physiognomical imagery, though most of these never found their way into his published works.[31]

Often, as in "My Kinsman, Major Molineux," physiognomy functions as a means of connecting two characters of a tale, whose similar faces suggest deeper similarities of motive or circumstance. Many of these Doppelgänger effects are mere gothic gestures, intended only to heighten the sense of mystery. Young Goodman Brown's companion in the forest is the devil in the guise of Brown's grandfather; the resemblance hints that Brown's vision of sin is self-imposed, but it also suggests that Brown represents all men in all generations; as usual, Hawthorne's purposes are served by either interpretation, and the touch is so light that neither seems quite over the boundary between realism and allegory.

The numerous thematic possibilities of encountering one's own image are sketched out in Hawthorne's "fantastic musings" on "Monsieur du Miroir" (1837), a whole catalogue of serious and silly puns growing out of the central visual pun on oneself. For the most part, these self-reflexive images seem to interest Hawthorne as curious phenomena of consciousness. An entry in the notebooks (1838) shows this fascination:

> A Perception, for a moment, of one's eventual and moral self, as if it were another person,—the observant faculty being separated, and looking intently at the qualities of the character. There is a surprise when this happens,—this getting out of one's self,—and then the observer sees how queer a fellow he is. (*AN* 178)

Many of Hawthorne's tales revolve around this sense of double consciousness, of looking at oneself and being looked at by oneself. In "The Minister's Black Veil" Mr. Hooper fears to see his masked face in the mirror, yet he wears his veil precisely to provoke anxious self-awareness in his congregation. The motive of Wakefield's eccentric disappearance and surveillance of his own absence is "a morbid vanity"; he wants to see "how the little sphere of creatures and circumstances, in which he was a central object, will be affected by his removal" (*TTT* 134). The narrator of "The Vision of the Fountain" "withdrew into an inner world, where my thoughts lived and breathed, and the Vision in the midst of them. Without intending it, I became at once the author and hero of a romance, conjuring up rivals, imagining events, the actions of others and my own"—all as a result of his gazing into "the watery mirror" of a fountain pool (*TTT* 216-17).

In these examples no particular effort is made to characterize the protagonists by description of their physiognomies. Indeed, Mr. Hooper's character depends on the impossibility of seeing his face at all. This restraint may seem surprising, given the obvious usefulness of physiognomical lore in conveying the thoughts and feelings of characters without seeming to violate the realistic facade of mere physical description.[32] Hawthorne was not reluctant to take advantage of these possibilities—as we shall see—but the absence of such effects in the tales just cited should warn us not to be satisfied with any simple or obvious account of his uses of physiognomical imagery. He never descended to the crudities of a Maria McIntosh, who endowed one of her characters with a mouth "which Lavater would have pronounced decidedly sensual," and a head "which would have attracted the attention of a phrenologist" because of its unusual fullness "in the region of ideality."[33] Hawthorne's own methods of characterization were much subtler, even when they depended on physiognomical effects.

For example, in "The Prophetic Pictures" and "Edward Randolph's Portrait" physiognomic character reading is central in the plots, yet never thrust before the reader in any of its vulgar detail. Both tales bring the divinatory powers of physiognomy into play. In "The Prophetic Pictures" an artist is hired to paint separate wedding portraits of a couple, but covertly sketches them in tableau as well. Years later the artist returns, to discover that the separate portraits now wear the candid expressions he had secretly sketched. When he comes upon his subjects, he finds them in precisely the pose he had imagined, that is, the husband threatening his wife with a dagger.

"Edward Randolph's Portrait" is similarly prophetic. An age-blackened portrait of a former New England governor, notorious as "the destroyer of our liberties" (*TTT* 262), is magically restored, so that the present governor, Thomas Hutchinson, may see his predecessor's agonized face and be warned off a similar course: "Behold his punishment—and avoid a crime like his!" (*TTT* 268). In spite of the explicitness of this warning, interpreted by his niece

Alice Vane (the portrait restorer), Hutchinson betrays the colonists and ends his days "choking with the blood of the Boston Massacre," and wearing a "frenzied look" similar to the "awful visage of Edward Randolph" (*TTT* 269).

In "The Prophetic Pictures" the artist-physiognomist makes a prediction about the future of his subjects on the basis of their faces; he has the gift "to see the inmost soul" (*TTT* 175), which, buried somewhere in the present countenance, will work itself out in the features and character until it finally takes full possession of both. In "Edward Randolph's Portrait" Hutchinson's fate appears not in his own face but in that of Randolph, "the torture of [whose] soul had come forth upon the countenance . . . as if the picture, while hidden behind the cloud of immemorial years, had been all the time acquiring an intenser depth and darkness of expression. . . ." (*TTT* 267). In both tales the face ultimately mirrors the soul, but in "The Prophetic Pictures" the artist's prediction is based on elements of character—"secret sentiments" (*TTT* 167)—seen already working in the subjects, whereas Alice Vane's prophecy seems more interpretive and conditional, depending first on the conjecture about Randolph, and then on Hutchinson's obduracy. Hutchinson is not doomed to the "People's curse" (*TTT* 269) endured by Randolph; rather he is willing to risk it.

Strictly speaking there is room in both tales for some doubt as to the inevitability of these physiognomic prophecies. The characters of "The Prophetic Pictures" do not enact the final catastrophe. "Our fate is upon us!" Walter cries, but when the painter reappears to prevent the murder, he complains, "Does Fate impede its own decree?" Apparently so. Moreover, the painter then addresses Elinor, "Did I not warn you?" implying that she might have avoided the fate he read in her face. Hawthorne then draws his moral: "Could the result of one, or all our deeds, be shadowed forth and set before us, some would call it Fate, and hurry onward—others be swept along by their passionate desires—and none be turned aside by the PROPHETIC PICTURES" (*TTT* 181-82).

Hawthorne's final word has this ambiguity, not to say inconsistency: while on the one hand he suggests that a person's fate may be read in his face, on the other hand he regards this fate as avoidable, since the physiognomic reading is to be taken as admonition rather than decree. This ambiguity, weighted on the side of free will, gives an almost transcendental turn to stories that, in the hands of

Poe, would merely be inexorable marches into the abyss. On its surface Hawthorne's moral is not much more convincing than the argument of those phrenologists who dodged the accusation of materialism by suggesting that a man might enlarge an underdeveloped faculty—and thus, presumably, its cranial manifestation—through exercise.[34] A careful reading of Hawthorne, however, reveals neither horror at the punctuality of fate, nor easy belief in a genial Providence skipping through the nineteenth century hand in hand with progress. He has a more Calvinistic message, psychologized in accordance with the tastes of his age: a man who labors under a curse does so through his own continual choice, recommiting in character and deed the sin for which he and his ancestors were first condemned. Hutchinson earns the fate of Randolph for himself by disregarding his example and repeating his sin. Similarly Elinor is told that "it is not yet too late to alter" the portraits, and thus her fate, "if your heart does not see itself reflected in your own portrait—if you have no secret cause to trust my delineation of the other" (*TTT* 175-76). The portraits in both tales represent final states into which the characters gradually settle, each responsible—because forewarned—for his own countenance as it ultimately appears.

Despite these reiterated indictments of his characters, Hawthorne is equally aware of their apparent helplessness to avoid the fates in store for them—"and *none* be turned aside" he notes at the end of "The Prophetic Pictures." Free will notwithstanding, Hutchinson seems predestined to betray "the People" in the manner of Randolph, as if "the People's curse" were on him from the outset. Walter and Elinor appear even less in control of their characters or destinies. The moody observations they exchange in front of their portraits imply some prior acquiescence in the fates depicted there. They are more to blame, one almost thinks, for tempting fate: in Hawthorne, as in most gothic writers, to have one's portrait painted is to invite a curse—or, at the very least, a prophecy—to be fulfilled by one's descendants or oneself.

But if sitting for one's portrait is a risk, painting someone else's face is also dangerous, as the artist of the prophetic pictures comes to feel. Because he had taken the likenesses of Walter and Elinor, "he almost regarded them as creations of his own" (*TTT* 179). This leaves him open to the charge that his art was "an offence against the Mosaic law, and even a presumptuous mockery of the Creator"

(*TTT* 169), and the painter begins to see himself as "a chief agent of the coming evil" (*TTT* 181) instead of a mere interpreter of physiognomic signs.

This potential guilt of the artist is not always invoked in Hawthorne's tales. Alice Vane is not held responsible for the fate she forecasts for her uncle—but then she is a critic rather than a painter, and she only restores Edward Randolph's portrait to make her point. If she had painted Governor Hutchinson's features, things might have been different. As a general rule, Hawthorne's artists—including painters, sculptors, and writers—must assume a considerable degree of responsibility for their creations, and for the subsequent lives of the real people who furnish their subjects. The vulgar admirers of the painter in "The Prophetic Pictures" were right to fear that "after he has once got possession of a person's face and figure, he may paint him in any act or situation whatever—and the picture will be prophetic" (*TTT* 172).

Hawthorne had himself in mind when he characterized his artist figures as "insulated from the mass of humankind" (*TTT* 178). Although he sometimes thought of his solitary years as a terrible self-imprisonment, he also recognized the need for such an exactment. One of the reasons Hawthorne left Brook Farm, for instance, was that he missed "the sense of perfect seclusion, which has always been essential to my power of producing anything."[35] Yet however essential to a prophetic art, "it is not good for man to cherish a solitary ambition" (*TTT* 180), and prolonged separation from society could foster insanity as well as genius. Hawthorne's artists and scientists, from the painter of the prophetic pictures to Aylmer or Ethan Brand, are subject to this occupational hazard.

The source of such madness, according to phrenological theory, would have been the "excessive mental activity" of the artist. Hawthorne seems to accept this view, but he elaborates the etiology to suit his own themes. Thus in borrowing the anecdote from phrenologist Andrew Combe as part of the plot of "The Birthmark," Hawthorne shifts the emphasis from the catalogue of artificial stimulants in the original to the fact that the experimenter had "shut himself up" with his books and test tubes. Even the resultant madness is different. Instead of a "fit of frenzy, which terminated in mania," Aylmer's insanity is "moral," the inability to distinguish good and evil—a new category being developed in medical jurisprudence by Bowdoin graduate and phrenological sympathizer Isaac Ray.[36] Just as the source of Aylmer's derangement is overindulgence in study and solitude, so it manifests itself in an interest in forbidden knowledge that will alienate him still further from humanity, a desire to "create" life and "perfect" nature. These are not the ordinary symptoms of lunacy, but they are typical of Hawthorne's mad artists and scientists.

Of course artists were not the only men prone to madness. Their sitters were often susceptible as well—as were the subjects of experiments pursued by Hawthorne's scientists. Edward Randolph's features were so "tortured" that Hutchinson, imagining a similar fate, cried, "'Twould drive me mad—that awful face!" (*TTT* 268). It is worth noting that madness is regularly revealed through the face, thus making the artist an appropriate diagnostician. In fact, the idea for "The Prophetic Pictures" came from a story Hawthorne chanced upon in a work of art history, which reported how an artist had discovered incipient insanity in his subject's physiognomy:

> Lord Mulgrave, whose name was *Phipps,* employed [Gilbert Charles] Stuart to paint the portrait of his brother, General Phipps, previous to his going abroad. On seeing the picture, which he did not until it was finished, Mulgrave exclaimed, "What is this?—this is very strange!" and stood gazing at the portrait. "I have painted your brother as I saw him," said the artist. "I see insanity in that face," was the brother's remark. The general went to India, and the first account his brother had of him was that of suicide from insanity. He went mad and cut his throat. It is thus that the real portrait painter dives into the recesses of his sitters' minds. . . .[37]

In adapting this idea, Hawthorne shifted some of the imputation of insanity from the sitter to the artist, who, reading "other bosoms, with an acuteness almost preternatural, . . . failed to see the disorder of his own" (*TTT* 180). Both Walter and the painter are called "madman" in the course of the story.

In general Hawthorne's artists and scientists become sinful or mad chiefly because of their interest in the sin or madness of others. The classic case is Ethan Brand, whose solitary musings in front of his lime kiln led to his search for the unpardonable sin, the self-destructive quest that ended in madness and despair. What he sought in others he produced in himself—a fact which, characteristically enough, his countenance revealed: "an indescribable something in that thin, rugged, thoughtful visage, with the grizzled hair hanging wildly about it, and those deeply sunken eyes, which gleamed like fires within the entrance of a mysterious cavern" (*SI* 86).

Not every solitary brooder ended up a madman. In a story written about the same time as "Ethan Brand"—indeed, it is best regarded as a companion piece—Hawthorne offered an alternative outcome to intense and long-continued meditation. "The Great Stone Face" shows how, by thinking only of others and never of himself, the lonely and reflective man may arrive at philosophic wisdom instead of forbidden knowledge. The hero Ernest "loved to go apart and gaze and meditate upon the Great Stone Face. According to [the other inhabitants of the valley] it was a folly, indeed, but pardonable, inasmuch as Ernest was industrious, kind, and neighborly, and neglected no duty for the sake of indulging this idle habit. They knew not that the Great Stone Face had become a teacher to him, and that the sentiment which was expressed in it would enlarge the young man's heart and fill it with wider and deeper sympathies than other hearts. They knew not that hence would come a better wisdom than could be learned from books, and a better life than could be moulded on the defaced example of other human lives" (*SI* 33). At last it is revealed that Ernest himself is the fulfillment of the prophecy, "the greatest and noblest personage of his time, . . . whose countenance, in manhood, should bear an exact resemblance to the Great Stone Face" (*SI* 28). Unlike Walter and Governor Hutchinson, Ernest ages gracefully into his fated physiognomy, and unlike the prophetic painter or Ethan Brand, he keeps his sanity, even grows wise, in solitude. Nevertheless, the story of Ernest is just another modification of the basic plot of "The Prophetic Pictures" and "Edward Randolph's Portrait"—that is, the working out of a prophecy by virtue of a character's face coming, over a period of time, to resemble a portrait or effigy somehow connected with his fate. This plot appealed to Hawthorne enormously and gave him repeated opportunities to explore the possibilities of the themes that we have identified as growing out of his interest in phrenology and physiognomy—the reading of character in the face, the risks taken by the artist who exercises his skill in character reading, and the various "magical" and "supernatural" phenomena, especially prophecies and curses, that might be associated with such feats. All these themes are elaborated most fully in the novel that Hawthorne wrote not long after "The Great Stone Face" and "Ethan Brand," *The House of the Seven Gables.*

iii

In May 1850, having completed *The Scarlet Letter* but not yet having begun *The House of the Seven Gables,* Hawthorne moved from Salem to Lenox, Massachusetts. Hawthorne had planned the move for a somewhat later date, but the exodus from Salem was advanced by several months when, as a result of the "Custom-House" chapter of *The Scarlet Letter,* he found himself rather unpopular in his native town. Accordingly, the Hawthornes spent a few weeks in Boston until their new home in the Berkshires was ready for them; Sophia and the children stayed with her relatives while Hawthorne lived in a nearby boarding house. As was his habit when not writing fiction, he kept a journal during this period, and it furnished several details for the novel that he began in September. But more interesting than these bits of description is the record he made of his sittings with the artist C. G. Thompson, "who had requested to paint my picture" (*AN* 491). Although nothing specific from these notes seems to have gone into *The House of the Seven Gables,* the attitudes revealed in them will help us understand its deepest themes.

After the second sitting, Hawthorne commented on his previous experience with painters. "I have had three portraits taken before this; a picture, a miniature, and a crayon-sketch; neither of them satisfactory to those most familiar with my phiz. In fact, there is no such thing as a true portrait; they are all delusions; and I never saw any two alike, nor, hardly, any two that I could recognize, merely by the portraits themselves, as being of the same man" (*AN* 491). The following day he had decided "it will be a good picture; but I see no assurance, as yet, of the likeness." He described the "artist's apartment," and ended by stating that portrait painting, whatever its insufficiencies, "has always interested my imagination more than any other [pursuit], and I remember, before having my first portrait taken, there was a great bewitchery in the idea, as if it were a magic process. Even now, it is not without interest for me"

(*AN* 492-93). And at the next sitting—the last recorded—Hawthorne and Thompson "talked of physiognomy and impressions of character—first impressions—and how apt they are to come right, in the face of the closest subsequent observation" (*AN* 498).[38]

These opinions—the delusory aspect of portraiture, its "bewitchery" and "magic," and especially its physiognomical application to the reading of characters—have been found in the tales already discussed. What is new is the opportunity to see Hawthorne thinking about them completely aside from any qualifying purposes, whether the popular taste of a magazine audience or the thematic necessities of a fiction. Whatever he might have thought worth saying, in jest or in earnest, to the readers of the *American Magazine of Useful and Entertaining Knowledge,* here we see that he was a believer in physiognomy—not the science, of course, but the art—and his interest in portraiture seems to have been related to that belief, not only as a convenience of plot in his tales, but also as a mode of perception in ordinary life. Not surprisingly, since it was on his mind, Hawthorne's notebooks for this period are full of physiognomical observations on the people he sees—in the boarding house, on the street, at the theater, the stables, the library. He even made some reciprocative sketches of the features of Thompson while the artist was attempting his. Although there is nothing unusual about any of these notations, it may be useful to quote a few, to get the feel of Hawthorne's physiognomical perceptions uncolored by the requirements of fiction:

> The artist is a man not far from forty, middle-sized, thin, a little stooping, with a quick, nervous movement. He has black hair, rather thin; a beard under his chin, grizzled; a small head, but well developed forehead, black eye-brows, eyes keen, but kindly, and a dark face, not indicating robust health, but agreeable in its expression.

> At dinner, to-day, our two other boarders appeared. One a clerk, I believe, in some bank; a middle-aged man with a dark, sallow complexion, black hair, and a great black beard and whiskers, bushy and shadowy enough for a ruffian. There is nothing ruffianly, however, about the personage in question; nor anything particularly

> marked. He seems to be fond of music, and attended the opera frequently; he is rather precisely accurate in his address and pronunciation, and somewhat scrupulously polite at table,—at least, it appears so, among such an unceremonious group as we make—and I know nothing else of him. There was likewise a young Frenchman . . . ; a young man of eighteen or thereabouts, with smooth black hair, neatly dressed, and a face showing a good disposition, but with nothing of intellect or character.
>
> [Another boarder was] a young lady, from the country. . . . She was not very pretty; a brunette, without force or character of face, with rather a silly smile breaking out without much aptness.
>
> In the next box to me were two young women. . . . One was a large, plump girl, with a heavy face, a snub nose, coarse looking, but good-natured, and with no traits of evil; save, indeed, that she had on the vilest gown—of dirty white cotton, so pervadingly dingy that it was white no longer, as it seemed to me—the sleeves short, and ragged at the borders—and an old faded shawl, which she took off on account of the heat—the shabbiest and dirtiest dress, in a word, that I ever saw a woman wear. Yet she was plump, as aforesaid, and looked comfortable in body and mind. . . . The other girl seemed as young, or younger than herself; she was small, with a particularly intelligent and pleasant face, not handsome, perhaps, but as good or better than if it were. It was mobile with whatever sentiment chanced to be in her mind; as quick and vivacious a face in its movement as I have ever seen; cheerful, too, and indicative of a sunny, though I should think it might be a hasty temper. She was dressed in a dark gown, (chintz, I suppose the women call it,) a good homely dress, proper enough for the fireside, but a strange one to appear at a theatre in. Both these girls appeared to enjoy themselves very much; the large and heavy one, in her own duller mode; the smaller manifesting her interest by gestures, pointing at the stage, and so vivid a talk of countenance that I could sympathize precisely as well as if she had spoken. She was not a brunette; and this made her vivacity of expression the more agreeable. Her companion, on the other hand, was so dark that I rather suspected her to have a tinge of African blood. (*AN* 499-503)

All these are perfectly ordinary observations, nothing "magical" or "divinatory" about them—though at the end of his notes on the "two young women" Hawthorne wondered "who they are—of what condition in life—and whether reputable as members of the class to which they belong. My own judgement is, that they are so."

Although Hawthorne sometimes borrowed such jottings from his journals for his fiction, he did so rarely, since the chief literary use of his notebooks was as a treasury of plots for his tales. Nor is there anything sufficiently striking about the people he describes to explain his interest in them. The only oddity of these passages of physiognomical observation is that they occur in the space of so very few pages, a partial report of two days' experience. Although other details of description and event appear there as well, physiognomy is the major concern, as if Hawthorne were experimenting with the technique not merely as a method of characterization, but as a mode of literary consciousness. Everything he notices about these various persons—dress, conversation, behavior, companions—is referred back and dovetailed with the primary index of character, the form and expressions of the face. Thus the bank clerk is genteel in spite of his "ruffianly" countenance, while the girls, as their expressions betoken, are at home and "comfortable" in the theatre regardless of their inappropriate dress.

When we turn from these life sketches to the imaginative renderings of characters in *The House of the Seven Gables*—as Hawthorne himself did—we can see how thoroughly this mode of literary consciousness had taken over his art. In representing actual persons and faces in his notebook, he was obliged to wrestle with innumerable details of perception that figured in reality as loose ends and untidy irrelevancies, to be tucked into a impression only by an effort of concentration. One feels it immediately, in contrast to the ease and variety Hawthorne commands when inventing his subjects. In his novel the use of physiognomy as a focus of attitude and motive is even more thoroughgoing, but depends less on narrowly descriptive passages punctuated by conjecture. Instead we find generous elaborations suggestive of personality and intimate circumstances.

On first acquaintance each character is described both physically and spiritually in terms of physiognomy. Hepzibah, for example:

> We must linger, a moment, on this unfortunate expression of poor Hepzibah's brow. Her scowl—as the world, or such part of it as sometimes caught a transitory glimpse of her at the window,

> wickedly persisted in calling it—her scowl had done Miss Hepzibah a very ill-office, in establishing her character as an ill-tempered old maid; nor does it appear improbable, that, by often gazing at herself in a dim looking-glass, and perpetually encountering her own frown within its ghostly sphere, she had been led to interpret the expression almost as unjustly as the world did. —"How miserably cross I look!"—she must often have whispered to herself;—and ultimately have fancied herself so, by a sense of inevitable doom. But her heart never frowned. It was naturally tender, sensitive, and full of little tremors and palpitations: all of which weaknesses it retained, while her visage was growing so perversely stern, and even fierce. (*HSG* 34)

Holgrave:

> It was a slender young man, not more than one or two and twenty years old, with rather and grave a thoughtful expression, for his years, but likewise a springy alacrity and vigor. These qualities were not only perceptible, physically, in his make and motions, but made themselves felt, almost immediately, in his character. A brown beard, not too silken in its texture, fringed his chin, but as yet without completely hiding it; he wore a short moustache, too; and his dark, high-featured countenance looked all the better for these natural ornaments. As for his dress, it was of the simplest kind; a summer sack of cheap and ordinary material, thin checkered pantaloons, and a straw hat, by no means of the finest braid. Oak-hall might have supplied his entire equipment. He was chiefly marked as a gentleman—if such, indeed, he made any claim to be—by the remarkable whiteness and nicety of his clean linen. (*HSG* 43)

Clifford:

> It is the likeness of a young man, in a silken dressing-gown of an old fashion, the soft richness of which is well adapted to the countenance of reverie, with its full, tender lips, and beautiful eyes, that seem to indicate not so much capacity of thought, as gentle and voluptuous emotion. Of the possessor of such features we should have a right to ask nothing, except that he would take the rude world easily, and make himself happy in it. (*HSG* 31-32)

Sometimes, as in Holgrave's case, subsequent observation merely confirms the initial reading of character. There is something opaque about him, a hint at his secret identity as a descendant of Matthew Maule. Clean shirts cover a variety of interesting potentialities in Hawthorne. Holgrave's peculiar combination of gravity and vigor, like his linen supply, is never exhausted, though "in the artist's deep, thoughtful, all-observant eyes, there was now-and-then an expression, not sinister, but questionable; as if he had some other interest in the scene than a stranger, a youthful and unconnected adventurer, might be supposed to have" (*HSG* 156). Even at Holgrave's climactic moment—his discovery of Judge Pyncheon's body, which constitutes a sort of triumph for the Maules—he retains his customary self-control: "The artist looked paler than ordinary; there was a thoughtful and severe contraction of his forehead, tracing a deep, vertical line between the eyebrows." For a moment pleasure and relief at Phoebe's return light up his face: "His smile, however, was full of genuine warmth, and had in it a joy, by far the most vivid expression that Phoebe had ever witnessed, shining out of the New England reserve with which Holgrave habitually masked whatever lay near his heart" (*HSG* 300-1). This constancy of character and physiognomy is more significant than might at first appear. As we will see in a moment, not every figure in the novel keeps in countenance so easily, and this helps to mark Holgrave as the hero, just as Phoebe, also a fixed quantity, must be the herione.

Other characters in *The Seven Gables* have more complex psychic organizations, also revealed largely through physiognomy. In his youth Clifford had a happy face, but thirty years of prison have blurred his features and "half-extinguished" the intelligence and sensitivity that once shown there. "The expression of his countenance—while, notwithstanding, it had the light of reason in it—seemed to waver, and glimmer, and nearly to die away, and feebly to recover itself again" (*HSG* 104). Much of the chapter titled "The Guest" is devoted to the comings and goings of sensibility in his faded visage, which not only reveal his character and its blighted fate, but even seem to hint at the causes of his catastrophe—"Then his face darkened, as if the shadow of a cavern or a dungeon had come over it; there was no more light in its expression than might have come through the iron grates of a prison-window" (*HSG* 110). At other times an effect still more magical seems to occur. Under Phoebe's health-giving influence,

> A beauty—not precisely real, even in its utmost manifestation, and which a painter would have watched long to seize, and fix upon his canvass, and, after all, in vain—beauty, nevertheless, that was not a mere dream, would sometimes play upon and illuminate his face. It did more than to illuminate; it transfigured him with an expression that could only be interpreted as the glow of an exquisite and happy spirit. That gray hair, and those furrows—with their record of infinite sorrow, so deeply written across his brow, and so compressed, as with a futile effort to crowd in all the tale, that the whole inscription was made illegible—these, for the moment, vanished. An eye, at once tender and acute, might have beheld in the man some shadow of what he was meant to be. (*HSG* 139)

This last phenomenon—as Hawthorne says, "not precisely real"—is characteristic of the physiognomical "bewitchery" that operates with several other figures, notably Hepzibah and Jaffrey. We have already seen Hepzibah's scowl, and discovered that, far from being a true reflection of her inner state, it is the reverse. Jaffrey, at the opposite pole, wears a smile that conceals his true nature, stern and cruel.

The relation between Hepzibah's character and her countenance is not simply a matter of inversion. For one thing, although her face has so dreadful a scowl that she must literally hide it from Clifford, her love for him is so great that it sometimes transforms even her ugliness. First her voice develops, on Clifford's arrival, "a certain rich depth and moisture, as if the words, common-place as they were, had been steeped in the warmth of her heart" (*HSG* 95). Unfortunately, this softness is only temporary, for when Hepzibah attempts to read aloud to her brother, he recoils as if he had "heard" her scowl. "His sister's voice, too, naturally harsh, had, in the course of her sorrowful lifetime, contracted a kind of croak, which, when it once gets into the human throat, is as ineradicable as sin" (*HSG* 134). Finally, just as her voice sometimes softened with love, so too her scowl could magically vanish in the right circumstance: "at the indistinct murmur of his words, her whole face grew tender, and even lovely, with sorrowful affection; the harshness of her features disappeared, as it were, behind the warm and misty glow" (*HSG* 106). There is something less consistent in this ebb and flow of love, perhaps, than in Clifford's waxing and waning sensibility, but the point seems to be the same—that while the countenance ordinarily mirrors the character, for a proper reading of the physiognomical signs it may sometimes be necessary to wait for the right moment.

Having established his characters as a collection of physiognomical surfaces, representing attitude and motive, Hawthorne handles their lives and natures almost as a painter might, in a series of tableaux that juxtapose moral and psychological as well as merely physical "faces." The confrontation of Hepzibah and Jaffrey in the chapter called "The Scowl and the Smile" is a good example. In their first encounter, at the same doorway earlier in the novel, Hepzibah had seemed "a perfect picture of Prohibition, at full length, in the dark frame of the door-way." Her perpetual frown, which could soften and melt for Clifford, became a true scowl for the judge—"too fierce, at this moment, to pass itself off on the innocent score of near-sightedness" (*HSG* 127). One is reminded of the Pre-Raphaelite paintings Hawthorne later learned to admire, where time stops, catching the figures in emblematic attitudes. Now, in her final struggle with her cousin, Hepzibah's "wrath" goes beyond mere appearance, and erupts in several paragraphs of outraged vituperation. "Without premeditation, to her own surprise, and indeed terror, she had given vent, for once, to the inveteracy of her resentment, cherished against this kinsman, for thirty years" (*HSG* 232).

For his part, the judge had maintained to this point his usual smiling aspect, expressing "mild forbearance—grave and almost gentle deprecation of his cousin's unbecoming violence—free and christianlike forgiveness of the wrong inflicted by her words."

> But, when those words were irrevocably spoken, his look assumed sternness, the sense of power, and immitigable resolve; and this with so natural and imperceptible a change, that it seemed as if the iron man had stood there from the first, and the meek man not at all. The effect was as when the light vapory clouds, with their soft coloring, suddenly vanish from the stony brow of a precipitous mountain, and leave there the frown which you at once feel to be eternal. Hepzibah almost adopted the insane belief, that it was her old Puritan ancestor, and not the modern Judge, on whom she had just been wreaking the bitterness of her heart. Never did a man show stronger proof of the lineage attributed to him, than Judge Pyncheon, at this crisis, by his unmistakeable resemblance to the picture in the inner room. (*HSG* 232)

Here physiognomy opens up moral vistas in several dimensions at once. Jaffrey, like Hepzibah, is not what he ordinarily seems. He wears a mask by choice, but it slips aside in his agitation, just as her involuntary frown was supplanted by a genuine grimace of indignation. Thus their countenances operate upon each other, uncovering hidden passions.

This is typical of Hawthorne's use of the tableau, a means of achieving a kind of psychological depth and ethical significance that depends neither on symbolic action in the plot nor on a Jamesian narrative consciousness. Of course the basis of the scene is an encounter, an event in the plot, but the action is not so much a development as an illustration, an emblematic juxtaposition of tendencies and intentions residing in the characters, fixed and unchanging. Hawthorne's technique is to present a series of such moments, with the same few characters juxtaposed in different moral attitudes, until he has exhausted the possibilities of combination given in their original dispositions.

The progress of such a narrative cannot have anything like the pace and sense of eventuation of ordinary novels, where one thing leads to another and characters learn from experience. Another sort of rhythm and pattern organizes *The Seven Gables.* This too is seen in the passage just quoted, and is a further use of physiognomy in Hawthorne. Hepzibah's "insane belief" that Jaffrey was "her old Puritan ancestor," whose portrait hung in the parlor, is based on her sudden perception of his resemblance to the old colonel. Jaffrey's "sultry smile" usually hides his true character, but its "painted" surface is thin, and, like the famous diorama of Louis Daguerre's illusionist theater, may be lit from within to reveal a totally different aspect.

This two-facedness may be uncovered in a fit of passion, or it may appear through more extraordinary means. Holgrave's daguerreotypy penetrates Jaffrey's hidden nature, like the paintings in "The Prophetic Pictures" or "Edward Randolph's Portrait." "There is a wonderful insight in heaven's broad and simple sunshine," Holgrave explains rather mystically. "While we give it credit only for depicting the merest surface, it actually brings out the secret character with a truth that no painter would ever venture upon, even could he detect it" (*HSG* 91). Moreover, in *The House of the Seven Gables* the Pyncheon curse is not laid on a single individual but a whole family, through several centuries, and is depicted in both family portraits and modern daguerreotypes. This curse and its fulfillment take the place of plot in this novel, and are worked out almost entirely in physiognomical terms.

The judge's resemblance to the colonel implies that they share the same character and fate. Like Jaffrey, the founder of the family also wore a mask—not so sociable and beaming, but nonetheless a mask. The old portrait in the back parlor has slowly unveiled his secret character, just as Holgrave's daguerreotype instantly pierces Jaffrey's false front.

> In one sense, this picture had almost faded into the canvass, and hidden itself behind the duskiness of age; in another, [Hepzibah] could not but fancy that it had been growing more prominent, and strikingly expressive, ever since her earliest familiarity with it, as a child. For, while the physical outline and substance were darkening away from the beholder's eye, the bold, hard, and, at the same time, indirect character of the man seemed to be brought out in a kind of spiritual relief. Such an effect may occasionally be observed in pictures of antique date. They acquire a look which an artist (if he have anything like the complaisancy of artists now-a-days) would never dream of presenting to a patron as his own characteristic expression, but which, nevertheless, we at once recognize as reflecting the unlovely truth of a human soul. In such cases, the painter's deep conception of his subject's inward traits has wrought itself into the essence of the picture, and is seen after the superficial coloring has been rubbed off by time. (*HSG* 58-59)

This is much like the gradual altering of the portraits of Walter and Elinor in "The Prophetic Pictures." And, as in "Edward Randolph's Portrait," the old painting hints obscurely at the doom of some modern figure, who deserves the fate of his predecessor because he has inherited from him not only his physiognomy but also his character—as well as the tendency to apoplexy that forms the physiological basis of the Pyncheon curse. Hepzibah makes the accusation explicit: "Alas, Cousin Jaffrey, this hard and grasping spirit has run in our blood, these two hundred years! You are but doing over again, in another shape, what your ancestor before you did, and sending down to your posterity the curse inherited from him!" (*HSG* 237). Hawthorne underscored the point more than once, since it constituted both theme and plot of his romance:

> . . . the weaknesses and defects, the bad passions, the mean tendencies, and the moral diseases which lead to crime, are handed down from one generation to another, by a far surer process of transmission than human law has been able to establish, in respect to the riches and honors which it seeks to entail upon posterity. (*HSG* 119)

> Nay; we could almost venture to say farther, that a daily guilt might have been acted by him, continually renewed, and reddening forth afresh, like the miraculous blood-stain of a murder, without his necessarily, and at every moment, being aware of it. (*HSG* 229)

The story will be over when the judge dies, just as the colonel did, sitting in the same room, in the same chair, facing the same portrait, guilty of the same sins, and punished by the same apoplectic stroke. The plot is not so much an unfolding of events leading up to this moment as it is an uncovering of the judge's character and a displaying of his multiple resemblances to his ancestor. Scenes are not "dramatic" opportunities for characters to interact and forward the action, but rather tableaux, in which one after another we are shown a series of moral configurations, each superimposed on the others—the career of the old colonel, the tale of Alice Pyncheon, Clifford's catastrophe, Hepzibah's thirty years of seclusion—all details in the indictment of the judge, who stands for the entire evil side of the Pyncheon family in its modern incarnation.

This is not the whole of the plot, but it is the only strand of it that runs all the way through the novel, from the opening chapter on the old colonel and his mansion to the final denouement and the abandonment of the house. Other strands are carefully woven into this basic physiognomic pattern. Clifford, for example, is first introduced through a portrait painted of him in his youth. When he later appears in the flesh, his present nature is given largely by contrast with the "Malbone miniature." And Clifford's slow recovery of his wits (which constitutes his own plot) is measured by the return of those old intellectual lights to his countenance.

Clifford's part in the central narrative, that is, in Jaffrey's plot, consists in the gradual sketching in, by physiognomical hint and conjecture, of the thirty years in prison that have all but obliterated his youthful delicacy of feature. This blotting out of his cousin's life and prospects constitutes Jaffrey's sin, the modern equivalent of Colonel Pyncheon's "legal murder" of Matthew Maule as a witch.

Much of the central portion of the novel is therefore devoted to the story that can be read in Clifford's face.

Other tributaries of the plot are equally dependent on physiognomy. We have already seen Hepzibah's contribution, as foe and foil to Jaffrey, scowl to his smile. Phoebe partly serves to cheer up Hepzibah and Clifford, so the images associated with her appearance are accordingly airy and spiritual. She is described in terms of sunshine and light, music and perfume, all rather unphysiognomical traits. But she also has a role in the "love story" of the novel, and so she too is given a face that can undergo temporal change. When we first meet her she is still a girl—"almost childlike"—and this characterless virginity is part of what Clifford finds so appealing in her. "Thus, his sentiment for Phoebe, without being paternal, was not less chaste than if she had been his daughter. . . . He read Phoebe, as he would a sweet and simple story; he listened to her, as if she were a verse of household poetry" (*HSG* 141-42). As her acquaintance with Holgrave deepens, her amorphous girlishness disappears. Before she leaves for a brief absence, Clifford calls her to him for a farewell inspection:

> "Close!—closer!—and look me in the face!"
>
> Phoebe put one of her small hands on each elbow of his chair, and leaned her face towards him, so that he might peruse it as carefully as he would. It is probable that the latent emotions of this parting hour had revived, in some degree, his bedimmed and enfeebled faculties. At any rate, Phoebe soon felt that, if not the profound insight of a seer, yet a more than feminine delicacy of appreciation was making her heart the subject of its regard. A moment before, she had known nothing which she would have sought to hide. Now, as if some secret were hinted to her own consciousness through the medium of another's perception, she was fain to let her eyelids droop beneath Clifford's gaze. A blush, too—the redder, because she strove hard to keep it down—ascended higher and higher, in a tide of fitful progress, until even her brow was all suffused with it.
>
> "It is enough, Phoebe!" said Clifford, with a melancholy smile. "When I first saw you, you were the prettiest little maiden in the world; and now you have deepened into beauty! Girlhood has passed into womanhood; the bud is a bloom! Go, now! I feel lonelier than I did." (*HSG* 220)

This constitutes Phoebe's major physiognomical development in the book. As it happens, her face also has a connection with the past, though not quite in the manner of Jaffrey's doomed countenance. In the interpolated story, "Alice Pyncheon," Holgrave's ancestor Matthew Maule mesmerizes Alice in an unsuccessful attempt to discover the missing deed to the Pyncheon lands in Maine. Although the somnambulatory quest fails—much to the annoyance of Alice's greedy father—the trance itself turns out to be fatal for Alice, who becomes henceforth a "spiritual slave" to Maule. Just as Clifford requests Phoebe to look into his eyes, Matthew Maule had begun his experiment by directing Alice to "fix your eyes on mine!"

> Alice complied. She was very proud. Setting aside all advantages of rank, this fair girl deemed herself conscious of a power—combined of beauty, high, unsullied purity, and the preservative force of womanhood—that could make her sphere impenetrable, unless betrayed by treachery within. She instinctively knew, it may be, that some sinister or evil potency was now striving to pass her barriers; nor would she decline the contest. So Alice put woman's might against man's might; a match not often equal, on the part of woman. (*HSG* 203)

Maule succeeds in "penetrating" her "barriers"—the sexual imagery is unrestrained—and "A power, that she little dreamed of, had laid its grasp upon her maiden soul. A will, most unlike her own, constrained her to do its grotesque and fantastic bidding. . . . Thus all the dignity of life was lost. She felt herself too much abased, and longed to change natures with some worm! . . . so lost from self-control, she would have deemed it a sin to marry. . . . " (*HSG* 208-9).

There is a relationship between Alice's "loss" and Phoebe's blush under Clifford's questioning gaze. Phoebe, no longer a child, closes her "maiden soul" even to Clifford. Alice was too bold and proud to avert her gaze in this way; she had too much of the old Pyncheon in her. The connection is further borne out after Holgrave finishes reading this object lesson of "Alice Pyncheon" to Phoebe. He discovers that his own hereditary mesmeric power, though exerted merely to illustrate Maule's methods and gestures in the tale, has brought Phoebe herself to the verge of trance. "It was evident, that, with but one wave of his hand and a corresponding effort of his will, he could complete his mastery over Phoebe's yet free and virgin spirit: he could establish an influence over this good, pure, and simple child, as dangerous, and perhaps as disastrous, as that which the carpenter of his legend had acquired and exercised over the ill-fated Alice." Once again the sexual connotations are emphasized in the diction: "To a disposition like Holgrave's, at once speculative and active, there is no temptation so great as the opportunity of acquiring empire over the human spirit; nor any idea more seductive to a young man, than to become the arbiter of a young girl's destiny" (HSG 211-12). Here again, as in Alice's less fortunate encounter with the "Maule eye" and in Phoebe's blushing modesty with Clifford, both plot and theme depend on the physiognomical notion of the eye as the window of the soul, an entrance to private and even sacred precincts of the self—with metaphoric implications for the sexual being as well as the spiritual.

It is appropriate that the most important feature of Phoebe's face should also be the most important in Holgrave's. The "Maule eye," however, is not so much a physiognomical sign as it is a means of reading such signs. Little is said about Holgrave's eye once its mesmeric power is asserted. Even so, the "Maule eye" does double duty, both as an organ of "penetrating" dominance over other consciousnesses, and as a "deep, thoughtful, all-observant" instrument of physiognomical perception. It is important to keep these two functions separate.

Phoebe thinks Holgrave "too calm and cool an observer" and is disturbed by his interest in "fathoming Clifford to the full depth of my plummet-line!" Not possessing his mysterious insight, she is unable to understand either his interest or his ability to gratify it—"I cannot see his thoughts!" she says. "How should I?" (*HSG* 177-78). This ability to "see" into another's thoughts may seem a mesmeric effect to modern readers, familiar with the mind-reading feats of hypnotic entertainments, but in Hawthorne's day the mesmerist's entry into another consciousness was either to exert his will there, or, in certain cases, to utilize the somnambulist as a medium for further seeing across time and space, not into minds but into other cities, or even into the ailing bodies of patients. Accordingly, although all the Maules including Holgrave have the reputation of being able to influence the dreams of the Pyncheons, none but Holgrave has the skill to read character and motive in their faces. He alone is an artist as well as a mesmerist, a seer as well as a spellbinder. For purposes of Hawthorne's plot, the division between these powers is convenient, since the physiognomical sensitivity of the "Maule eye" cannot be exercised until the present generation of Pyncheons arrives on the scene, offering masks of scowls and smiles to be deciphered by their ancient enemies. The plot then consists in laying bare the "inner Pyncheon," who is also the "ancient Pyncheon"—"the original perpetrator and father of this mischief [who] appears to have perpetuated himself, and still walks the street—at least, his very image, in mind and body" (*HSG* 185).

Partly to legitimate this psychic talent, Hawthorne makes Holgrave a daguerreotypist, so that his ultramodern profession (scarcely a dozen years old by 1851[39]) may "scientifically" supplement the mystical expertise he inherits. His profession is an advantage when it comes time to jettison all Holgrave's shady past and turn him into a gentleman for Phoebe, for a mere vocation can be renounced as a mystic power cannot. This serves to detach him somewhat from his slightly "questionable" role as greedy audience to the tragic drama of the Pyncheon family. Whatever Holgrave's own purposes and loyalties, "pictures never lie"—or as he puts it, the daguerreotype "brings out the secret character with a truth that no painter would ever venture upon." Thus he is not guilty of the sin of the painter of "The Prophetic Pictures," and his prying into the secrets of his subjects is in no way responsible for their living up to his discoveries.

Other aspects of the story display similarities to "The Prophetic Pictures." At one point, for example, the difference between Jaffrey's public and private faces is compared with the "vast discrepancy between portraits intended for engraving, and the pencil-sketches that pass from hand to hand, behind the original's back" (*HSG* 122)—an obvious backward glance at "The Prophetic Pictures." And the main plot strand of *The Seven Gables*—the Pyncheon curse—is the same working out of a prophecy by virtue of a living man coming to resemble a portrait. Most interesting of all is the comparison of the two artists, Holgrave and the prophetic painter, both solitary types, more or less friendless as well as homeless, and both able to divine a man's character from his face, even to the extent of being able to predict his fate. Although both are also called to account for unnatural probing into the souls of their subjects, Holgrave is finally cleared of this charge, as we have just seen. In part Holgrave is insulated by his technology, since he cannot be blamed for the "insights" that the sun itself "paints." Even more important is his renunciation of power at the crucial moment—when Phoebe begins to go under his mesmeric spell. The guilt of the artist or scientist lies in his influence on his subjects, not merely in his reading of their inner thoughts and propensities. At least in Holgrave's case, it is only the mesmeric aspect of the "Maule eye" that is evil, and unlike his ancestors, he forbears its use to control the lives of the Pyncheons.

Matthew Maule, on the other hand, indulges his power over Alice to make her do his "grotesque and fantastic bidding." Like the painter of "The Prophetic Pictures," who "pryed into" his subjects' souls so deeply that "he almost regarded them as creations of his own" (*TTT* 179), Maule robs Alice of her "self-control," her will. The traditional power of the Maules to control the dreams of the Pyncheons is extended to Alice's waking life as well—everyday reality becomes for her the world of nightmare and somnambulism. The terms of this dominance—"fantasies," "dreams," "creatures"—suggest the way in which its source, whether physiognomic or mesmeric, lies in the imagination of the artist. Obviously these painters and portrait takers are stand-ins for the author himself. Indeed, Holgrave is a writer as well as a daguerreotypist, and publishes in the very magazines that Hawthorne had written for. The story of "Alice Pyncheon" has two authors, Holgrave and Hawthorne; and if there is "something of the hawk-eye" about Hawthorne, as Lawyer Haynes remarked, there is something of the "Maule eye" about him too.

As we have already observed, according to contemporary psychological theory, the main risk any artist runs is "excessive mental activity," that is, the overstimulation of the imagination. Thus the prophetic painter becomes so involved in the souls of others that he fails "to see the disorder of his own." This is a kind of lunacy, not so different from the more violent madness of his subject, Walter, who at the beginning of the tale is also accused, by his fiancée, of "paint[ing] my face with your own fantasies" (*TTT* 167). In Hawthorne's fiction insanity almost invariably results from the misuse of the imagination. "Keep the imagination sane," was his warning to Sophia when she first broached her interest in mesmerism.

Clifford and Hepzibah represent two extremes of the imagination run wild in *The Seven Gables*. Hepzibah sometimes "appeared to be walking in a dream; or, more truly, the vivid life and reality, assumed by her emotions, made all outward occurrences unsubstantial, like the teasing phantasms of a half-conscious slumber. . . . There is sad confusion, indeed, when the spirit thus flits away into the past, or into the more awful future, or, in any manner, steps across the spaceless boundary betwixt its own region and the actual world" (*HSG* 66-67). Clifford, on the other hand, as a result of his long imprisonment, draws another sort of blank: "With a mysterious and terrible Past, which had annihilated his memory, and a blank Future before him, he had only this visionary and impalpable Now, which, if you once look closely at it, is nothing" (*HSG* 149). Because he has lost his chance at reality, Clifford must live entirely in the imagination. Even this is possible only through the mediation of Phoebe, who "was not an actual fact for him, but the interpretation of all that he had lacked on earth, brought warmly home to his conception; so that this mere symbol or lifelike picture had almost the comfort of reality" (*HSG* 142).

These old "owls" have lived too long in their imaginations, too little among men. Again the point is forced into a physiognomic mold. When Clifford gazes into the bubbling waters of Maule's well, "faces looked upward to him there—beautiful faces, arrayed in bewitching smiles—each momentary face so fair and rosy, and every smile so sunny, that he felt wronged at its departure, until the same flitting witchcraft made a new one. But sometimes he would suddenly cry out—'The dark face gazes at me!'—and be miserable, the whole day afterwards. . . . The truth was, however, that his fancy—reviving faster than his will and judgement, and always stronger than they—created shapes of loveliness that were symbolic of his native character, and now and then a stern and dreadful shape that typified his fate" (*HSG* 154).

Hawthorne's view—a rather curious one for a writer—seems to be that Clifford should renounce the fancies that threaten his sanity, and compound with reality for whatever shreds of solid existence it may offer. Hawthorne apostrophizes Clifford:

> Alas, poor Clifford! You are old, and worn with troubles that ought never to have befallen you. You are partly crazy, and partly imbecile; a ruin, a failure, as almost everybody is—though some in

> less degree, or less perceptibly, than their fellows. Fate has no happiness in store for you; unless your quiet home in the old family residence, with the faithful Hepzibah, and your long summer-afternoons with Phoebe, and these Sabbath festivals with Uncle Venner and the Daguerreotypist, deserve to be called happiness! Why not? If not the thing itself, it is marvellously like it, and the more so for that ethereal and intangible quality, which causes it all to vanish, at too close an introspection. Take it, therefore, while you may. (*HSG* 157-58)

Decisive as this advice may appear, it is easy enough to find passages of seeming opposite tendency. Jaffrey, for example, is criticized for overvaluing the public realities, taking "hold of everything as if it were real" (*HSG* 316). He was apparently not imaginative enough to tell a fiction or a fantasy from the truth, and so he had mistaken Clifford's "fairy tale" of the portrait's secret treasure for a clue to their uncle's supposed hidden wealth. Jaffrey even managed to convince himself that he was a respectable citizen, by scrupulous attention to every outward sign of propriety and social substance. Falling back once again on the physiognomic metaphor, Hawthorne accuses him of painting his own portrait in false colors. He asks ironically, "what room could possibly be found for darker traits, in a portrait made up of lineaments like these! This proper face was what he beheld in the looking-glass. This admirably arranged life was what he was conscious of, in the progress of every day. Then, might not he claim to be its result and sum, and say to himself and the community—'Behold Judge Pyncheon, there'?" (*HSG* 231). If Hepzibah "needed a walk along the noonday street, to keep her sane" (*HSG* 59), and if Clifford ought to avoid "too close an introspection" into his own state of mind, Jaffrey seems to require opposite counsel—he is too much involved in worldly matters, and not introspective enough. But of course this too is a failure of the imagination, though of a different sort from Hepzibah or Clifford's delusions.

Where does this leave the artists, Holgrave and Hawthorne? The lesson seems to be that all uses of the imagination are dangerous, whether as a tool of art or as a means of coping with everyday reality. In one sense, then, it is perfectly reasonable for Holgrave to break his wand like Prospero at the end of the novel, and retire to a quiet life in the country—living off the Pyncheon estates! Like the characters in the earliest tales—Roger Malvin, the narrator of "The Vision of the Fountain," or M. Miroir—Holgrave is pushed toward a self-recognition—one that would surely involve Hawthorne as well. What does Ethan Brand see in the Wandering Jew's "diorama"? Is it not a picture similar to the images of "Fancy's Show-Box," in which "Mr. Smith was invariably haunted by his own lineaments" (TTT 224), just as Clifford gazes at the imaginary faces in Maule's well, reflecting only his own mind, confused and bedazzled? One sees oneself in these mirrors of consciousness.

Holgrave begins to understand, in his tale of his ancestor and Alice, and so he avoids a similar outcome for himself and Phoebe. But he carries his recognition no further; the implications for art itself are dodged. The conclusion to "Fancy's Show-Box" is more frank. There the case of Mr. Smith and his life of guilty though unacted desires is explicitly compared to that of the author:

> A scheme of guilt, till it be put in execution, greatly resembles a train of incidents in a projected tale. The latter, in order to produce a sense of reality in the reader's mind, must be conceived with such proportionate strength by the author as to seem, in the glow of fancy, more like truth, past, present, or to come, than purely fiction. The prospective sinner, on the other hand, weaves his plot of crime, but seldom or never feels a perfect certainty that it will be executed. There is a dreaminess diffused about his thoughts; in a dream, as it were, he strikes the death-blow into his victim's heart, and starts to find an indelible blood-stain on his hand. Thus a novel-writer, or a dramatist, in creating a villain of romance, and fitting him with evil deeds, and the villain of actual life, in projecting crimes that will be perpetrated, may almost meet each other, half-way between reality and fancy. (*TTT* 225-226)

Hawthorne goes on to say hopefully that only enacted evil is truly sinful, thus absolving the artist of his guilty imaginings. Yet his final word in this sketch is admonitory: "Man must not disclaim his brotherhood, even with the guiltiest, since, though his hand be clean, his heart has surely been polluted by the flitting phantoms of iniquity" (*TTT* 226). One wishes he had been able to take his novels more openly into the territory he so often claimed for them in his prefaces, "half-way between reality and fancy." *The Seven Gables,* for example, would have benefited from a more sophisticated version of the ending of "The Great Stone Face," one that would explore the discovery that the artist is his own subject and paints his own fate. As we have already seen in our discussion of Holgrave as a mesmerist, the conception he needed lay unused in Hawthorne's notebooks:

> A person to be writing a tale, and to find that it shapes itself against his intentions; that the characters act otherwise than he thought; that unforeseen events occur; and a catastrophe comes which he strives in vain to avert. It might shadow forth his own fate,—he having made himself one of the personages. (*AN* 16)

Much of Hawthorne's fiction seems to consist in attempts to avoid writing this story, to turn away at the last moment from his own countenance as it stared up at him from the page.

Four

Homoeopathy

> "You're dying now," says Una, "so you must lie still." "I shall walk, if I'm dying," answers Julian; whereupon he gets up, and stumps about the room with heavy step. Meantime, Una lies down on the couch, and is again grandmamma, stretching out her hand, in search of some tender grasp, to assure herself that she is still on the hither side of the grave. All of a sudden, Julian is Dr. Pearson, and Una is apparently mamma, receiving him, and making excuses for not ushering him into the sick-chamber. Here ensues a long talk about the patient's condition, and symptoms. Una tells the Doctor plainly, that she thinks we had better have Dr. Cummins, whereupon, Doctor Pearson replies, "We can't have any more talking. I must go!" The next instant, Una transforms him into Dr. Cummins—one of the greatest miracles that was ever performed, this instantaneous conversion from allopathy to homeopathy.(*AN* 431- 32)

HAWTHORNE WROTE this description of his children playing "doctor" in his jounal for July 30, 1849. The next day his mother died in the room where she had kept to herself so long, the most reclusive of a family that knew how to appreciate a closed door. Though he "did not expect to be much moved at the time," Hawthorne found himself sobbing at his mother's bedside; it was, he said, "the darkest hour I ever lived" (*AN* 429); yet, in the midst of these scenes of sorrow and death, he had an ear for the voices of his children merrily imitating the follies of the sickroom. The contrast was precisely in Hawthorne's mode.

Something of Una's impishness in grave contexts enlivens the behavior of Pearl in *The Scarlet Letter,* the novel that Hawthorne began shortly after his mother's death. Hawthorne often found his eldest child a bit eerie (see *AN* 270, 551-52), in much the way that Hester and Dimmesdale are struck by their daughter's quirkiness. Still more interesting—though no such easy line of connection can be drawn—is the appearance in *The Scarlet Letter* of a medical practitioner whose bedside manner owes something to the homoeopathic controversies that Una and Julian mimicked in their play. Hawthorne's conception of Roger Chillingworth, the sinister old alchemist-turned-physician of seventeenth-century Boston, has much in common with the nineteenth-century pseudoscientists who were making such a fuss over the proper gathering and purification of their drugs, and whose successful cures seemed to have an air of "modern necromancy" about them.

Chillingworth was a prototype of the homoeopathist, not only in his patient researches into the virtues of the herbs he collected in the forest, but also in his insistence on treating Dimmesdale's peculiar disease at its sources: "A bodily disease, which we look upon as whole and entire within itself, may, after all, be but a symptom of some ailment in the spiritual part" (*SL* 136). His counterpart in Hawthorne's day likewise attempted to treat the whole man, body and soul. Hahnemann's *Organon of the Art of Healing,* the homoeopathist's bible, made no distinction between "that morbidly altered, spirit-like dynamis (vital force) animating our body, and residing unseen in its interior, and the complex of externally perceptible symptoms caused by that power in the organism, and representing the actual disease." According to homoeopathy they "constitute a whole—one and the same."[1]

Although Chillingworth thus recognizes the necessity for the physician to take both body and soul into account in prescribing for his patient, he uses this knowledge in Dimmesdale's case only to destroy him, to set body and soul at war with one another. When Chillingworth claims that without his medicinal aid Dimmesdale would have succumbed to his ailment long ago (*SL* 171), he hides the true nature of his treatment: his medicines and counsels constituted a "secret poison" through which his patient's "conscience had been kept in an irritated state, the tendency of which was, not to cure by wholesome pain, but to disorganize and corrupt his spiritual being" (*SL* 193). Though his ethics are therefore in question, once again

Chillingworth's therapeutics are quite in line with the doctines of nineteenth-century homoeopathy: his avoidance of the stringencies of ordinary medicine—the lancet, the bolus, the purgative, all of which were part of Puritan as well as nineteenth-century allopathic orthodoxy—in favor of the subtler and more artful palliatives available in a new pharmacopia of poisons—belladonna, wolfsbane, hemlock, poison oak, and the like, administered in dilutions whose efficacy was in dispute.

It remains to be seen whether Hawthorne was taking sides in the great dispute between the allopaths and the homoeopaths—medical traditionalists vs. the "irregulars" and reformers. When he speaks of "wholesome pain," he surely has something different in mind than the famous Magendie, who argued against anesthetics on the grounds that pain was the healthy body's defense, or the "school doctors" like David M. Reese, who believed that blistering, cupping, and bloodletting were among the most potent resources in the physician's black bag. Significant as such questions might be, Hawthorne's interest was in something else. As he put it in his journal, he wished to explore the notion of a "physician for the cure of moral diseases" (*AN* 235). Chillingworth was an example of the problems of medical ethics entailed in such a conception. What is the responsibility of the physician? "Who art thou," Dimmesdale demands, "that dares thrust himself between the sufferer and his God?" (*SL* 137). Of such questions homoeopathy had little to say. Nonetheless, a careful examination of the nature of homoeopathic doctrine and of Hawthorne's own contacts with both homoeopathic and allopathic doctors will tell us a surprising amount about Chillingworth and his fellow physicians, apothecaries, and mad scientists.

Homoeopathy was one of the *Humbugs of New-York* pilloried in David Reese's book—a "stupendous humbug" that "might fitly be included in the chapter devoted to quackery, yet because of the prominence it has attained, the prodigious pretensions it has set up, deserves to be singled out for separate animadversion."[2] Why, the allopathic Dr. Reese asked himself, have the homoeopathists become so popular? First of all was the gullibility of "the multitude," the foundation of every humbug in Reese's rogue's gallery. "Add to this the popular prejudice against *mercury,* by reason of its empirical abuse, and the outcry made against *bleeding* by the Thomsonians, who with their illustrious master most sagely argue, that 'if God

Almighty intended any blood to be taken out of the human body, he would have left an opening somewhere on the surface for the purpose, and a cork to stop it.'"[3] Such fads, Reese maintained, could appeal only to the ignorant. "Familiar with the potency and success of his lancet in subduing a pleurisy or frenzy, and having proven by numerous examples in himself and others the innocence and safety of a depletion," no competent allopathic physician would be fooled for a moment by the claims of the upstart homoeopaths.[4]

Of course Dr. Reese was partly right, though not in the way he thought. Much of the success of the new practice was simply due to the unwillingness of the homoeopaths to bleed their patients to death or to poison them with "heroic" doses of calomel (mercurous chloride) and other fatal remedies, the standbys of physicians since Chillingworth's time.[5] As Hawthorne caused a character in *The Seven Gables* to say, "We are sick of Dead Men's diseases, physical and moral, and die of the same remedies with which dead doctors killed their patients!" (*HSG* 183). Any medical doctrine that merely abstained from a few such murderous therapies would quickly gain a reputation for a higher rate of cure than its competitors. According to Oliver Wendell Holmes, who had come to his own reckoning with the new practitioners in *Homoeopathy and its Kindred Delusions* (1842), all or nearly all the successes of homoeopathy were negative in precisely this way. "Suppose then a physician who has a hundred patients prescribes to each of them pills made of some entirely inert substance, as starch, for instance.—Ninety of them get well, or if he chooses to use such language, he cures ninety of them. It is evident according to the doctrine of chances, that there must be a considerable number of coincidences between the relief of the patient and the administration of the remedy."[6] *Natura sanat,* and if a homoeopathist happened to have dispensed one of his "microscopic sugar-plums" at the right time, the credit would go to him.

In the medical context of 1842—before asepsis, before anesthesia, before any systematic pathology of disease—the safest treatment for almost any illness was to do nothing. If a new school combined some good advice with its placebos—counseling cleanliness, or temperance, or fresh air and exercise—success was assured. One after another—Thomsonianism, Eclecticism, Hydropathy—opposed venesection and "dosing" and substituted their own, usually less harmful concoctions along with homely wisdom about diet and hygiene. Homoeopathy was the most popular of these competing medical reforms.

Like its sister sciences mesmerism and phrenology, homoeopathic medicine was the discovery of a single man—Samuel Hahnemann. And like so many of the new doctrines (here one thinks of Priessnitz and Jahn as well as Mesmer, Gall, and Lavater), homoeopathy's native tongue was German and its early adherents were Central Europeans. By 1819 it was important enough to be banned in Vienna, as phrenology had been a dozen years earlier, and animal magnetism before that. The first immigrant homoeopath arrived in New York City about 1825, and as with other pseudoscientific imports, there were soon more practitioners and enthusiasts in the United States than in any European country.[7] There were American editions of Hahnemann's *Organon* in 1836, 1843, and 1848, and an edition of the *Lesser Writings* in 1852. The *Index-Catalogue of the Library of the Surgeon General of the United States Army* lists seventeen separate journals devoted to homoeopathy between 1840 and 1860, and well over 100 separate books and pamphlets published in this country during the same period. Hahnemann's star continued to rise in the United States until the end of the century, when it was estimated that sixteen homoeopathic medical schools had produced some twelve thousand practicing physicians.[8]

Among the early believers in homoeopathy was Dr. Nathaniel Peabody, father of Hawthorne's future wife. Dr. Peabody had begun his career as a schoolteacher, but after his marriage he took up medicine, and ultimately dentistry. (As a boy Hawthorne himself is said to have been treated by him for lameness, but this would have been long before his conversion to homoeopathy. Perhaps he was the doctor who recommended pouring cold water on Hawthorne's foot from a second-story window; if so, he was an embryonic hydropath as well as a homoeopath.[9]) Dr. Peabody's son Nathaniel followed in his father's footsteps, setting up shop as a homoeopathic druggist, for a time in the same rooms as his father's office. An allopathic view of medical ethics might regard this doctor-and-pharmacist family relationship as a bit too cozy, but it was well within the limits of good homoeopathic practice. Indeed, every homoeopathist might properly be expected to serve as his own druggist, in imitation of Hahnemann, who found that he could not trust conventional pharmacists to give him honest drugs, let alone drugs triturated and diluted to their correct homoeopathic potencies.

Homoeopathic theory in fact was largely devoted to the description of drugs and to the rationale for their selection, preparation, and administration. The guiding principle of its elaborate pharmacopia was *similia similibus curantur* (like cures like), an insight that had come to Hahnemann in 1790 when he discovered that doses of quinine produced intermittent fever in his healthy body, the very symptom that it cured in malaria or Roman fever. On this and a few other seminal examples, such as inoculation for smallpox, the entire *materia medica* of homoeopathy was founded.

An immediate corollary was the "proving" of drugs, testing out their virtues by administering doses to healthy subjects and noting any changes in their physical or mental states. Typically, proving was done in the family. Hahnemann used himself and his wife and children to ascertain the powers of substances like hensbane, sumach, and ipecacuanha root.[10] Most doses were too small to do any harm, but at least one homoeopathist was charged with manslaughter in the early 1860s, when he gave thirty-five drops of tincture of gelseminum (yellow jasmine) as a proving, and his subject died an hour and a half later.[11]

It is not recorded that Dr. Peabody or his son the druggist ever proved their medicines on anybody, but Sophia Peabody's medical history had plenty of shocking experimentation in it, though not perpetrated by homoeopaths. As an infant Sophia had been given allopathic doses of paregoric during her particularly difficult teething. From his later homoeopathic vantage point Dr. Peabody regretted the measure. He feared the sedative had contributed to the general debility of her adolescence, and especially to the chronic headaches that developed when she was fifteen.[12] For a long time after this she was in the clutches of Boston allopaths, who, "one after another, tried their hands at curing her." As her sister Elizabeth recalled years later, "she went through courses of their poisons, each one bringing her to death's door, and leaving her less able to cope with the pain they did not reach. But the endurance of her physical constitution defied all the poisons of the *materia medica,* mercury, arsenic, opium, hyoscyamus, and all."[13] It is not surprising that in her adult life Sophia was a steadfast believer in the infinitesimal doses of the homoeopathists—not for the sake of her father or brother so much as herself.

The typical dose recommended by Hahnemann was a "dynamization" raised to "the 30th potency"; that is, "two drops of fresh vegetable juice mixed with an equal proportion of alcohol, are diluted with 98 drops of alcohol, and potentiated by two succusions of the hand; this is the first development of power (potency). The same process is then to be repeated with 29 successive vials, each vial to contain 99 drops of alcohol, filling three-quarters of the vial; this second vial is then to be shaken twice, and so on to the 30th development of power; this is the potentiated decillion-fold dilution, and the one to be commonly used."[14] If such a subtle dose was unlikely to do much good, at least it was equally unlikely to do much harm. For an ailment like Sophia's, there was probably nothing better than a well-trusted placebo—unless it might be mesmeric passes, the efficacy of which Hahnemann was early to endorse, explaining that the process "acts in part homoeopathically."[15]

These were the primary rules of homoeopathic pharmacology: Drugs were to be derived from pure ingredients, animal, vegetable, and mineral—often from substances regarded as poison in ordinary quantities. Their potencies, which grew stronger, not weaker, through dilution, were to be carefully controlled by the doctor; the average dose was infinitesimally smaller than an allopathic pill. The virtues of each drug were to be ascertained by experimentally proving its effects on healthy subjects. The matching of remedy to illness was to be made on the principle of similarity of symptoms; a drug was prescribed in each case that would produce a simulacrum of the disease in a healthy body.

In addition, the homoeopathist did not accept the traditional names or classifications of disease. During the later years of his career Hahnemann ascribed all illness to three underlying or "primary maladies"—syphilis, sycosis, and psora—of which the third, "the itch," was held responsible for seven-eighths of all chronic disease. The problem, he explained, was not so much the disease itself as the suppression of its ordinary symptoms by allopathic treatment, thus producing the great variety and virulence of symptoms gone "underground" and erupting in apparently unrelated ways elsewhere in the system. Few of Hahnemann's followers accepted this doctrine; his earlier insistence on the uniqueness of every case of disease remained the rule for American homoeopaths. In this insistence Hahnemann had done a service to medicine, for pathology had not yet approached a reliable nosology, and the hypotheses that held sway in school medicine—"repletion" "depletion," "aggravations," "constipations," "fevers" and "consumptions"—were as mythical as any pseudoscientific dogma of "the itch." Hahnemann thrust aside all such "falsely empiric" notions: "diseases are never to be discerned or cured according to the similarity of names which refer to single symptoms, but in conformity with the totality of every symptom of the particular condition peculiar to each patient, whose suffering must be accurately investigated, but never hypothetically assumed."[18]

This new concern for the individual patient and his unique illness gave much greater weight to the sufferer's own account of his symptoms. Here, for example, is a fictional report of a homoeopathic interview which purportedly took place in New England at mid-century; although part of a larger burlesque, the general outlines of this excerpt are accurate, and not only show homoeopathy "in practice" but also indicate, in the diagnosis which follows, something of its relation with other pseudosciences:

> Her exact age was first marked; then the peculiarities of her constitution, as they had been revealed from birth to the present time, were elicited. An account of her habits of life was also demanded. The homoeopathist was evidently a close observer. He noticed, with a critical eye, the configuration of the head, and the general physical organization of his patient. Then, the kinds of food that best suited her palate were discussed, and the various effects which each article produced. By turns, the German mentioned the brain, the nerves, the spine, the lungs, the heart, etc.; made sundry investigations, and learned as well as he could, the condition of each organ, and the state of its functions.[17]

The subject of this examination, Miss Delia Thornton, is what later physicians were to call "neurasthenic," and the homoeopathist here consulted is merely one in a long line of *Delia's Doctors*—allopaths, homoeopaths, hydropaths, mesmerists, and so on—with whose advice and prescriptions the young lady is never satisfied. The homoeopathic Dr. Liston, for example, loses her confidence when he forbids all her favorite foods—limes, pickles, currants, lemonade, honey, coffee, tea, pastry, hard-boiled eggs, pork, figs, raisins, spices and condiments, eels, clams, oysters, lobsters, and so on. But the final straw for Delia is the discovery of Dr. Liston's notes on her case, written in phonographic script (which one of the other characters in the novel obligingly translates):

> Size of the head, full. Temperament, a combination of the nervous and the lymphatic. The latter predominant. The former developed by circumstances. Much revealed by the organs of the head, more than by her answers. Perceptive faculties better developed than the reflective. Appearance of the head singular, from the unusual prominence of some organs, and the defective size of others. *Combativeness* wanting, hardly force enough to resist either disease or danger. *Alimentiveness* excessive for a young lady. *Firmness,* minus. *Hope,* ditto. *Individuality,* very prominent. *Form,* so prominent that the distance between the eyes is quite startling. A striking, but not a good head. Figure, too slender for health or beauty. No definite disease, but a general want of tone to the system. Pulse, weak; complexion, inclining to sallow; manner of speaking, languid; expression of countenance, listless. Needs some incitement to mental and bodily action, rather than any course of medicine. So feeble, however, has the frame been rendered by bad habits, that some medicine is needed. Tendency to incipient diseases must also be counteracted by the application of remedies. Tedious case in perspective.
>
> Delia Thornton, nineteen years, three months.[18]

This parody—by Salem schoolteacher Hannah G. Creamer—is remarkably true to its orginals. Delia is not much more than a frilly excuse for the satire, yet if one imagines a more authentic type as the patient—say Sophia Peabody—the phrenological jargon, the homoeopathic emphasis on diet and general health, even the transcription of the diagnosis in phonography, will all ring absolutely true. This was a typical melange of pseudoscience as it tended to combine in the United States, and Miss Creamer merely pushes it gently to the edge of folly.

Even in satire, though the means by which Dr. Liston arrived at his diagnosis are scarcely trustworthy, still the character reading itself is presented as accurate enough. Similar cases occurred outside fiction. What is most significant is not the accuracy, but the fact that character reading played so large a part in a medical diagnosis. This was the specifically homoeopathic contribution to Delia's case, and it is to the author's credit that she understood the medical scene well enough to recognize what many professional observers missed.

It was appropriate that phrenology be linked with homoeopathy in such a context, for these two were the pseudosciences that most insisted on regarding disease from a moral or psychological as well as a physiological perspective. According to the phrenologists the brain was the organ of the mind, subject to disease like any other part of the body. They maintained that a person could not be held responsible for the effects of "moral insanity" any more than for the results of smallpox. As one hostile commentator put it, phrenology considered crime "a physiological malady, cured by dietetic regimen, treated in hospitals and asylums, soothed into repentance with music, and flowers, and fetes, instead of whips and prisons and gallows."[19] This was the beginning of psychotherapy in America.

Homoeopathy came at the same problem from the other side. It too maintained that most of "the so-called diseases of the mind are in reality bodily diseases," but where the phrenologist identified psychic disturbance with some malfunction of the brain, the homoeopathist argued that all physical ailments produced some mental aberration. Indeed, Hahnemann claimed that the "effect upon the state of mind and disposition is the principal feature of all diseases." In many cases "a slight degree of mental disturbance is enlarged into the main symptom, which henceforth serves as a substitute for the rest of the physical symptoms, and palliates their violence."[20]

Ultimately this view was at odds with the more familiar psychosomatic theory of phrenology and later psychiatry. Yet Hahnemann also recognized some mental diseases of nonbodily origin. For the majority of cases he recommended homoeopathic medicines, since they were merely disguised physical illnesses; for the few genuinely mental disturbances, he advised "psychical treatment; gentleness, kind admonition, appeals to reason," and so on.[21] He was one of the first advocates of humane treatment of the insane, and was himself the proprietor of a small experimental sanitarium (he had but one patient) where all the rules of enlightened care could be seen in successful operation decades before the advent of "moral treatment" in conventional asylums.[22] In the *Organon* Hahnemann gave his principles for the handling of mental cases (including those of physiological origin): "Raving madness should be met by calm fearlessness and firmness of will; painfully plaintive melancholy should be soothed by silent compassion conveyed by gestures and expression of countenance; silly loquacity should be listened to in silence, but with some degree of attention; indecent behavior and obscene language are to be treated with indifference. The destruction and injury of objects should be simply prevented by placing them out of reach, *without reproaching the patient for his conduct;* furthermore, the treatment should be conducted with a view to the absolute avoidance of corporeal punishment or torture."[23] All this is most enlightened, and it is curious to find it in combination with the dogmatic belief that in most mental cases, minute doses of belladonna, aconite, or hyoscyanus would ultimately effect a cure.[24] If phrenology was the beginning of psychotherapy, homoeopathy was an early prototype of chemotherapy.

It is ironic that these two, among so many medical pseudosciences, should prove most attentive to the subjective condition of their patients, for no doctrines could be more materialistically inclined in their initial premises than phrenology and homoeopathy. The phrenologist's obsession with the cranium parallels the homoeopathist's fetishism of drugs. Yet in practice both were known for their intuitive understanding of the psychological dimension of disease. Even their opponents felt obliged to account for the success of their practice while despising their theory. As we have seen, Oliver Wendell Holmes attributed homoeopathic cures to the placebo, which let nature take its course, aided by the faith of the patient. Not that he approved of such methods, but he recognized the component of psychological medicine in them and in the "kindred delusions" of quackery. Similarly, he winnowed the chaff out of phrenology: "Its maps of the surface of the head are, I feel sure, founded on a delusion, but its studies of individual character are always interesting and instructive."[25] Of course it was just this combination of material means and transcendental ends that made the pseudosciences so popular in the United States. Nothing could have suited the national temperament better.

ii

As a writer of romance, Hawthorne had special need for emblems of the sort that homoeopathy and its kindred delusions provided the masses. Mesmerism gave him a symbol of practical, "scientific" power brought to bear on the human spirit; phrenology and physiognomy offered a method of reading character, and even fate, in the physical human countenance. Although he could not use homoeopathy so boldly as he did these others—for it would have been indelicate to make free with the profession of his wife's father and brother—nonetheless he found ways of incorporating many details of homoeopathic lore and practice into his work.

A particularly striking example is *The Scarlet Letter,* in which Roger Chillingworth anachronistically borrows homoeopathic techniques to treat both body and soul of his patient Arthur Dimmesdale. The very title of the book refers, among other things, to Dimmesdale's bizarre psychosomatic complaint, at once a physical symptom and a literary emblem of the spiritual source of his disease. His physician, like the homoeopathist of Hawthorne's day, lays stress on the patient's full report of his symptoms and of the state of his soul. And the curative methods that Chillingworth applies to his case, though their precise nature is hidden from us, are clearly derived from arcane pharmacological researches not unlike those of Hahnemann and his disciples.

Even in Puritan New England it was possible to be a doctrinaire physician. Chillingworth is apparently a follower of Galen rather than Paracelsus—that is, a believer in botanical rather than chemical drugs.[28] Although trained in a German university (*SL* 121) and expert in alchemy as well as medicine (*SL* 75), Chillingworth seems to prefer herbal remedies to the mineral "miracle drugs" that were coming into vogue during the last half of the seventeenth century. True, he mentions Parcelsus favorably (*SL* 72) and his laboratory apparatus is designed for chemical as well as botanical concoction (*SL* 126), but the emphasis is clearly laid on the herbs and roots that he gathers in the forest and prepares, it is hinted, according to primitive recipes acquired from "medicine men" during his Indian captivity (*SL* 70-72, 119-21, 131). Hawthorne does not attempt to draw any analogy between the botanical/chemical rivalry of the seventeenth century and the homoeopathic/allopathic antagonisms of the nineteenth, but he does make it plain that Chillingworth was a recreant from "school medicine" in his high estimation of Indian remedies. In a contemporary setting, this bias would have been homoeopathic—for the allopaths swore by mercury and other Paracelsian panaceas, while their opponents favored botanical drugs. But for Hawthorne's literary purposes that is neither here nor there. His aim was simply to characterize Chillingworth as learned, and as unorthodox in his learning. This sets the stage for the revelation of Dimmesdale's ailment, far more esoteric than any technique Chillingworth has of treating it. It also establishes Chillingworth as another of Hawthorne's "mad scientists," whose delving into forbidden knowledge—he "had enlarged his medical attainments by joining in the incantations of the savage priests" (*SL* 127)—is punished by the loss of his soul.

This Faustian motif is explored as the relationship between Chillingworth and Dimmesdale unfolds. The physician's prying into his patient's conscience and unearthing his secret guilt, again repeats the pattern Hawthorne called "the unpardonable sin"—"a want of love and reverence for the Human Soul; in consequence of which, the investigator pried into its dark depths, not with a hope of making it better, but from a cold philosophical curiosity" (*AN* 251). "A rare case!" Chillingworth muses over his victim's condition, "I must needs look deeper into it. A strange sympathy betwixt soul and body! Were it only for the art's sake, I must search the matter to the bottom" (*SL* 138). Thus Chillingworth—whose primary motive had been revenge—becomes so dehumanized by his experiments with Dimmesdale's sick conscience that he forfeits his own "human heart" and becomes "a fiend" (*SL* 172). When he discovers the scarlet letter on Dimmesdale's breast, his "ghastly rapture" exactly mimicks that of Satan "when a precious human soul is lost to heaven, and won into his kingdom" (*SL* 138).

The pattern, whether on this grand scale or in the details of Chillingworth's medical research, leaves no doubt that Hawthorne disapproved of his "physician for the cure of moral diseases." However humanitarian it might appear at the outset, that ambition invariably ended in mischief—the "separation of the intellect from the heart" (*AN* 251). Chillingworth had once been studious of his art, not for revenge nor out of "cold philosophical curiosity," but "for the advancement of human welfare" (*SL* 172). As Hawthorne was fond of pointing out, "from the very gate of heaven, there is a by-way to the pit!" (*BR* 243). This was part of his attitude toward pseudoscience, especially those doctrines that prided themselves on their philanthropic intentions. Sometimes a secret motive lurked among the flowers of altruism, as in the case of a Doctor Grimshawe; sometimes the pursuit of human improvement or perfection seemed to harbor the seed of evil in its very goal, as with Aylmer's ambition in "The Birthmark," or Doctor Dolliver's quest in *The Dolliver Romance.*

Of course there is more to *The Scarlet Letter* than Chillingworth's sinister nursing of the soul-sick minister. Hester and Pearl have their places in the story as well. Yet however much they dominate the scenes, the plot revolves around "the leech and his patient." A central chapter of the book is given that title, surely with awareness of the literal meaning of the term applied to Chillingworth—who, though he does not bleed his patient, sucks him dry nonetheless. Through most of the novel Hester is merely a horrified bystander, watching her lover grow pale and sickly while Chillingworth looms to gothic proportions, an Ethan Brand or Dr. Rappaccini of Puritan times.

The structural centrality of Chillingworth in *The Scarlet Letter* is in large part a function of the role he plays as spy on Dimmesdale's secret guilt. Since the emergence of this guilt into the light of day constitutes the plot of the novel, Chillingworth holds a privileged position in the narrative, not a protagonist but an evil chorus figure whose perspective has much in common with that of the reader and the author. His nearest analogues in Hawthorne's other novels are not the villains, Judge Pyncheon or Professor Westervelt, but the outsiders and onlookers, Holgrave and Coverdale. These are the author surrogates in the other novels, and it is interesting to think of Chillingworth in a similar light, as a facet of Hawthorne's authorial consciousness.

Perhaps all of Hawthorne's mad scientists and evil doctors can best be understood as projections of his own pervasive artist guilt. Like Chillingworth they are all plotters and connivers, attempting to snare others in their webs of cause and effect. Dr. Rappaccini makes Giovanni the subject of one of his experiments and Dr. Baglioni plots a counterexperiment. Dr. Heidegger plays a rather literary trick on his friends, then sits back to watch them in their illusory roles. "The Haunted Quack" imagines himself into his mentor's practice. Doctor Grimshawe is a "dark, subtle manager, for the love of managing, like a spider sitting in the centre of his web" (*DGS* 122). Dr. Portsoaken schemes Septimius Felton's death. Dr. Dolliver, as he becomes progressively younger, develops the tendency "to make matter of observation of everything," until like Chillingworth "he finds himself growing to be a devil by force of solitude and long life" (*LP* 126). All these figures are veiled artists, manipulating others as a novelist controls his characters and their interactions. Grimshawe is perhaps the clearest example, for he not only plots a revenge, like Chillingworth, but actually fabricates a plausible story to accomplish it—the false genealogy of young Etherege. Sitting in his Salem study, he contrives the events of the story that will go forward in England—the "self-imprisonment" of his old enemy, the machinations of his henchman Hammond, the ambitions of Etherege himself—until finally "they are set at liberty by the death of the magician who originally enthralled them" (*DGS* 164; cf. 125, 150).

Most of these doctors originally meant to benefit others, not to harm them, by their experiments and plots. Their objectives are typically humanitarian—a "magic clue by which mankind was to be rescued from all its errors" (*DGS* 45), "a way to clear disease out of the world" (*LP* 133), "the reformation of the world, . . . war, intemperance, slavery, all manner of crime brought to an end" (*LP* 112). Like Chillingworth's ambition, these rosy ideals quickly fade in practice.

Hawthorne frequently complained that his romances turned out darker and gloomier than he planned, just as these altruistic careers issue in sin. Again *Doctor Grimshawe's Secret* offers a beautifully detailed example. In its several sketches and drafts one may watch the whole process by which Hawthorne's sunnier intentions were slowly eclipsed by his deeper pessimism. Grimshawe first appears as a genial old man, shuffling and a bit daffy, the perfect companion for the two children who are his wards. But with these premises the story will not flow; again and again the characters must be reconsidered, the plot doctored and revised. By the time Hawthorne gave up the novel in frustration, Grimshawe had become a brandy-soaked monster of intrigue and vengeance, using his wards as mere instruments in his evil plot. His beloved spider webs, which initially were to provide a panacea for humanity, end up a symbol of his perversion—"making tissues of cobweb out of men's life-threads"—while the "great spider shall be an emblem of the Doctor himself . . . the one . . . growing more swollen with spite and the other with venom" (*DGS* 122-23). Thus vanished the more cheerful, humanitarian mood of both character and author.

Why, it should be asked, did Hawthorne so often fix on doctors and scientists for his models of such patterns of disintegration and sin? The literature of his day tended, if anything, to idealize the physician, concentrating on his eligibility as a husband for spirited but impoverished heroines. To attempt an answer to this question, it may be useful to look more carefully at one of Hawthorne's closest approaches to such a romantic plot, "The Birthmark," where Aylmer's experiment is performed on his own bride, out of his desire to perfect her already considerable charms.

Of all these mad scientists, Aylmer is perhaps the least reproachable for his motives, the least guilty of the unpardonable sin. His whole life has been devoted to lofty scientific ideals, and even his frantic desire to rid Georgiana of her birthmark may be supposed admirable on the face of it, an obsession with perfection.

His motives are not so pure as he thinks. "I feel myself fully competent to render this dear cheek as faultless as its fellow," he tells Georgiana; "and then, most beloved, what will be my triumph, when I shall have corrected what Nature left imperfect, in her fairest work!" (*MOM* 41). There is hubris here. And in the crucial moments of his experiment, Aylmer reveals once again that his ambition is stronger than his love. As he sits by Georgiana's side, "watching her aspect with the emotions proper to a man, the whole value of whose existence was involved in the process now to be tested," he does not fail to take note of "the minutest symptom" and record it in his book of experiments, "the history and emblem of his ardent, ambitious, imaginative, yet practical and laborious, life" (*MOM* 49, 54). The irony needs no further underlining.

Up until his marriage to Georgiana, Aylmer has spent his life filling that "large folio" with descriptions of his experiments; his "brightest years" have been passed in "recondite pursuits" in his laboratory (*MOM* 44). He entertains Georgiana with the fruits of some of his labors—a magic lantern show, a camera obscura, a daguerreotype—all mere illusions, it may be observed, rather than substantial accomplishments. Still another exhibition is even more ominous. Aylmer displays "a small crystal globe, containing a gold-colored liquid," so beautiful that Georgiana wonders if it might be "the Elixir of Life." Aylmer explains that the liquid is a powerful poison, yet in minute doses it has a "virtuous potency," the ability to remove freckles "as easily as the hands are cleansed." Georgiana asks if this is the medicine to be applied to her birthmark; Aylmer answers darkly that it is too "superficial" a remedy for her case (*MOM* 47). When the time comes, of course, it is a similar elixir that fulfills the threat implied: Georgiana drinks, the birthmark fades, but with it she too perishes. Aylmer's drug—it was also a liquor "bright enough to be the draught of immortality" (*MOM* 53)—has proved a poison rather than a panacea.

It is significant that Aylmer's means of treating Georgiana should be pharmaceutical. Both the method and the terminology of his earlier exhibition, the cosmetic poison, are almost certainly derived from homoeopathy. In their raw state all homoeopathic drugs, even those manufactured from the most innocent herbs, were considered poisons. Allopaths like Oliver Wendell Holmes were agreed that certain substances—smallpox vaccine for instance—owed their homoeopathic-like efficacy in minute doses to their character as "morbid poison," but in their view this was a special category, comprising but a few cases.[27] Hahnemann *defined* medicines as "artificial morbific potencies."[28] "Potency" is also the term that Hahnemann used to name the virtue that his medicines acquired when diluted sufficiently for therapeutic purposes. Thus Aylmer's phrase "virtuous potency," though redundant, is homoeopathically precise.

Moreover, just before explaining the powers of his crystal globe of poison, Aylmer shows Georgiana a small vial of perfume, "gentle yet . . . capable of impregnating all the breezes that blow across a kingdom" (*MOM* 47). This juxtaposition with the homoeopathic poison may be accidental, but it is worth recalling that, after the comparison with vaccines, the favorite analogy adduced in defense of extreme dilutions was to this very property of some substances to diffuse their odors over surprisingly great expanses. This argument too was popular enough to draw fire from Holmes in *Homoeopathy and its Kindred Delusions,* so it was quite possibly known to Hawthorne.[29]

There is even reason to think that Holmes' spartisan tract may itself have contributed something to "The Birthmark," and that Hawthorne's paired references to the vial of perfume and the globe of poison were his muted way of acknowledging the debt. The first edition of *Homoeopathy and its Kindred Delusions* appeared early in 1842; Hawthorne wrote "The Birthmark" during the last half of January 1843, and it was published in March. At the time Holmes's pamphlet caused no little stir in medical circles. By the end of 1842 three replies to it were already in print. One of these was by Dr. Robert Wesselhoeft, who seems to have been the Peabody family physician (Dr. Peabody having completely abandoned medicine for dentistry).[30] Thus it is possible that Hawthorne had heard of *Homoeopathy and its Kindred Delusions* through acquaintance with its critic if not its author (his friendship with Holmes dates from a later period, when they were summer neighbors in the Berkshires).

If Hawthorne was tempted to read Holmes's essay, he must have paid special attention to an early section, devoted not to homoeopathy but to "Perkins metallic tractors," a pseudoscientific craze that had developed about the turn of the century and was now quite defunct. The "tractors," as Holmes describes them, were "two pieces of metal, one apparently iron and the other brass, about three inches long, blunt at one end and pointed at the other. These instruments were applied for the cure of different complaints, as rheumatism, local pains, inflammations and even tumors, by drawing them over the affected part very lightly for about twenty minutes."[31] Hawthorne would have been interested because a few years earlier he had become friendly with a well-known believer in Perkins' tractors, Thomas Green Fessenden, who was the author of a satiric poem in defense of their virtues, "Terrible Tractoration." Hawthorne lived with the Fessenden family during the six months he spent in Boston in 1836 editing the *American Magazine of Useful and Entertaining Knowledge,* and when Fessenden died the following year, he wrote a memorial sketch of his life, including some discussion of Perkinism (XII 246-63).

Although never mentioning Fessenden by name, Holmes devotes some space to his poem, and if Hawthorne read *Homoeopathy and its Kindred Delusions,* he surely paid particular attention to the passages on Perkinism, including Holmes' humorous case history:

> A certain lady had the misfortune to have a spot as big as a silver penny at the corner of her eye, caused by a bruise, or some such injury. Now, another lady, who was a friend of hers, and a strong believer in Perkinism, was very anxious to try the effects of tractoration upon this unfortunate blemish. The patient consented; the lady "produced the instruments, and, after drawing them four of five times over the spot, declared that it changed to a paler color, and on repeating the use of them a few minutes longer, that it had almost vanished, and was scarcely visible, and departed in high triumph at her success." The lady who underwent the operation, assured the narrator "that she looked in the glass immediately after, and that not the least visible alteration had taken place."[32]

We cannot be sure that Hawthorne read this anecdote, with its upshot so different from his own dismal moral in "The Birthmark," but there is nothing to disprove the borrowing. The notion of a man destroying "his beloved in trying to raise her to more than mortal perfection" had been in Hawthorne's notebook for several years (*AN* 20, 165, 184); perhaps the anecdote of the blemish "cured" by pseudoscience gave him the emblem he needed to embody that conception.

Even if these conjectures are wrong, and Hawthorne never read Holmes's tract, it is still likely that homoeopathy contributed to Aylmer's treatment of his wife's facial blemish. The diction and dosage of the first, "gold-colored" concoction are thoroughly Hahnemannean, and the effects of the still more potent second draught suggest a typically Hawthornesque inversion of homoeopathic doctrine: if poisons diluted to the proper "potency" are medicines, then why may not medicines turn out to be poison? This motif of the "fatal potion" was a favorite with him, appearing at crucial moments in "The Birthmark," "Rappaccini's Daughter," "The Haunted Quack," *The Dolliver Romance,* and twice in *Septimius Felton. Dolliver* provides the most convincing evidence of a homoeopathic source for the motif: Colonel Dabney is poisoned by Dolliver's *genuine* elixir of life because he fails to limit himself to the proper dilute dose of a single drop.

No doubt all of these fatalities would retain much the same significance for a modern reader had there never been a pseudoscience prescribing infinitesimal doses of "poison." The ironies that Hawthorne is after do not depend on a reader's acquaintance with the doctrine of Hahnemann. His morals never need a gloss of this sort. Nonetheless, there is something almost obsessional about Hawthorne's use of the fatal potion, his fondness for plots involving experimental pharmacologists concocting mysterious elixirs and testing them on their families and friends. Their individual meanings in particular stories are one thing; their overall relevance in his art is another.

iii

Unlike his wife, who before and after their marriage suffered from various chronic ailments, Hawthorne was remarkably healthy; with him, Sophia rhapsodized, "earth's maladies have nothing to do."[33] During the Roman winter of 1859, when he caught "the severest cold he ever had," Hawthorne's family was shocked to see him confined to his bed and obliged to consult a doctor for the first time since boyhood.[34] A few years later, in his final illness, he chafed at the loss of the vigor he had always taken for granted. "Why does Nature treat us like little children!" he exclaimed to his friend Fields—a remarkable outcry from a man who never complained.[35]

The comparison to "little children" may serve to remind us that although healthy in its middle span, Hawthorne's life was rounded at both ends with seriously incapacitating illness; it would be no surprise if the invalidism of his sixtieth year recalled the lameness that had struck him at nine. An injury to his foot, sustained while playing "bat-and-ball," threatened for a time to leave him permanently crippled, and it was three years before he was fully recovered.[36] During this long convalescence Hawthorne had his own youthful experience of physicians and medicines, not so grim perhaps as Sophia's extended sufferings—nor so paradigmatic as those of the fictional Delia Thornton—but nonetheless marked and revealing.

The earliest known letter from Hawthorne (December 9, 1813) reports to his Uncle Robert that his foot is no better, and that a new doctor is to be consulted: ". . . and maybe he will do some good for Doctor Barstow has not and I dont know as Doctor Kitridge will . . . ."[37] As with Sophia's headaches, there were many doctors (including Nathaniel Peabody himself) and the usual range of ineffectual remedies. But whereas his wife's experience embittered her only against allopaths (she swore by her homoeopaths), Hawthorne seems to have learned to distrust all physicians, of whatever stripe. This is not to say that he completely renounced medicine. He was fascinated as well as revolted by the subject. At Bowdoin, for example, he was friendly with the medical students, and even enrolled himself in a medical course on human physiology his senior year. Yet this special knowledge of the profession did not win him over; on the contrary, he summed up his feelings in a letter to his mother from college: "I should not like to live by the diseases and infirmities of my fellow creatures."[38]

Hawthorne indulged Sophia's preferences to the extent of allowing the children to be treated homoeopathically for the diseases that befell them. He gave Julian "two globules of Aconite" for a wasp sting (*AN* 458), and took the children to a Boston homoeopath, who prescribed belladonna for scarlet fever.[39] When the children came down with measles during their London residence, the famous Swedenborgian homoeopathist J. J. Garth Wilkinson was called in. Hawthorne noted in his journal that the doctor was a believer in spiritualism as well as homoeopathy. Although impressed by Wilkinson's learning and his standing in the intellectual community (Wilkinson gave him a letter of introduction to Coventry Patmore), Hawthorne could not swallow the stories of "ghostly hands" and came away feeling "a sluggish disgust" (*EN* 616-17). Yet for a mere case of measles, learned quackery of Dr. Wilkinson's sort could probably do little harm.

When it came to more serious illness, Hawthorne wavered strangely. A year earlier Sophia had acute bronchitis so severely that she and the children ended up moving to Lisbon for six months to recuperate from the English climate. As usual, she consulted only homoeopathic physicians, and Hawthorne was obviously relieved at the intervention, contrived by a friend, of an orthodox practitioner. In his journal he recorded Sophia's "scruples of conscience and judgment" about taking allopathic medicines, but "for my part, I am inclined to put faith in what is tangible" (*EN* 374). This is the view of homoeopathy that seems most characteristic of him. Yet given his skepticism, one cannot help wondering why he had to wait for a friend's initiative to bring Sophia to allopathic advice. The explanation is probably that he put so little faith in any physician that he was unwilling to contend with his wife's strong belief.

When their fourteen-year-old daughter Una came down with Roman fever in 1858, it was again Sophia who chose the doctor, "the most prominent homeopathic physician in Rome."[40] Fortunately, homoeopaths and allopaths agreed on the use of quinine, in sufficient doses, for the treatment of malaria. Even so, Una's fate hung in the balance for many months. The prognosis was first optimistic, then grave; long afterwards, Sophia told her son Julian that Hawthorne "had never taken a hopeful view of the case. The grief he felt at the idea that perhaps his daughter might die was so keen that he could not endure the alternations of hope and fear, and therefore had settled with himself not to hope at all."[41] Given this defensive pessimism, it is less surprising that he did not insist on an allopathic physician: why quibble over rival quackeries, when the consequence was to be fatal in any case?

His own last illness was much the same. As his health failed rapidly, he seemed to make up his mind to die. "I am not low-spirited, nor fanci[f]ul, nor freakish," he wrote to Fields, "but look what seem to be realities in the face, and am ready to take whatever may come."[42] He permitted Sophia to treat a "cold in the neck" with belladonna, but refused to see her latest "Homoeopathic Sage," Dr. Vandersende. A change of scene was arranged instead, and his publisher and friend George Ticknor agreed to accompany him to Cuba. Bad weather forced them to Philadelphia instead, but for a few days Hawthorne did seem to improve in appetite and spirits. Then suddenly Ticknor himself fell ill with pneumonia, and died before any of his family could arrive to relieve Hawthorne from the duties of nurse and comforter. This ordeal "told upon him," as he admitted to Sophia.[43] Not the least of it was the allopathic cure applied to Ticknor, with Hawthorne's horrified but helpless acquiescence. The doctor "belabored with pills and powders of various kinds, and then proceeded to cup, and poultice, and blister, according to the ancient rule of that tribe of savages."[44] No wonder that he feared to consult a physician himself. The homoeopaths were quacks, the allopaths witch doctors.

His condition grew dramatically worse, yet he still refused to seek medical advice. Sophia would not have him "take any of the allopathic poisonous drugs for the world. I am sure he could not survive calomel, blue pill and such horrors."[45] But when she decided that "it is only to a homoeopathic physician he has an objection," she quickly changed her opinion: "learned doctors in these days of whatever belief, do not drug their patients as absurdly as they did in old times."[46] Whether Hawthorne really had an aversion only to homoeopathic treatment (after his experience with Ticknor's case that seems unlikely), he finally did agree to see his old acquaintance Oliver Wendell Holmes in a semiprofessional way—more to please Sophia, who contrived the meeting, than out of any hope for himself. The examination was painless enough, consisting of a half hour's stroll on a Boston street. Holmes later reported Hawthorne "docile" to his counsel, but completely without hope of recovering his health.[47] Although he did not say so, the doctor agreed with this prognosis. Holmes took his patient to a nearby pharmacy "and treated him to simple medicine as we treat each other to ice cream," but his private word to Hawthorne's friends was that "the shark's tooth is upon him."[48] In eight days he was dead.

Hawthorne had begun to die when he returned to America in the summer of 1860. The entire family perceived the transformation, though none spoke of it. As his younger daughter later wrote, it was "like an instant's change in the atmosphere from sunshine to dusky cold."[49] The signs of decrepitude forced themselves on Hawthorne's awareness, and he seemed more and more drawn to literary subjects that reflected his condition. The unfinished romances of the 1860's—*Doctor Grimshawe's Secret, Septimius Felton,* and *The Dolliver Romance*—all revolve around emblems of aging, decay, and death. Not only do these novels clearly reveal his struggle to accept his fate, but they also show his revulsion from the medical profession that made a living out of death. Hawthorne's doctors and scientists had never been very admirable; now they became ghouls digging in the grave for the secret of immortality. Una's Dr. Franco and Sophia's Drs. Wesselhoeft, Esterbrook, and Vandersende reappear as Grimshawe, Portsoaken, and Dolliver; aconite and belladonna become the elixir of life—and the deadliest of poisons.

Hawthorne began each of his last romances by attempting once again to write a "sunny" book. But the images that usurped his consciousness were of bloody footsteps, spiders, poisons, graveyards and coffins, and strange flowers growing from buried hearts. He struggled with these, trying to find a plot that would encompass them. The shadows lengthened, the characters grew as sinister as their settings. He wondered at himself: "Seriously, my mind has, for the present, lost its temper and its fine edge, and I have an instinct that I had better keep quiet."[50] His greatest anxiety, he told Holmes in their last interview, was that his sanity might go. It had always been a disturbing thought, that "excessive mental activity" might lead to madness, one of the more fearful "disorders of literary men" he had read about. Now his physical constitution was undermined—that was clear. Whatever he thought of the pseudosciences, he knew their doctrine of the psychological consequences of physiological disease. His extraordinary difficulty in completing a novel during these last years must have seemed an ominous counterpoint to his failing digestion and the wasting of his flesh.

There may be some special significance in the fact that Oliver Wendell Holmes was the authority to whom Hawthorne applied for an opinion of his case. The relation of spiritual and physical disease interested Holmes very much, and it may even be that

Hawthorne knew this when he agreed to consult him, for Holmes had written on the subject. Whether or not Hawthorne ever read Holmes's tract on homoeopathy of 1842, it is hard to imagine that he did not know *Elsie Venner,* Holmes's "medicated novel" of 1861, which had been serialized in Hawthorne's own magazine outlet, the *Atlantic Monthly,* and appeared as a book with the imprint of Hawthorne's publishers, Ticknor and Fields. *Elsie Venner* explored questions that Hawthorne had himself asked in many of his own "medical fictions" and was returning to in his new romances: Was sin a disease, like small pox or scarlet fever? Was immorality merely a form of insanity? Could there be a "physician for the cure of moral diseases"? In *Elsie Venner* Holmes caused one of his characters to assert for the medical profession that "our notions of bodily and moral disease, or sin, are apt to go together." He points out that "a large class of persons" are "condemned as sinners by theologians, but considered by us as invalids."[51]

His purpose, Holmes announced in the preface to a later edition, was "to test the doctrine of 'original sin.'" Almost in the same breath, he hastens to assert that Hawthorne's *Marble Faun* had appeared too late to influence his theme, and that his idea came from "no fable or romance, but in a physiological conception fertilized by a theological dogma."[52] Hawthorne's own interests in the physiology of sin and the psychology of guilt were extremely close to those of Holmes, and though *The Marble Faun* contributed nothing to *Elsie Venner,* much else in Hawthorne's work did. Quite possibly Hawthorne got the idea of "The Birthmark" from *Homoeopathy and its Kindred Delusions;* almost certainly "The Birthmark" repaid the debt by supplying Holmes with several hints for Elsie Venner. She too has a birthmark, which symbolizes *her* earthly imperfection—a ring about her neck like the band or marking of a rattlesnake. In Elsie's last illness, it turns out that the "lower nature" symbolized by her birthmark reaches like Georgiana's "hand," to "the centres of life," so that her snake self cannot die without her human self also expiring.[53] After she is dead, her birthmark vanishes—just as Georgiana's did.

Elsie Venner contains innumerable other little touches and borrowings from Hawthorne. The anecdote of Alexander and the poisoned slave girl is retold here, from "Rappaccini's Daughter"; echoes of "Egotism; or, The Bosom Serpent" are obvious; and the avalanche at the end of the novel is specifically compared to the disaster at Crawford's Notch that Hawthorne recounted in "The

Ambitious Guest." Yet with all this connection and indebtedness, *Elsie Venner* ultimately propounds a moral much at odds with Hawthorne's opinions on the diseases of the spirit.

Holmes was a thoroughly modern type after all, a professor and an experimenter who proved himself, at least to Sophia Hawthorne's satisfaction, quite as much a Paul Pry as any of her husband's evil scientists. Sophia would never have encouraged Hawthorne to consult the genial allopath if she had known that Holmes would publish, before her husband was cold in his grave, the indelicate details of his symptoms. She had only just managed to get the *Atlantic Monthly* to suppress the worst revelation—his fear that he might lose his mind—when she discovered that Holmes was being proposed to write a life of Hawthorne. Her husband had spent his last days burning old letters, had emphasized "his dislike of biographies," and "forbade any such matter in connection with himself in any distance of the future."[54] Holmes was an opportunist, a dabbler, without taste or principles. Nothing so harsh was said perhaps, but the moral distance could not have seemed wider to Sophia, and she gave notice of total noncooperation.

This is not to say that Hawthorne would have disapproved of *Elsie Venner,* but only that Holmes's novel, while much in Hawthorne's vein, was far from him in attitude or message. Where Hawthorne would have had an evil scientist, Holmes has a whole collection of wise and compassionate physicians—the young hero, the kindly local practitioner, the learned professor at Harvard. And Holmes handles his Beatrice/Georgiana figure differently too. Elsie Venner is not totally innocent of evil impulses and deeds, as her prototypes surely were. Yet in spite of her murderous streak Holmes finally defends Elsie, explaining that her darker nature is hereditary and therefore as much out of her control as the birthmark that is its emblem. Holmes's theory of the "limitations of human responsibility" is borrowed, as he admits, directly from the phrenologists, whose "great doctrine of moral insanity" he applauds while pooh-poohing its pseudoscientific origins. The lesson is the same, regardless of its source: *"Treat bad men as if they were insane,"* is the advice of the professor. "They are *in-sane,* out of health, morally."[55]

However antipathetic to pseudoscience Holmes supposed himself, his novel is really quite faddish in its science. There is this deep bow to phrenology, a still more respectful reference to James

Braid's academic version of mesmerism—hypnotism—and even a faintly conciliatory gesture in the direction of homoeopathy—"We don't look at sickness as we used to, and try to poison it with everything that is offensive."[56] Most of all, the chief doctrine of the novel, Holmes's answer to original sin, is the hereditary transmission of moral propensities—a relatively new pseudoscience that was developing out of various phrenological and other theories.

As early as 1843 Orson Fowler had published his *Hereditary Descent* (at the end of volume V of the *American Phrenological Journal*), and as late as 1877 Fowler and Wells were still printing books like Georgiana Bruce Kirby's *Transmission; or, Variation of Character through the Mother*. In 1851 Mrs. Hester Pendleton (again through Fowler and Wells) presented *The Parents' Guide for the Transmission of Desired Qualities to Offspring*, while Henry C. Wright's *Marriage and Parentage* (1854) asserted that "parents, alone, are responsible for the existence, the organization and constitutional tendencies of the bodies and souls of their children."[57] Andrew Jackson Davis, the spiritualist and trance speaker of the 1840s and 1850s, published his own pseudoscientific novel in 1869, based on the same phenomenon of hereditary transmission of sin— ". . . by this mysterious and immutable law of phreno-electrotyping, so to call it, which is outwrought in the sensitive surfaces of, and by the means of the psycho-dynamical forces at work within the unborn brain, the offspring could, and absolutely does, mentally inherit a predisposition to particular vices and crimes, as easily as to be born with cross-eyes, red-hair, far-sightedness. . . ."[58]

Holmes's less flamboyant theorizing is just as pseudoscientific as Davis's. Elsie, whose mother was bitten by a snake during her pregnancy, was thereby imbued with qualities that belonged to another species: "an ante-natal impression . . . had mingled an alien element in her nature."[59] This snake-like nature pervades her physique and behavior, even to the extent of giving her a peculiar power over her "cousin-species." With this fanciful set of notions Holmes purports to disprove the doctrine of original sin, the "inherited moral responsibility for other people's misbehavior."[60] What the author of *The House of the Seven Gables* would have thought of such deductions can easily be imagined. Like the pseudoscientists he claimed to despise, Holmes really seems to have believed that sin might be cured by a proper dose of something.

What "might seem to a minister a good example of total depravity" can be treated with "iron and valerian," and exercise "on horseback."[61]

Hawthorne might be said to hold precisely the contrary view, and in his last books particularly, the imbibing of medication seems a sure way to nurture evil rather than eradicate it. Homoeopathists believed that all true medicines were "poisons"—indeed, as late as 1952 the *Journal of the American Institute of Homoeopathy* was still publishing articles on the medicinal virtues of spider webs and venoms, a startling recrudescence of Doctor Grimshawe's theories.[62] Hawthorne merely took this principle more literally than any homoeopathist meant it. Accordingly, the elixir of life in most Hawthorne stories is just the opposite of what it claims to be. At first it seems to fulfill its promise. The initial effects of drinking it are euphoria and renewed energy—but these symptoms are followed almost immediately by the most painful death. Thus the concoction acts in accord with its "secret ingredient," typically an exotic flower which, on closer inspection, proves to be growing out of a grave.

The elixir of life is not the only fatal potion brewed by Hawthorne's mad scientists. Beatrice Rappaccini, for example, is herself a poisoned vessel devilishly prepared by her father. Her kiss is the most desirable, but also the most dangerous, of favors. And just as her breath is death to others, the strongest restorative is deadly poison to her. Indeed, no one in Hawthorne ever seems to be saved by medicine. Another fatal beauty, Lady Eleanor in the "Legends of the Province House," refuses an antidote that might save her, as does Richard Digby in "The Man of Adamant." These antidotes are genuine (so far as we can tell), yet they are spurned along with the lovers who offer them. Whenever a character does accept a supposed remedy for some condition, it always fails. Both Beatrice and Georgiana, and later Sybil Dacy in *Septimius Felton,* willingly drink false antidotes for the sake of their deluded lovers, who are not satisfied with mortal imperfection.

Still other characters suffer more or less accidental deaths from quaffing the elixir of life or some similar panacea. The "haunted quack" is pursued by the supposed ghost of a patient who took his prescription. Septimius Felton's Aunt Keziah dies in agony when her darling Seppy slips some of his graveyard blossoms into her favorite tonic: "What was the harm of that? Medical men, no doubt, are always doing so, and he was a medical man for the time. . . . Something must be risked in the cause of science" (XI 352, 362). Dr. Dolliver's grandson Edward died from testing his own exotic concoctions upon himself, and in one of the sketches for the rest of that romance an old "Indian Doctress," who knows or is trying to find out the secret of the elixir, poisons herself with her mysterious herbs (*LP* 126). In one of the projected plans for *Doctor Grimshawe's Secret,* the doctor is slated to die of the bite of his pet spider, whose webs or venom was to be the source of his universal remedy.

All of these patterns revolve around the same basic emblem—the fatal potion. The direction of its effect is always toward evil, even when the potion is only sought and has not yet been sipped. Although Septimius Felton follows an abstemious set of rules for purity of life as part of his pursuit of immortality, his "moral dietetics" (XI 339) lead him into evil rather than good. He becomes a self-centered isolate, coldly experimenting on others for the sake of his goal. And the one successful seeker after the elixir, Dr. Dolliver, is not satisfied with eternal youth, but begins a quest back into the past which eventually isolates him from human warmth and affection just as completely as Septimius's regimen.

This was the traditional theme of immortality myths, especially the gothic versions that Hawthorne knew, like Godwin's *St. Leon* and Maturin's *Melmoth the Wanderer,* in which the possessor of the secret cannot reveal it to anyone who is not willing to trade his mortality (and thus his soul) for eternal existence in this world.[63] The combination of secrecy and extraordinary longevity precludes the development of any enduring human attachments. Loves wither and die; "the undying man" outlives every mortal passion and principle. Mocking cynicism alternates in his character with the despair of fallen angels, eternal and unpardonable.

The *elixir vitae* thus becomes another *memento mori.* Far from Holmes's refutation of original sin, Hawthorne's interest in medical and scientific curiosities led to the reaffirmation of the darker side of human nature—the fall, expulsion from the garden, sin and death. In its earliest version, Holmes's snake was the Serpent and Hawthorne's elixir was the Apple.

Later redactions would include Stevenson's *Dr. Jekyll and Mr. Hyde* and perhaps *Edwin Drood* and *The Picture of Dorian Gray,* tales of dual personalities activated by drugs. After Hawthorne, however, there is an increasing perfunctoriness in these stories. The horror seems less horrifying as audiences grow accustomed to the new pseudoscientific view of man as a mechanism, his propensities for good and evil a function of heredity and chemistry. Nothing religious, or even magical, remains in the conceptions of schizophrenic characters and antisocial behavior induced by drugs. The marvelous becomes commonplace, and the symbolic manner is no longer so appropriate as flat naturalism. Thus we have novels about alcoholics and addicts, or utopias based on LSD.

Even within Hawthorne's thirty years as a writer, one can see shifts and trends in his handling of these themes. Tales like "Dr. Heidegger's Experiment," "The Birthmark," and "Rappaccini's Daughter" had introduced the theme of the elixir of life long before the last romances, so it is not correct to speak of new subject matter so much as a new emphasis. What one senses in the later work is a much closer identification with the characters, and a correspondingly greater difficulty for Hawthorne in imagining an appropriate history of their lives. The personages of a tale like "Dr. Heidegger's Experiment" are little more than stick figures illustrating a moral, and the moral itself is stiffly conceived, a schematic repetition of the old lesson that immortal youth is not what it's cracked up to be. It was easy to imagine behavior that might be typical of such purely emblematic characters. There is more complexity in the conception of Aylmer, although he too is handled distantly, a case study: something ambiguous clings to him, and the moral at the end seems unsatisfactory, too pat for Aylmer's experience.

In both "The Birthmark" and "Rappaccini's Daughter" the poisonous potion is administered to a victim, not gulped by its concoctor. The aim is to achieve power over nature or other people, rather than to escape from mortality altogether. A curious thing happens as this second goal comes to prominence in the late romances; in spite of this continuing condemnation of the mad scientist, Hawthorne seems more and more to project himself into just that figure. We watch over Septimius' shoulder as he brews his elixir; we are meant to follow Dr. Dolliver on his journey into a second youth; even in *Doctor Grimshawe's Secret,* the least overt of these private fantasies, we can trace lines of self-portraiture in the gloomy old doctor alone in his study. Old age brought Hawthorne closer, though unwillingly, to the mad scientist. At last it was he who had to drink the fatal potion.

As we have already seen, a major theme in Hawthorne's earlier treatment of the scientist had to do with the moral nature of disease. Most graphically in *The Scarlet Letter,* but no less clearly in "The Birthmark" or "Lady Eleanor's Mantle," the physical symptoms of disease always betray a spiritual source. These emblems—the "A" on Dimmesdale's breast, the hand on Georgiana's cheek, the pox on Lady Eleanor's face—are the wages of sin, the stamp of mortality. Rarely is there any question that they deserve such afflictions, for sin is as universal as Reverend Hooper or Young Goodman Brown imagine. At least that was always a possible view for Hawthorne, much as he condemned such despair in Hooper, Brown, or Ethan Brand. Indeed, the crux of many of his stories is just this: is the darker view of human nature not itself the blackest sin of all? Despair *was* the unpardonable sin, simply because there was no possibility of penitence; if faith was by grace, what remedy was there for despair, what medicine for the sick soul? This question took on new significance as Hawthorne found his own powers failing, his life itself fast waning.

In his earlier stories Hawthorne seems to play Ishmael to these Ahabs, counseling a passive, almost transcendental acceptance of the nature of things. In his later works—beginning perhaps with *The Marble Faun,* and most strikingly in the labyrinthine romances he could not find his way out of—he seems to come to the more desperate impasse of Melville's *Pierre.* Gradually he merges with his mad scientists, so that finally it is not the story of Grimshawe or Dolliver that he is writing, but "the larger book," as Pierre Glendinning called it, for his "own private shelf."[64] Perhaps the secret of Hawthorne's unfinished romances is that the putative narrative is really just a pretext for the narrative voice itself, which frequently breaks free of the story and confronts the very sources of the creative imagination. "Two books are being writ," Melville said about Pierre's novel, "of which the world shall only see one, and that the bungled one." Hawthorne too was at work on two books. The genuine account was written in the margins of the other, and records his desperate effort to find a set of meanings adequate to the emblems of decay and death that his imagination forced upon him. This meant searching out the disease of his own spirit.

In *The Scarlet Letter* Chillingworth's one great purpose is to discover Dimmesdale's secret, the moral equivalent of his physical illness. In the later romances these two figures, the physician and his patient, are conflated. Thus Dolliver administers the elixir to himself in order that, by "living back," he may "discover some secret, left unravelled in his previous youth—to study out some particular secret, of an earthly nature,—to effect something that shall give a substance to all his life. What? Something which, once effected, he feels as if he could die willingly, and with a sense of completeness" (*LP* 125). Hawthorne could never find the secret adequate to his conception, and it is not surprising that *The Dolliver Romance* petered out like all the others.

One is reminded of what Melville told Julian Hawthorne, "that he was convinced that there was some secret in my father's life which had never been revealed, and which accounted for the gloomy passages in his books."[65] Perhaps it was easy for Melville to imagine such secrets, but no conjecture can possibly bear the weight such a hypothesis throws on it. Melville was right only in this sense: that Hawthorne, especially in his last works, was himself in search of some such secret, that would "give a substance to all his life." But it was impossible to discover.

During the Christmas season of 1854, his first year in the Liverpool consulate, with more wealth and fame and ease than he had ever known, Hawthorne wrote in his journal:

> My early life was perhaps a good preparation for the declining half of life, it having been such a blank that any possible thereafter would compare favorably with it. For a long, long while, I have occasionally been visited with a singular dream; and I have an impression that I have dreamed it, even since I have been in England. It is, that I am still at college—or, sometimes, even at School—and there is a sense that I have been there unconscionably long, and have quite failed to make such progress in life as my contemporaries have; and I seem to meet some of them with a feeling of shame and depression that broods over me, when I think of it, even at this moment. This dream, recurring all through these twenty or thirty years, must be one of the effects of that heavy seclusion in which I shut myself up, for twelve years, after leaving college, when everybody moved onward and left me behind. How strange that it should come now, when I may call myself famous, and prosperous!—when I am happy, too!—still that same dream of life hopelessly a failure! (*EN* 98)

What Hawthorne seems here as elsewhere reluctant to face is that the solitude of his youth is not merely an unpleasant memory. It forms both literally and metaphorically the grounds of his art. Insofar as he now basked in social and civic rewards, it was at the expense of that art. His art had always been at the expense of his more genial nature, the side that could take comfort in family and friends, wealth and fame. When he decided to send Dolliver back into his youth, to seek he knew not what secret that might "give a substance to all his life," Hawthorne was once again reflecting unconsciously upon his own situation as a writer, launching himself wearily one last time into the region of the imagination where he was most completely alone. He was old and tired and sick. Writing no longer gave him joy. Yet he mixed the potion as best he could, trying to remember the ingredients and their order, and drank it off.

II

Five

Social Science

THE PSEUDOSCIENCES had no collective name at midcentury. David Reese might dub them all humbug, but for most people they were animal magnetism, phrenology, homoeopathy, watercure, grahamism, and so on. Yet shrewd observers could see that these fads and fanaticisms added up to a movement, and that their tendency would be to coalesce in some unitary science or philosophy. Emerson suggested the possibility in his journal as early as 1835:

> Ages hence, books that cannot now be written may be possible. For instance a cumulative moral & intellectual science. If I would know something of the elements & process of the Moral sublime where shall I now seek the analysis? If I would know the elementary distinction of spiritual & intellectual where shall I inquire? A sentence showing a tendency is all that a century contributes to psychology. Where shall I find the result of phrenology? of animal magnetism? of extacy?[1]

From a modern vantage point, it seems ironic that a philosopher like Emerson should be the one to call for such a science; but of course he could not predict the direction that pragmatism and behaviorism would push the analysis of the "Moral sublime" he proposed. In the late 1830s and early 1840s not only Emerson but even his more doctrinaire disciples Thoreau and Alcott were imagining the same value-free science of man. "Why always insist that men incline to the moral side of their being?" Thoreau wrote in his journal. "Our life is not all moral. Surely, its actual phenomena deserve to be studied impartially. The science of Human Nature has never been attempted, as the science of Nature has. The dry light has never shone on it. Neither physics nor metaphysics have touched it."[2] Like Emerson, Thoreau seemed to hanker after a sharper tool than ethics or religion to dissect human behavior. Alcott too, in his journal, had the same thought about the same time: "We want a pathology and diagnosis of sin as well as of physical disease. Physiology and psychology are one—polar effects of the Soul. And each has its therapeutics."[3] The idea was the same as Emerson's or Thoreau's, though Alcott put a utilitarian twist on it when he introduced the notion of a therapeutics as well as a pathology of sin. He was imagining something like the "physician for the cure of moral diseases" that Hawthorne had proposed in *his* journal (*AN* 235), a bare month before he married and went out to Concord to settle down in the midst of all these seasoned philosophers of the soul instead of the philanthropists and socialists at Brook Farm.

The difference between Hawthorne and his new neighbors was that he knew from the start that the new science of man would not satisfy him. His "physician" was an object of satire, not admiration. In this opinion he was out of step with the tendency of his age. It was no mere coincidence that the notion of a unitary "science of Human Nature" occurred at the same time to keepers of journals in Concord, Massachusetts. The same goal soon began to tease less fastidious minds in Boston and New York, and the decade that followed saw dozens of attempts to consolidate the pseudosciences and their stepsisters the philanthropies. What finally emerged in the 1850s pleased the transcendentalists as little as it did Hawthorne, though it did aspire to the title that they had offered ten or fifteen years earlier, "a cumulative moral & intellectual science." It was called "social science" by its enthusiasts, and depending on the breadth of their ambition, it included most of what we now call pseudoscience as well as a number of popular programs that ultimately developed, after many transformations, into modern sociology, psychology, and anthropology. But in 1852, when *The Blithedale Romance* first appeared satirizing the new sciences, it was not yet settled what was "social," what was "pseudo," and what fell between the stools into the abyss of philanthropy. To begin to sort these disciplines and dogmas out, let us look at some typical examples.

On the night of December 6, 1851, the first graduating class of the American Hydropathic Institute (Port Chester, Long Island) was sent on its way "to preach truth" with the following exhortation from the chief speaker of the occasion:

> . . . the science of the true social relations of mankind . . . the Science of Society is a legitimate and indispensable part of the science of medicine, and of the art of preventing and curing disease. . . . Sociology, the Science of Society, the science of true human relations and conditions, and of the means of securing them to all classes and individuals of the race, is part and parcel of your legitimate professional knowledge. . . .[4]

This repetitive voice belonged to Stephen Pearl Andrews, jack-of-all-reforms and friend of the proprietors of the Institute, Thomas L. and Mary S. Gove Nichols, a bohemian pair who were just getting their second wind in a long career of philanthropic endeavor. All three were currently helping to form Modern Times, a new utopian community on Long Island, where some of their ideas of "social science" would be put to the test. Even more than the nascent community, however, Andrews was plugging his new book, *The Science of Society*, in which he argued at greater length the "propriety of the use of the term 'Science' in such a connection":

> If researches into the habits of beetles and tadpoles, and their localities and conditions of existence, are entitled to the dignified appellation of Science, certainly similar researches into the nature, the wants, the adaptations, and, so to speak, into the true or requisite moral and social *habitat* of the spiritual animal called Man must be, if conducted according to the rigid methods of scientific induction from observed facts, equally entitled to that distinction.
>
> The series of works, of which this is the first in order, will deal in no vague aspirations after "the good time coming." They will propound definite principles which demand to be regarded as having all the validity of scientific truths, and which, taken in co-relation with each other, are adequate to the solution of the social problem.[5]

Far from Emerson's plodding psychology, adding a sentence a century to its repertoire, the ambition of the new science was to net and domesticate human nature and society overnight. In a course of twelve weeks the twenty graduating students of the Institute were certified to have "acquired such thorough knowledge of the Principles and Practice of Medicine, Surgery, and Obstetrics, as to merit confidence as a Water-Cure Physician." Social science, with its "definite principles . . . adequate to the solution of the social problem," was thrown in for good measure at the end of the semester.

Besides Andrews, other guest lecturers at the Institute included J.W. Redfield, the discoverer of "Comparative Physiognomy," and T.L. Harris, one of spiritualism's earliest spokesmen, who had seen "a paradisiacal city" in a vision the preceding year, and went on to found three cultist communities and produce many volumes of prophetic verse.[6] Animal magnetism and phrenology, hydropathy, comparative physiognomy, and "extacy" (to borrow Emerson's term for Harris's *forte*) all might huddle under the umbrella that Andrews raised in the name of "Sociology" or that his friend Nichols called "Esoteric Anthropology."[7]

Today social science consists of a number of relatively distinct disciplines—sociology, psychology, anthropology, and the like. Some of the names were the same in Hawthorne's time, and the fragmentation and specialization was even more elaborate, but along different lines, reflecting approach and technique rather than subject matter. Social science was an activist pursuit, and its adherents wanted to understand human nature chiefly in order to improve it. When Andrews addressed himself to the hydropathists, he assumed that as practicing physicians they ought to be social scientists, just as when he put on his hat as editor of the *Phonetic* (or *Fonetic*) *Propagandist,* another of his current projects, he considered himself devoted "to practical reforms, especially in matters of self-education," as well as "writing and spelling reformation."[8] Andrew's enthusiasm for Josiah Warren's community at Modern Times and his theory of Individual Sovereignty was similarly pragmatic. Individual Sovereignty was immediately practicable in human relations, and like phonography and hydropathy it would make a difference in men's lives. *The Science of Society* proclaimed it; Modern Times proved it.

The science of human nature was thus conceived as an applied science, a series of competing or compatible technologies of man. During the 1840s there had been several efforts to consolidate these sciences into a movement, a counterculture if you will. Various publicists and philanthropists tried to build a following or a newspaper on some amalgamation of causes. Lewis Ryckman, a leader at Brook Farm, agitated for a "union of all reforms" throughout 1845, and early in 1846 W. H. Channing issued a call in the Brook Farm *Harbinger* "To the Associationists of the United States," to join and support his newly formed American Union of Associationists, which had among its goals "to eradicate forever the inhumanities of Slavery, War, Legalized Murder, Cruelty to Criminals, Intemperance, Licentiousness, Poverty, Popular Ignorance, Commercial Fraud, Universal Competition. . . ."[9] But these attempts failed; there were too many "one-idea men," like Hollingsworth in *Blithedale,* unable to find common ground on anyone else's map of heaven.

Lacking such a consensus, philanthropy drifted along behind its most all-encompassing reformers—those who offered to provide a blueprint for the ideal community—so it was communitism that became known as *the* social science. There had been crazes that swept the country—phrenology in 1832, with J. G. Spurzheim's famous visit and demise in Boston, mesmerism in 1836, with Charles Poyen's whirl through New England—but the first stir of a major movement rather than a mere fad was the Fourierist campaign that began in 1840 with the publication of Albert Brisbane's *Social Destiny of Man.* Brisbane, who had himself dabbled in mesmerism and later took up spiritualism, recognized a call when he heard one, and understood how to promote an idea to an eager public. Almost singlehandedly he raised Charles Fourier to the position of a Gall or Mesmer and made his name the byword of the entire socialist movement in antebellum America. His method was shrewd; he sold Fourierism as a science. Before the work of Fourier, he announced in his best-selling book, " . . . in the field of *Social Science* nothing [had] been done . . . ":

> Philosophers have only given us theories on the generation of ideas, have only occupied themselves with metaphysical discussions on the nature of the conscience, of the will, &c., which are merely secondary, accessory questions. What we want, is a fundamental theory or science of the springs of action of the soul—the passions.[10]

Such a theory, Brisbane explained, was the basis of Fourier's plan for a new social order; the theory of "passional harmony" provided the rationale of "attractive industry." By coming to a scientific understanding of human desire, one could devise a perfectly articulated society, in which each individual would sustain precisely the roles to which his natural affinities disposed him. Thus, in the famous example, the little boys were delegated to collect the garbage and fertilize the fields. Where, Hawthorne must have wondered at Brook Farm, were the eager urchins to help him shovel the manure and clean the stables? But Brook Farm had not yet gone Fourierist in Hawthorne's season there, and the guiding concept of its early days was merely the bringing together in each member of intellectual and manual labor—a crude and individualistic analysis as compared to the delicate corporate anatomy of the phalanx that was instituted at West Roxbury in the winter of 1843-1844.

Not all communitists were "social scientists," much less Fourierists. John Humphrey Noyes's followers at Putney, Vermont—later the well-known Oneida Community, where the division of labor was carefully reconsidered without benefit of Fourier—advertised their caution: "We are attempting no scientific experiments in political economy nor in social science."[11] Later their social experiments in complex marriage, birth control, and eugenics made them notorious, but although they admired the Brook Farmers and their Fourierist journal *The Harbinger,* they always insisted that "the Fourierists have begun at the wrong end. . . . The great problems of our relation to God and of the relation of the sexes, which the Fourierists postpone as of no pressing importance, we consider the first to be solved."[12]

A similar position, at least on the religious side, was held by Adin Ballou, founder of the Hopedale Community of Practical Christians at Mendon, Massachusetts. Ballou too was friendly with the Brook Farmers—indeed, it was only his insistence on a membership creed that kept his followers apart from George Ripley's more eclectic communitists at the outset in 1841—but he could not "believe that there is any such absolute natural science of society as [Fourier] pretends to have discovered. His mathematical exactness and order of arrangement are too physical, too mechanical, too fanciful, too romantic, to be actualized by a race of beings, in whom matter and spirit are so mysteriously conjoined. The given terms will not produce the supposed results. Moral natures cannot be weighed, measured and gauged with any such scientific nicety. Something more simple and elastic is requisite for human nature."[13] To this the Brook Farmers responded emphatically, "we cannot hesitate for one moment, to believe that the harmonies of society in which the weal or woe of man is so essentially involved, are dependent on scientific laws, as rigid, as immutable, as absolute, to say the least, as those which determine the harmonies of mathematics or of music."[14]

Finally, at Modern Times one might find all these opinions and more. In addition to Josiah Warren and his Individual Sovereignty, with Andrews explaining it scientifically, and the Nichols bringing it into their hydropathic curriculum, there was Henry Edger, the "hierarch" of Positivism in the Western Hemisphere, there were refugees from Hopedale (who liked the sexual laissez-faire at Modern Times), there were homoeopaths and spiritualists, vegetarians and feminists and nudists. Only a thoroughly anarchist community could have held in solution all these fermenting philosophies of life. That Warren's Individual Sovereignty could coexist with the chief American outpost of Comte's Positivism is some sort of miracle of toleration, since both claimed to be *the* science of human nature.[15]

The foregoing arguments for and against the application of science to social life are the formulations of rival communitists, not utopians and anti-utopians, but they will serve equally well to indicate the essential issues debated between those even more deeply divided camps, and thus begin to bring Hawthorne's views into focus. On the one hand were the social scientists, whose millenium was to be a matter of the reassessment of human needs and desires, the discovery of the laws of human nature and society. On the other hand were the skeptics, who saw only old humbugs dressed up in the hocus-pocus of pseudoscience, and who, even if they thought man redeemable, expected the New Jerusalem to come in more traditional, not to say intelligible form. Hawthorne was one of the skeptics, and *The Blithedale Romance* was among the first and certainly the best of nineteenth-century anti-utopias, indicting the pretensions of a science of man that claimed to prescribe for his sins and sentiments as efficaciously as for his bodily ills. The laws of community were not to be so easily discovered, the passions so painlessly regulated, moral nostrums so confidently applied.

Just as among the welter of philanthropies and pseudosciences communitism was *the* social science, so too in fiction the utopian (or anti-utopian) theme tended to dominate; but other enthusiasms—especially the spiritualism and feminism of the 1850s—also played a part in bringing these antagonisms to a literary head. The anti-utopian novel might more properly be called "anti-philanthropic." Orestes Brownson's highest praise for *The Blithedale Romance* was to say that "perhaps nothing has been written among us better calculated to bring modern philanthropists into deserved disrepute, and to cure the young and enthusiastic of their socialistic tendencies and dreams of world reform."[16] When Brownson launched his own antiphilanthropic *Spirit-Rapper* (1854) in Hawthorne's wake, his targets included an even wider panoply of "seers and seeresses, enthusiasts and fanatics, socialists and communists, abolitionists and anti-hangmen, radicals and women's-rights men of both sexes."[17] And Hawthorne's fellow Salemite Hannah G. Creamer had worked still another, more light-hearted satire on the pseudo-sciences—mesmerism and hydropathy, phrenology and homoeopathy—in her *Delia's Doctors,* brought out the same year as *Blithedale.* (Significantly, the neurasthenic Delia is finally cured by feminism; the one good apple in Miss Creamer's barrel is the least "scientific.") Other exposés may have distributed praise and blame differently, but they all usually included the three major movements scrutinized in *Blithedale*—communitism, feminism, and mesmerism (or its offspring of the 1850s, spiritualism). Other hobbyhorses, like Hollingsworth's plan to reform criminals or Dr. Corning's "manigraph" theory in *The Spirit-Rapper* (that all social evil is the result of insanity), are mere also-rans in this field.[18]

Like Hawthorne, Brownson was especially censorious of the "one-idea man" who thought to save the world with his patented panacea. Years earlier, in a review of one of William Alcott's copious do-good tracts, Brownson had written, "All these classes of evils are mutually connected, and no one of them can be cured separately. The cause of them all lies deep in human nature, as now developed, and they must be regarded as inseparable from the present stage of human progress."[19] He called the random efforts of reformers like Alcott "ultraisms" and held out little hope for their success. By the time of *The Spirit-Rapper* a dozen years later, Brownson was taking these ultraisms as greater evils than the follies they pretended to reform. And though he now saw matters from a Catholic rather than a socialist point of view, he still considered them a single tree with many branches. "The connection of spirit-rapping, or the spirit-manifestations, with modern philanthropy, visionary reforms, socialism, and revolutionism, is not an imagination of my own," he argued. "It is historical, and asserted by the Spiritists, or Spiritualists themselves. . . ."[20] As Brownson's book progresses, we watch the narrator discover further connections, historical and imaginary, between spiritualism, socialism, and women's rights. The "good" religious characters in the novel warn him against pursuing his scientific investigations into these areas, but he ignores them until it is too late, when he finally realizes that all his science and philanthropy have been inspired by the devil, and all his reforms carried out by demons.

Although Brownson affirms a dark interplay between the chief enthusiasms under attack—utopian socialism, spiritualism/mesmerism, and feminism—he does not go much beyond the imputation of satanic agency in explaining their kinship. Nor is *The Blithedale Romance* any more specific in drawing the lines of force among its similar poles. Yet a pattern begins to emerge when *Blithedale, The Spirit-Rapper,* and other novels in the genre—if one may call it that—are placed side by side and their common features studied against the background of "historical" fact which, as Brownson argues, is the ultimate basis of these literary connections.

At one level, it is easy enough to see how a novelist like Hawthorne, having decided to satirize the philanthropies of his day, would find the materials for fiction in them: setting and theme came from Fourier, and from his own experience at Brook Farm in 1841; women's rights gave him the spice he wanted for the love interest; and mesmerism provided the melodramatic plot. Or, at a deeper level, one may glimpse a more mythic conception, in which the utopian dreams of the communitists, including the new sexual dispensation, turn out to be nothing more than the mesmeric hallucinations of a disordered imagination. Although never said in so many words, this is the structure of *The Spirit-Rapper.*

The possibility of viewing the utopian thinker as a self-entranced mesmerist probably occurred to Hawthorne; in *Blithedale* he marvels over the anomaly that Fourier, unlike most of his counterparts, never claimed to speak "with authority from above" (*BR* 54). But

Hawthorne's own conception of mesmerists and philanthropists is more complex, requiring a different character for each of the ultraisms that he introduces—Hollingsworth as philanthropist, Westervelt as mesmerist, Zenobia as feminist, and Coverdale himself, the ambivalent artist-as-communitist. This division, in conjunction with the fact that all four characters are in competition for the "sybilline" spirit of Blithedale, Priscilla, and thus more or less in arms against one another, prevents any easy literal identification of mesmerism as the source of reformist impulses in the novel.

In *The House of the Seven Gables* one figure, Holgrave, represented art, reform, and mesmerism. For another sort of novelist, that would have been an advantage in exploring the relations between them, but a symbolist like Hawthorne almost never enters into the consciousness of his characters in this way. In splitting the elements of Holgrave's character into three distinct personalities, Hawthorne has moved not further away but even closer to the problem.

A novelist like James—who complained that *Blithedale* was not realistic enough[21]—might read Hawthorne's novel as merely a "charming" portrayal of philanthropic types, like his own pigeonholing in *The Bostonians*. But whatever James's opinion, *The Blithedale Romance* was no simple confection of lightly satiric reminiscence, to be digested in a sitting. Its relation to other works in a new and uncertain genre was extremely problematic. Its foundations in Hawthorne's experiences at Brook Farm and in the popular social sciences of the day are equally complicated. To examine these sources and relations in greater detail, and with more attention to the texture and parts of the novel itself, let us now proceed to separate discussions of the four main characters and their respective "sciences": Coverdale and utopian communitism, Zenobia and feminism, Westervelt and spiritualism, and Hollingsworth and penal reform.

Six

Associationism

THE OVERALL EFFECT of *The Blithedale Romance,* whatever elements of plot and setting Hawthorne introduced, was finally determined by his decision to write in the first person, allowing the character of Coverdale to dominate the book. Everything in the novel is saturated with his consciousness. Other themes—Hollingsworth's monomania, Zenobia's self-dramatizing sexuality, Westervelt's sacrilegious science of the will—are absorbed by Coverdale's own "opera-glass" imagination, as Zenobia calls it (*BR* 170). No doubt all the characters, including Coverdale, are refractions of the author's mind, but Coverdale's special status as narrator gives him a strange ambiguity. Like Hawthorne himself, he observes that the other characters are merely products of his imagination, yet they are real too—"goblins of flesh and blood" (*BR* 157), in his careful phrase—and so Coverdale is not only an isolated fantast, like the Oberon of Hawthorne's early tales, but also an alienated artist like the wandering "story-teller" of "The Seven Vagabonds" or the "Passages from a Relinquished Work." Coverdale wavers between the feeling that his habits of observation and literary apprehension cut him off from any meaningful participation in life, and the opposite suspicion, that his entire story is imaginary and only he himself real.

"It had been nothing but dream-work and enchantment" (*BR* 207), Coverdale muses as he returns to Blithedale after a brief absence in the city. He finds his friends in costume, at a picnic masquerade, and comments oracularly, "I was like a mad poet hunted by chimaeras" (*BR* 211). In one sense Coverdale has imagined everything: he is right to wonder "whether the whole affair had been anything more than the thoughts of a speculative man" (*BR* 146). For the novel is, after all, a fiction, and Coverdale's solipsism could not be better founded; yet it is equally true that, within the story, Coverdale represents the mere onlooker of "affairs which were none of mine, and persons who cared little for me" (*BR* 157). At the end he points out that "I have made but a poor and dim figure in my own narrative, establishing no separate interest, and suffering my colorless life to take its hue from other lives" (*BR* 245). This picture of the alienated artist is at least as plausible as that of the solipsistic "epicure of my own emotions" (*BR* 146).

It is appropriate that the narrator of such a tale, at once art and projective revelation, should figure in his own plot as the brooding artist, self-appointed chronicler of the tragedy of his friends. Much of the novel is devoted to this theme. What is especially interesting is how this character type also serves as the proponent of utopian communitism in the book. What, one may ask, is the significance of this identification of the alienated or solipsistic artist with the utopian thinker?—for, in spite of Coverdale's reiterated ambivalence about the experiment, he is the only character in the story who has the least claim to the title of communitist. All the others are at Blithedale for frivolous if not downright subversive motives. Coverdale is the only one who can say at the end, albeit with the cynicism of hindsight, "I rejoice that I could once think better of the world's improvability than it deserved" (*BR* 20).

Part of the explanation for the choice of Coverdale as representative of the communitist impulse may be seen in such world-weary affirmations. "Yet, after all," he says at the outset,

> let us acknowledge it wiser, if not more sagacious, to follow out one's day-dream to its natural consummation, although, if the vision have been worth the having, it is certain never to be consummated otherwise than by a failure. And what of that? Its airiest fragments, impalpable as they may be, will possess a value that lurks not in the most ponderous realities of any practicable scheme. They are not the rubbish of the mind. Whatever else I may repent of, therefore, let it be reckoned neither among my sins nor follies, that I once had faith and force enough to form generous hopes of the world's destiny—yes!—and to do what in me lay for their accomplishment." (*BR* 10-11)

This vein leads into both his resigned utopianism and his conception of himself as voyeur of his own fantasies. Either posture involves an ambivalent recognition that reality is a mixture of convention and commitments, a faith in ideas that may at any moment recede, leaving the believer high and dry. "Blithedale was no longer what it had been," Coverdale announces immediately after the "tragic passage-at-arms" in which he cuts himself off from Hollingsworth's influence and friendship. "Everything was suddenly faded" (*BR* 137-38). Just at this point Coverdale leaves Blithedale and retreats deeper into his own imagination. Whatever tentative faith he had put in the community is withdrawn, and from this moment on the novel is scarcely at all concerned with the utopian theme.

Here then is one clear connection between the artistic and utopian imagination: the vision of an ideal community depends on the pull of social needs and expectations—bonds of love and friendship—that for the artist are never quite real, because of his literary habit "of insulating them from other relations," in order to keep them steadily present "upon my mental stage, as actors in a drama" (*BR* 156). The trouble, as Zenobia shrewdly divines, is that the artist of such a mental drama is likely to be too analytical and intellectual, and most of all, too much in love with his own creations to allow them any life outside his imagination: Coverdale is guilty of "a monstrous scepticism in regard to any conscience or any wisdom, except one's own; a most irreverent propensity to thrust Providence aside, and substitute one's self in its awful place" (*BR* 170).

Had anything of this sort presented itself to Hawthorne when he himself joined the founders of Brook Farm in the spring of 1841? Perhaps not in these terms, but certain issues involving the artist's life in society were sharply posed for him during his half year in communal life.

One of the chief aims of Brook Farm in its earliest stages was the integration of manual and intellectual labor, a "back to the land" mystique that has often characterized the reformist movements of industrial societies. George Ripley formulated the motives neatly in a letter inviting Emerson to join the community: "Our objects, as you know, are to insure a more natural union between intellectual and manual labor than now exists; to combine the thinker and the worker, as far as possible, in the same individual."[1] These intentions appealed to Emerson, who was already thinking of dosing his sedentary constitution with more physical labor, while at the same time reducing the burden of servants in his household.[2] But such goals might be accomplished without transplanting himself to West Roxbury, and so he declined to join Ripley.

It was probably on the issue of the social meaning of labor that the individualists were most at odds with the communitists. Ripley had proposed as the ultimate goal of Brook Farm "a society of liberal, intelligent, and cultivated persons, whose relations with each other would permit a more simple and wholesome life, than can be led amidst the pressure of our competitive institutions."[3] Emerson and his friends also saw the problem in social terms. The need "to begin the world anew, as he does who puts a spade into the ground for food," was the result of the corruption of society in the United States, especially of commerce and its conventions. So said Emerson in "Man the Reformer," published the year of Brook Farm's founding.[4] Similarly the Blithedale communitists "sought our profit by mutual aid, instead of wresting it by the strong hand from an enemy, or filching it craftily from those less shrewd than ourselves" (*BR* 19).

But whereas Ripley and the Brook Farmers hoped to reform society from without, by establishing a new social order that would serve as alternative and model for reform, the transcendentalists proposed a rebirth of the spirit, to precede a gradual regeneration of society from within. The distinction between "science" and "spirit" is relevant, for the communitists argued "scientifically" that to reform society one needed first to abolish all duplicated or competitive labor—in favor of a completely rationalized "associative industry." This was the road to prosperity, and until abundance was economically feasible, there could be no justice. Emerson thought such visions mere "arithmetic."[5] The issues were moral and spiritual, not economic or political.

Corollaries to these positions quickly began to signify more than the axioms. Thus at Brook Farm the question became not whether but how manual labor and intellectual activity might be combined. At first the division of labor fell out much as one would expect on a farm. Sophia Ripley reported during the first weeks, when the number for dinner was still only thirteen, that everyone was pitching in heroically. Her phrasing is noteworthy: William Allen and Frank Farley are praised for knowing "how to do everything" or being "practised in all kinds of labour," whereas Hawthorne is admired for "despising no labour"—the different emphasis highlighting the value, at this point, of all-round ability rather than any special skills. The exception was sexual. "House work" devolved on Mrs. Ripley herself and "a bright girl from Maine."[6]

Similarly at Blithedale the initial divisions are between experienced and inexperienced, and between men and women. Silas Foster, the only genuine farmer among them—"something of a dab" at all useful trades (*BR* 32)—reckons "three of you city-folks as worth one common field-hand (*BR* 20); unfortunately, he is himself only hired help, not a true communitist. And to the question, "have we our various parts assigned?" Zenobia replies, "Oh, we of the softer sex . . . will take the domestic and indoor part of the business, as a matter of course" (*BR* 16). Aside from these distinctions, no specialization of labor was encouraged in the early days. After all, the auspices were nominally so much the reverse.

Again the transcendentalists would approve. "Where is all this division of labor to end?" asked Thoreau in *Walden,* "and what object does it finally serve? No doubt another *may* also think for me; but it is not therefore desirable that he should do so to the exclusion of my thinking for myself."[7]

Thoreau's way of putting it is particularly appropriate, since it focuses the manual/intellectual dichotomy that concerned them all. But few experimenters, whether communitists or individualists, were long able to sustain both roles. Emerson soon had to admit in his journal that physical labor, even if undertaken alone in one's garden, "indisposes & disqualifies for intellectual exertion," and on the farm Hawthorne was complaining by mid-August that "labor is the curse of this world, and nobody can meddle with it, without becoming proportionately brutified."[8] Emerson further reported—on whose authority it is not known—that "the experience of Brook Farm was unanimous, 'We have no thoughts.'"[9] The feeling is echoed in Blithedale, where "The clods of earth, which we so constantly belabored and turned over and over, were never etherealized into thought. Our thoughts, on the contrary, were fast becoming cloddish. Our labor symbolized nothing, and left us mentally sluggish in the dusk of the evening. Intellectual activity is incompatible with any large amount of bodily exercise" (*BR* 66).

In the face of such a realization, several roads were open to the artist-utopian. He might continue, as Emerson did, to rely on the conventional social matrix for his sustenance and justification. He might adopt the expedient of Thoreau, who wanted less in order to need less, and worked but six weeks in the average year, so he maintained. Or one might combine with others in "industrial association," taking advantage of the economics of communal living, especially in the household, and also calling upon a "science of society" to furnish a theory for the division of labor that would spread the talents of the community more efficiently over its tasks. This was the choice of Brook Farm when it converted to Fourierism in the winter of 1843. Where before there had been little formal organization and, as Emerson judged, "no authority, but each master and mistress of their own actions,"[10] now there were group and series leaders for every facet of the community, Cadre and Echelons all modeled after Fourier's tables of organization of the ideal phalanx.

Hawthorne had left Brook Farm before any of this order was instituted, so its effect on *The Blithedale Romance* is limited, at least as far as explicit reference goes, to a single disparaging discussion of Fourier between Coverdale and Hollingsworth. But the issue is there in another form. Coverdale insists—and here he surely speaks for Hawthorne as well—that Fourierism and the original philosophy of Brook Farm "differed, as widely as the Zenith from the Nadir, in their main principles" (*BR* 53). It is obvious which of the two he prefers, and yet the truth of the matter is that Coverdale—and even more so Hawthorne—finds himself dissatisfied with precisely those principles that most distinguished Blithedale from a Fourierist phalanx, that is, the attempt to integrate manual and intellectual work and do away with the division of labor. If associationism did not seem an adequate solution, it was because it did not go far enough toward a division of labor that would free the thinker to think, the writer to write. Ordinary society, though not by any means ideal, came closer than any utopian scheme to providing a way for men to live by their wits alone.

Hawthorne's own solution to the labor problem was like Emerson's, a gradual return to conventional life. First he arranged with George Ripley to be responsible for little or no manual labor after the heavy effort of getting the crops in—to be, in essence, a boarder rather than a member. The labor quota for each member was ten hours a day in the summer, eight hours in the winter, six days a week all the year round. In the later period at Brook Farm, after the establishment of Fourierism, the labor records show a much shorter average working day, but this was when the membership had passed 100.[11] In Hawthorne's time ten hours was probably not an unusual stint at pitchfork or ploughshare. It is hard to understand how the Brook Farmers thought there would be any energy left over for intellectual pursuits. If Thoreau managed to hear the clang of Trojan armor as he hoed his beans, it was surely because he had not been at it all day. At Blithedale too, "each stroke of the hoe was to uncover some aromatic root of wisdom, heretofore hidden from the sun. . . . In this point of view, matters did not turn out quite so well as we anticipated" (*BR* 65-66).

However it was, Hawthorne's new leisure in September and October did not seem to free him for writing. He acted like a man between jobs—as in fact he was, although he hadn't quite decided it. He paced, he rambled the countryside, carrying his notebook with him, and entering long passages of description—"going through the motions," as he always did when he was not actively producing stories. On September 28 he was elected a trustee of the community and, ironically, to the committee on finance. He had already informed Ripley that he would not stay the winter and might not be back in the spring, so it looks as if the communitists were making one last attempt to win him into the fold by bestowing honors and responsibilities. The effort was futile, for soon the chairman of the committee on finance was trying, with little success, to get back his investment in the community.[12]

At some point Hawthorne had recognized that the problem was not merely the lack of time and energy for writing, but the want of mental space. He had come with a mistaken notion of the psychic economy of utopia—his desire to build a little honeymoon cottage betrays his "individualistic" attitude—and he now discovered that the very premises of communal life were death to his creative impulse. "I have not the sense of perfect seclusion," he wrote Sophia, "which has always been essential to my power of producing anything. It is true, nobody intrudes into my room; but still I cannot be quiet. Nothing here is settled. . . . My mind will not be abstracted."[13]

The total commitment of life in utopia can be a mixed blessing. On the one hand, faith and fervor run high in an experimental community, so that there is plenty of excitement and, at least in the early stages, the sense of new purity and powers. Binding oneself over to the communal good involves much soul searching and sloughing off outworn opinion and the eccentricities of private life, the sort of thing that Coverdale congratulates himself on (*BR* 61). On the other hand, this same enthusiasm can work as an oppressive force in a community, most of all on members whose inner sense of grace remains in doubt. Once confirmed by time and experience in its bonds of brotherhood, such a group tends more and more to enforce the letter as the spirit recedes, until only the forms of the love feast remain, dietary laws, ritual affirmations, taboos.

Little if any such complication rises to the surface of *The Blithedale Romance,* nor was it so very apparent at Brook Farm itself, where the creed was no-creed, and the culture cosmopolitan. Yet one can feel the collective will lurking in both the actual and the fictive communities. One notices it in the unsigned (though identifiable) articles for *The Harbinger*—especially after Fourierization—where every voice finds the choral harmony, or in the collectivization of labor that also followed the conversion to phalanx.

In Blithedale the evidence is subtler and still more indirect. What emerges is a sense of background pressure—the indistinct solidarities that are being undermined and abrogated by Zenobia's dilletantism, Hollingsworth's secret plans for a takeover, and Coverdale's mental reservations. Against whom are such sins, venial or not, committed? The community is like the walls of a room, perceived as a set of constraints by the major characters. We are never presented with corporate Blithedale, so there is no way of pinning down this communal spirit. After the early chapters the utopian features of setting and theme quickly subside into the merest excuse for getting the leading characters together at suppertime.

Blithedale was "pretty well agreed as to the inexpediency of lumbering along with the old system any farther" (*BR* 63), but its members found themselves therefore in a kind of dilemma. In withdrawing from "the weary tread-mill of the established system. . . , for the sake of showing mankind the example of a life governed by other than the false and cruel principles, on which human society has all along been based," the Blithedale enthusiasts soon discovered that, "as regarded society at large, we stood in a position of new hostility, rather than new brotherhood"—and this "in pretty fair proportion with the strictness of our mutual bond among ourselves" (*BR* 19-21). Coverdale cites the community's need to compete with its neighbors for a market for its cash crops; at his most skeptical, he even accuses himself of taking the food "out of some wretch's mouth, into whose vocation I had thrust myself" (*BR* 40). Lesss obvious sources of irritation are only hinted at in *Blithedale,* but were also causes of estrangement. Coverdale reports the good-natured needling by neighbors on the subject of gentlemen farmers; there was also gossip about sexual unconventionalities that, in the actual case of Brook Farm, was much more vicious.

Moreover, this same spirit of mockery works both ways at Blithedale; Silas Foster, the hired hand, is the butt of any number of snide and condescending witticisms, especially on the part of Zenobia. Similarly, Coverdale notes—rather too complacently, a modern reader may find—a number of class differences apparent among the members. Some of them, he suggests, might not have "so quietly taken our places among these good people"—namely the crude Silas, his "rotund helpmate," and two serving-girls—"save for the cherished consciousness that it was not by necessity, but by choice" (*BR* 24). In short, the elitism of members like Zenobia or Coverdale (and, in a slightly different way, Hollingsworth) soured things within, much as the community's zealous condescension tended to poison its relations with society as a whole.

Nor is it clear that any of this was avoidable. If, as Coverdale asserts, the hostility of society seemed to be a function of "the strictness of our mutual bond among ourselves," it might have been argued just as convincingly—and perhaps more crucially—that that same hostility was necessary to the development of internal solidarity at Blithedale. To identify oneself so closely and finally with the community, it was essential to expose or invent a common enemy, an establishment from which one had seceded and against which one could define oneself and friends.

Hints of the intense "moral atmosphere of the Community" appear here and there, as in the immediate effect on the whole membership of the quarrel between Hollingsworth and Coverdale. "It was incidental to the closeness of relationship, into which we had brought ourselves, that an unfriendly state of feeling could not occur between any two members, without the whole society being more or less commoted and made uncomfortable thereby" (*BR* 139).

The phenomenon—a "species of nervous sympathy" Hawthorne calls it—is met within communities where social life is not only more regimented, but also usurps a larger part of the total activity of the members. Primitive tribes are a good example. Their premium on order and conformity produces group behavior so perfected as to seem almost instinctual to an outsider. Among communal experiments, religious societies have most closely approached this sort of tribal unanimity. Primitive Christianity is like primitive culture in many ways. The backwardness is not always an ingredient, but sometimes accompanies a special innocence, as well as the typical predominance of the group over the individual will.

In the Shaker villages, for instance, observers noted something much akin to the "nervous sympathy" Hawthorne imputed to Blithedale. It was a phenomemon that interested Emerson too, and he reports it in his journal: "C[harles] L[ane] describes the action of the Shakers in reference to all their daily arrangements as nervous. Without any formal communication they coincide, and when one is ready, others are, and the cart & the horse also."[14] Emerson's reaction to the Shakers' "nervous arrangements" was not unmixed. He investigated further, and found the members "cleanly & industrious but stupid," "peasants, with a squalid contentment."[15] The judgment, one supposes, implied a comparison to the cosmopolitan society at Brook Farm, where Emerson had noted the lack of authority, "each master and mistress of their own actions." Obviously Emerson knew which he preferred and what he was prepared to pay for it. At Brook Farm they were not so clear about the alternatives or the price. Perhaps because their own style was so civilized and individualist, some members seemed to admire the more instinctual community, where all could agree on values and activities in common, without the necessity of the cumbersome, often oppressive, institutions of modern life.

It is interesting to note that Melville's *Typee* was reviewed in the Brook Farm *Harbinger* soon after it came out, and these same communal traits in the Marquesan Islanders were singled out for praise. The reviewer, Charles Dana, quoted several passages marvelling at the "harmony and smoothness" of life in the valley. Melville was especially enthusiastic about "the unanimity of feeling" among the Typee. "With them there hardly appeared to be any difference of opinion upon any subject whatever. They all thought and acted alike." Dana has nothing but praise for such communal virtues; instead of wondering what it might be like to live in this heaven of collective consciousness, he has eyes only for the means of getting there: "The peace and good will of that South Sea valley are as possible here as they are there. . . . we must have a social system which will produce and distribute to every member of society a complete abundance as the result of a healthy amount of labor."[16] Here again is the "arithmetic and comfort" that Emerson complained of in the original conception of Brook Farm, an emphasis on goals and instrumentalities that ignored too many of the costs.

Of course Brook Farm never attained to the "nervous arrangements" of the Shakers, let alone the unanimity of the Typee. Nonetheless, it must have been a milder version of the same moral atmosphere that kept Hawthorne incapacitated for art during his months at West Roxbury, especially after he had renounced manual labor and was thus presumably free to write. "My mind will not be abstracted," he said, and one is reminded of the little fold-down desk he built for himself the following year in the Old Manse, with its face to the wall rather than the window. Certain kinds of intellectual activity might mesh well enough with hard physical labor, so long as there was not too much of either; but the art of fiction could not flourish in paradise. The unmediated enjoyment of the natural and social orders—work, companionship, and love—seemed to obviate meditation or fantasy, continuously drawing the mind out rather than forcing it back upon itself. Thus Hawthorne was known as a recluse among his friends (Alcott saw him once in a season when they lived next door to each other) and he viewed himself as an "owl" or "captive" self-immured in a "dungeon."[17] It was the same instinct of consciousness that made Emerson exclaim against company—"in all mere mortal parties, I take the contagion of their views & lose my own. . . . As soon as they are gone, the muse returns"—and the same that gave rise to Thoreau's dictum, "Friends will be much apart; they will respect more each other's privacy than their communion. . . . "[18]

When Ripley invited Emerson, and when Alcott's friends at Fruitlands invited Thoreau, to join with them in communal life, their responses were emphatic. The business they had to transact was private and could best be pursued in study or shack. Hawthorne's opinion was more divided, or he would never have joined Brook Farm to start with, but finally he too regarded his privacy as essential to his art. On his return from Europe in 1860, when he could finally afford it, he too built a retreat, the "tower" in the Wayside at Concord.

Perhaps the difference between these neighbors had to do with the kinds of writing they did. As a moralist, Emerson was often of two minds about a subject, but he rarely entertained both possibilities at once. His attitude toward manual labor, for example, did an about-face in the early 1840s, and his journals record first one position, then the other, with equal certainty. Thoreau handled ambivalence with paradox. But as a storyteller, Hawthorne developed modes of irony and doubleness that raised dubiety to an artistic and even a moral virtue. In his work the imagination is a no man's land of attitude and belief. His heroes are chameleons like Holgrave, or sophisticates like Kenyon. His villains are the characters who cannot persevere in mixed ethical circumstances—Aylmer, Giovanni, Young Goodman Brown, Ethan Brand—but demand a clear-cut case and final solution to all human problems.

In *Blithedale*—a relatively late work after all—Hawthorne has taken this tolerance for ambiguity to a stage quite beyond even the risk taking of his Brook Farm days. But at the same time that his fiction has grown to include more of his sense of the possibilities of life, the valves seem to have been closed down considerably in the life itself. Perhaps this was the lesson that Brook Farm taught—that the freedom of the imagination was a function of the social space it preempted, the elbow-room that was lacking in the community. Conventional married life was his version of Walden Pond, as solitary and inward an existence as his bachelorhood in Salem.

The Blithedale Romance deals with such alternatives—the choices of his own early manhood—in an astonishingly forthright manner, considering that all the decisions and commitments had been settled years before. Not that Hawthorne allows communal life to emerge as much of an alternative—there is in fact scarcely even a caricature of it, aside from the attack on Fourierism—but neither is the domestic option that he finally picked up given the emphasis one might have expected. A novel like James Fenimore Cooper's *The Crater* (1847) could depict a utopian community almost solely to prove the impossibility of any egalitarian society and the preferability of institutions like the nuclear family, the self-made man, and the traditional social order. The same set of values wins out in *Blithedale,* but the victory is pyrrhic at best, and the failure of the community is not an occasion for gloating as it is in Cooper. No one really wins in *Blithedale,* and of the losers, perhaps the artist figure, the surrogate of the author, forfeited the most. The reservations about communal life that Coverdale brings with him to Blithedale are profoundly intertwined with his literary consciousness. It is because he regards his friends as actors in a drama taking place on the private stage of his own imagination that he cannot become one of them and enter into their feelings directly. He is an outsider, a "chorus" to the tragedy, as a function of his art. Hollingsworth, Zenobia, Priscilla, Westervelt, and even Old Moodie are regarded as a "knot of characters, whom a real intricacy of events, greatly assisted by my method of insulating them from other relations, had kept so long upon my mental stage, as actors in a drama" (*BR* 156).

It is interesting that both of Hawthorne's Concord neighbors, Emerson and Thoreau, had identified this same antisocial propensity in themselves, even so far as to have chosen the same metaphor to describe it. In *Walden* Thoreau had also used terms borrowed from the stage to explain his conception of consciousness and reality:

> By a conscious effort of the mind we can stand aloof from actions and their consequences; and all things, good and bad, go by us like a torrent. . . . I only know myself as a human entity; the scene, so to speak, of thoughts and affections; and am sensible of a certain doubleness by which I can stand as remote from myself as from another. However intense my experience, I am conscious of the presence and criticism of a part of me, which, as it were, is not a part of me, but spectator, sharing no experience, but taking note of it; and that is no more I than it is you. When the play, it may be the tragedy, of life is over, the spectator goes his way. It was a kind of fiction, a work of the imagination only, so far as he was concerned. This doubleness may easily make us poor neighbors and friends sometimes.[19]

There is a matching passage in Emerson's journals, written not long after Thoreau went out to Walden:

> Men go through the world each musing on a great fable dramatically pictured & rehearsed before him. If you speak to the man, he turns his eyes from his own scene, & slower or faster endeavors to com-

> prehend what you say. When you have done speaking, he returns to his private music. Men generally attempt early in life to make their brothers first, afterwards their wives, acquainted with what is going forward in their private theatre, but they soon desist from the attempt on finding that they also have some farce or perhaps some ear & heart-rending tragedy forward on their secret boards on which they are intent, and all parties acquiesce at last in a private box with the whole play performed before himself *solus*[20]

These views are remarkably similar in terms and application, and it is only in the degree of acquiescence in such a private life of the imagination that the three differ. Thoreau, the most willful and the most solitary, is also the most comfortable with a "double consciousness." Emerson was less happy with the "private box," and part of his account is a description of efforts to share it with others. Of the three Hawthorne is most uneasy with this vision of life and thinks it not so much the temptation of all men as the peculiar vice of the artist. Holgrave, the artist figure of *The Seven Gables,* is accused of treating his friends as characters in a "tragedy"—"played exclusively for your amusement" (HSG 217). These are obviously echoes of self-reproach, and reveal a guilty obsession with the antisocial—one may say, anticommunal—nature of the literary imagination. Where Thoreau and Emerson seem to think their literary habit of mind can hurt no one but themselves, Hawthorne conceives of it as a more active, meddling mode of consciousness, dangerous to the social fabric that it not only calls into question symbolically, but also directly interferes with. Hawthorne summed up his misgivings when he had Coverdale say:

> It is not, I apprehend, a healthy kind of mental occupation, to devote ourselves too exclusively to the study of individual men and women. If the person under examination be one's self, the result is pretty certain to be diseased action of the heart, almost before we can snatch a second glance. Or, if we take the freedom to put a friend under our microscope, we thereby insulate him from many of his true relations, magnify his peculiarities, inevitably tear him into parts, and, of course, patch him very clumsily together again. What wonder, then, should we be frightened by the aspect of a monster, which, after all—though we can point to every feature of his deformity in the real personage—may be said to have been created mainly by ourselves! (*BR* 69)

This "prying into . . . character" is the unpardonable sin everywhere in Hawthorne. *The Blithedale Romance* is a daring book because in it Hawthorne tried for once to face directly the almost metaphysical anxiety that the practice of his art seemed to arouse in him. By planting Coverdale precisely in the center of his dilemma—the antithetical claims of social conscience and literary consciousness—and especially by writing in the first person, with material from his own life at Brook Farm, Hawthorne reopened all the old issues that two dozen stories and as many years had served to smooth over and neutralize in habitual formulations. It was the last great book he wrote, the culmination of three hard years of imaginative work in a genre that forced him beyond the easier answers of shorter fiction, where an emblem or metaphor might serve instead of analysis. Coverdale left him no such dodges; he was a character not many writers would have dared create.

Seven

Spiritualism

ANOTHER WAY OF describing how Coverdale's literary consciousness prevents his participation in the community or the drama of its members is to point out the difficulty of being a character in a story one is narrating. Coverdale is peculiarly both in and out of the novel, since he is not only character and narrator, but also, quite frequently, the author himself, Hawthorne in mood and voice. This is spreading Coverdale rather thin, of course, and the novel suffers for it on the realistic level. But as Hawthorne makes clear enough in his preface, realism is not his literary manner. His habitual stance is symbolism, and what he attempts with Coverdale is an extremely interesting experiment in symbolic fiction, the embodiment within a narrative of the psychic phenomenon of narration itself. Hawthorne understood—partly, one supposes, through the gothic tradition, partly through his own experience—how the characters in a novel work as projections of the author's own inner life. In *The Blithedale Romance* he set out to catch the imagination in the act of this sort of projection. This accounts for Coverdale's repeated intimations that, although completely outside the valences of his friends' affairs, he nonetheless is somehow deeply responsible for them, and, lacking a career of his own, lives vicariously in their acts, brooding only over their destinies.

In *The House of the Seven Gables* Holgrave is unmistakably a representation of facets Hawthorne could identify in himself—writer, reformer, spellbinder. Other characters—Phoebe,

Clifford, Hepzibah, and Jaffrey—comprise the required cast for Hawthorne's favorite fantasies, not so much embodiments of his own nature as materials for "dream-work." *The Blithedale Romance* investigates these very processes of identification and fantasy. The chief male characters are refractions of the Holgrave/Hawthorne personality—Coverdale the writer, Hollingsworth the reformer, and Westervelt the mesmerist. As narrator Coverdale is treated as both fantast and participant in his own fantasies, while the others help him act them out.

The structural method of *Blithedale* thus necessarily differs from that of *The Seven Gables.* In the earlier novel the plot moved in two directions: one within the advancing present, reported by the narrator (Hawthorne himself) along the lines of conventional probability and expectation; the other oscillating back and forth in the Pyncheon family history, partly controlled by Holgrave, whose tale of Alice Pyncheon exposes an abyss of symbolic meanings behind the events and relations of the surface plot. In *Blithedale* all such choices of scene and subject are much more palpably occurring in the mind of the narrator, whose tone colors everything and whose opinions invariably accompany each detail or event. As in *The Seven Gables* the plot is implied rather than unfolded; the progress is marked by tableaux rather than dramatized in scenes. In *Blithedale,* however, the access to each stage is through Coverdale's consciousness, in ways that make every "event" and its setting appear at once part of a realistic plot and part of a projected fantasy. Some obvious examples are the many peephole scenes, in which Coverdale observes or "seems to remember" observing the interplay of his friends from secret, distant vantage points—the grape arbor "hermitage," the boardinghouse window, and so on. These perspectives not only underline the "realistic" situation of Coverdale—his alienation from his world—but also suggest that the entire story is, on another level, merely the product of the narrator's imagination. "By long brooding over our recollections, we subtilize them into something akin to imaginary stuff, and hardly capable of being distinguished from it," he admits at one point (*BR* 104-5). Such frequent hints leave the reader little choice but to take the next step and consider the possibility that all is mere fantasy.

Hawthorne is not the only American writer of his day to play such games with narrative stance, though perhaps he was the most in earnest. Poe liked to toy with his readers, leaving them in doubt whether the tellers of his tales actually suffered all the horrors they report, or merely hallucinated them. And much more seriously, Melville experimented with the same problems of narrative illusion, beginning with the teasing ambiguity that led readers to doubt the authenticity of his Marquesan adventures, and culminating in the imaginings come to life of his writer-hero Pierre Glendenning.

Pierre is as dark and complex a book as *Blithedale* itself—too much so to furnish any pat examples of the symbolic mode as Melville had come to practice it in 1852. But from the very beginning of his career Melville had been tempted into symbolic episodes in his fiction, and there is a passage in *Typee* (a book Hawthorne admired) that will serve for comparison with a characteristic scene in *Blithedale.* It provides a particularly clear example of the way that realistic prose can suddenly shift gears and become thoroughly symbolic in intent, all the while retaining its veneer of verisimilitude.

After jumping ship and making their way far into the interior of the island, Tommo (Melville) and his friend Toby have found their adventure turning into more of an ordeal than a lark. They have run out of food, worn themselves out on the rugged countryside, and finally are drenched by rain. Tommo develops a fever and a curious symbolic "wound" that stays with him throughout the novel: " . . . one of my legs was swelled to such a degree, and pained me so acutely, that I half suspected I had been bitten by some venomous reptile, the congenial inhabitant of the chasm from which we had lately emerged."[1] The sexual implications of this wound are clear enough and are tied to other symbolic meanings that go deep into the problems of living in Paradise which the novel treats. There are no serpents in Paradise but one, and it is a major aim of *Typee* to explore that single sinful potentiality. This is scarcely evident on the surface of the prose, but passages like this one and the paragraph that immediately follows it tell us how to read the rest:

> As the feverish sensation increased upon me, I tossed about, still unwilling to disturb my slumbering companion, from whose side I removed two or three yards. I chanced to push aside a branch, and by so doing suddenly disclosed to my view a scene which even now I can recall with all the vividness of the first impression. Had a glimpse of the garden of Paradise been revealed to me I could scarcely have been more ravished with the sight.

There ensues a description of the beauties of the Typee valley—the "palmetto-thatched houses," the "universal verdure," the "hushed repose, which I almost feared to break lest, like the enchanted gardens in the fairy tale, a single syllable might dissolve the spell."

Melville's narrator Tommo is in much the same position as Coverdale, subject and object of his story, and these first glimpses of Typee paradise provide the clue to the symbolic method into which Melville seems to be drifting. The whole adventure that follows is both real and imaginary, a genuine experience and a novel. Its earliest readers saw this paradox as the problem of the book, and the controversy over whether any of it really happened is famous. Even more interesting to a reader of *The Blithedale Romance* is the connection between this ambiguous stance and the problems of communal life—in brief, the problem of consciousness in paradise, or the problem of faith.

As we have already seen in discussing the choice of Coverdale as representative of both literary consciousness and the utopian impulse, the dilemmas and impasses built into this situation are not easily solved. As we now come to focus on Westervelt—that avatar of the author whose essence is out-and-out antisocial, and whose very profession is spiritual delusion—we get a still closer look at this same problem of consciousness in paradise, from the point of view of the Evil One himself, irresistible whisperer in the ear of faith.

In the scene of the first meeting between Coverdale and Westervelt, Hawthorne moves with marvelous ease and deftness into a symbolic mode, through which we begin to gather that Coverdale and Westervelt are antithetical alter egos, Coverdale all the while being somehow prior to Westervelt, the ultimate source of his enemy-double. The chapter called "The Wood-Path" opens the second main section of the novel. "Paradise," insofar as Blithedale represents it, has already been described with much irony, including an embarrassing caricature of Zenobia as Eve. In spite of the anxiety and apprehension betrayed in these tones, the bond between Coverdale and Hollingsworth has not yet been broken, and Blithedale is still a brotherhood aspiring to the communal virtues of the tribe, the total family of *Typee.* Now enters the villain, the tempter in Eden, Westervelt, who carries a cane "with a wooden head, carved in vivid imitation of that of a serpent" (*BR* 92), and who, like "the black man" Goodman Brown meets on *his* wood-path, is obviously the devil in disguise.

As Coverdale begins to describe his walk in the woods, he makes a point of explaining that he wants to escape from the social pressures of Blithedale. These are not specified much further, but enough to show that they are the same factors that kept Hawthorne from being able to write at Brook Farm:

> Unless renewed by a yet farther withdrawal towards the inner circle of self-communion, I lost the better part of my individuality. My thoughts became of little worth, and my sensibilities grew as arid as a tuft of moss. . . . (*BR* 89)

As Coverdale penetrates deeper into the woods, his "individuality" returns, and we begin to see what he means by that. In a beautifully paced and modulated passage reminiscent of *Typee,* Coverdale tells us that we are entering a symbolic region—not "Paradise" in this case, but another interior landscape:

> At first, I walked very swiftly, as if the heavy floodtide of social life were roaring at my heels, and would outstrip and overwhelm me, without all the better diligence in my escape. But, threading the more distant windings of the track, I abated my pace and looked about me for some side-aisle, that should admit me into the innermost sanctuary of this green cathedral; just as, in human acquaintanceship, a casual opening sometimes lets us, all of a sudden, into the long-sought intimacy of a mysterious heart. (*BR* 89-90)

Next comes the encounter with Westervelt—the "casual opening" that lets us see into Coverdale's own "mysterious heart." In the dark forest, away from his ostensible hopes and attachments to society, Coverdale is accosted by a strange, dreamlike figure costumed for the stage, his behavior so mannered and his appearance so contrived (his smile reveals that his gleaming teeth are false) that Coverdale conjectures that he must be a "goblin"—that is, from the reader's point of view, a demon conjured up by Coverdale's imagination.

> So much was I absorbed in my reflections—or rather, in my mood, the substance of which was as yet too shapeless to be called

> thought—that footsteps rustled on the leaves, and a figure passed me by, almost without impressing either the sound or sight upon my consciousness.
>
> A moment afterwards, I heard a voice. . . . (*BR* 90)

As so often in Hawthorne, this account may be read in two ways: as a realistic detailing of an event or as a subtle analysis of a hallucination. Or, perhaps most helpfully, Westervelt may be viewed as a sort of Doppelgänger for Coverdale, both real and imaginary, the evil materialization of his "individuality" without any redeeming social ties. How else is Coverdale's instant dislike of Westervelt to be explained? Certainly not by his own absurd justification, his supposed offense at being addressed as "friend" by a stranger. As their conversation proceeds, it gradually dawns on the reader that Westervelt is expressing, with pointed irony, Coverdale's own hostile feelings about his friends, Zenobia, Hollingsworth, and Priscilla. Westervelt has an uncanny way of giving the nasty twist of public gossip to every one of Coverdale's private reservations.

Immediately after the interview, Coverdale retreats to his "hermitage," the bower of grape vines which he has discovered in a pine tree; his "one exclusive possession, while I counted myself a brother of the socialists." Here he has arrived at the center of his inwardness: "It symbolized my individuality, and aided me in keeping it inviolate" (*BR* 99). Perched high enough to make his friends' problems and aspirations seem "ridiculous," Coverdale begins to realize that his attitude has taken its coloration from Westervelt: "I recognized, as chiefly due to this man's influence, the sceptical and sneering view which, just now, had filled my mental vision in regard to all life's better purposes. And it was through his eyes, more than my own, that I was looking at Hollingsworth, with his glorious, if impracticable dream, and at the noble earthliness of Zenobia's character, and even at Priscilla, whose impalpable grace lay so singularly between disease and beauty" (*BR* 101). Coverdale blames his own "cold scepticism" on Westervelt, or the Westervelt in himself—"a part of my own nature showed itself responsive to him" (*BR* 102)—but the reader of the symbolic level may take the analysis a step further and see how Westervelt's very existence as a character is being proposed as tentative and illusory. "Was it a vision that I had witnessed in the wood?" Coverdale exclaims a few chapters later. "Was Westervelt a goblin?" (*BR* 127).

ii

If calling Westervelt a "goblin" warns the reader to think of him as a symbolic figure, a projection of the narrator's own fantasies, it is also true that terms like "goblin," "fiend," "enchantment," "possession," and so on cast shadows of gothic mystery over all such techniques and apprehensions. The supernatural is familiar enough in Hawthorne, of course, but in *Blithedale* the emphasis is unusual because its peculiar aura derives as much from the new spiritualism popular in the 1850s as from the ancient varieties of demonology. Westervelt is not only a mesmerist, but also a spiritualist, and Priscilla is both somnambulist and medium. These latter-day traits and terms are interwoven with more traditional features of the supernatural, and all are embedded in a narrative based on actual persons and places.

The Westervelt thread of the plot presents at least one rather mystifying set of supernatural allusions. In "Zenobia's Legend" the magician who exhibited the Veiled Lady—that is, Westervelt—is said to have "bartered his own soul for seven years' possession of a familiar fiend," and we are told "that the last year of the contract was wearing towards its close" (*BR* 110). The Veiled Lady describes herself as "a sad and lonely prisoner, in a bondage which is worse to me than death" (*BR* 112-13). At the end of the legend, when the Zenobia figure has betrayed the Priscilla figure, "the dark Magician, who had bartered away his soul . . . threw his arms around the Veiled Lady; and she was his bond-slave, forever more!" (*BR* 116).

This thread is more than supernatural embroidery on the character of Westervelt. At several other points in the novel the mesmerist is called a "goblin," and it is easy enough to connect the "Magician" of "Zenobia's Legend" with the "wizard" of Fauntleroy's tale, who "subjected" Priscilla "as his familiar spirit, through whose medium he gained cognizance of whatever happened, in regions near or remote" (*BR* 188). In that same story the "wizard" is revealed as a "demon" (that is, a "goblin") and his "semblance of a human body . . . only a necromantic, or perhaps a mechanical contrivance" (*BR* 188). Priscilla is here again described as "enthralled in an intolerable bondage" (*BR* 190). All this will hold together well enough, though it constitutes a lump more than a leavening in an otherwise realistically presented story. But this is not the end of it.

In the final chapters, when Zenobia has been supplanted by Priscilla as legend foretold—"In love, in worldly fortune, in all your pursuit of happiness" (*BR* 115)—it is not Westervelt who is accused of being "a monster," a "cold, heartless, self-beginning and self-ending piece of mechanism," but Hollingsworth; while instead of Priscilla, Zenobia herself is now described as "an hereditary bond-slave," at last "awake, disenchanted, disenthralled" (*BR* 217-18). Still more confusing, Zenobia alludes to the "fiend" and the "seven years" that appeared earlier in her legend: "The fiend, I doubt not, has made his choicest mirth of you [that is, Hollingsworth], these seven years past, and especially in the mad summer which we have spent together." This "fiend" cannot be the "monster" Hollingsworth, nor even the "familiar fiend" Priscilla in her mediumistic role as Veiled Lady; perhaps it is the "goblin" and "demon" Westervelt, though it may be some higher ranking devil still, assumed to be at the heart of all the evil influences of the novel—perhaps Satan himself. (It is noteworthy that Westervelt is typically referred to as a "goblin" and not a fiend.")

Finally—to present all the complications before attempting to unravel any of them—even Coverdale is implicated in this knot of supernatural intrigue. Early in the book, before any character has been proposed as "fiend" or seven years' "bond-slave," Coverdale attempts to poison Priscilla's mind against Hollingsworth and Zenobia, who he hints—quite correctly as it turns out—will ultimately betray her. "It had taken me nearly seven years of worldly life," he announces with curiously irrelevant specificity, "to hive up the bitter honey which I here offered to Priscilla." When Priscilla rejects his worldly wisdom and goes to sit at the feet of Hollingsworth, Coverdale notes that love is a kind of magnetism or spiritualism that "transports" its victims "to the seventh heaven; and if you ask what brought them thither, they neither can tell nor care to learn, but cherish an ecstatic faith that there they shall abide forever" (*BR* 76-77). Thus Coverdale too, although a skeptic in matters of ecstasy and the spiritualistic spheres, is nonetheless part of the seven years' supernatural compact that lies mysteriously behind all these passages.

Hawthorne's use of such materials can be rationalized without much difficulty. It is only the ambiguity of their application to different characters that presents problems. The "Village-Hall" chapter of *Blithedale* clears up a good deal of the demonological theory behind Hawthorne's "goblins" and "fiends." First of all, a distinction is made there between the old spiritualism—really mesmerism—of the "singular age" (circa 1841) that serves as background to the story, and the modern spiritualism of ten years later, the "epoch of rapping spirits." The former is characterized chiefly as a matter of "the miraculous power of one human being over the will and passions of another," whereas the latter involves "intercourse with spirits, . . . goblins, . . . shadows of past mortality" (*BR* 198-99). The first sort of supernaturalism is thus explicitly located in Westervelt's evil powers, whereas the second is treated as a later discovery or elaboration of such powers, not part of the plot but only a kind of elucidation of it, from Coverdale's vantage-point of hindsight.

This second passage gives us a clue as to how to interpret the application of the term "goblin" rather than "fiend" to Westervelt. As a "goblin" he is to be viewed as a "shadow," of an "order" of spirits "below humanity," not a power such as a "fiend" might be, perhaps nothing but an illusion that may not "exist at all" (*BR* 199)—and thus, symbolically, a kind of figment of the imagination. As another writer, less skeptical about such matters than Hawthorne, said in a book exactly contemporaneous with *Blithedale,* these rapping spirits "are the gossips of ghost land, poor, frivolous, flimsy wretches, who receive the shreds of thought here, and the shadows only of thought in the spirit world. . . . They have a restless desire for tangibility, and are perpetually trying to command material objects in a way to make themselves known."[2]

Although careful to make the distinction between mesmerism and spiritualism—the opening pages of the novel give additional criteria, mesmerism being more a matter of mystification, spiritualism affecting "the simplicity and openness of scientific experiment"—Hawthorne in fact presents a mixed genre in his account of the Veiled Lady's performances. Like the early somnambulists, Priscilla is entirely subject to her operator's will and cannot perceive anything except at his behest. Several "deep-lunged country-fellows" are encouraged to yell in her ears and beat "upon the floor with bludgeons," to demonstrate her deafness to all but Westervelt's call, and finally they "laid hold of the great chair" and lifted her high in the air, without disturbing her composure (*BR* 202). Such tests were commonplace in the early days of mesmeric demonstrations, and Hawthorne may have watched, for example, the exhibitions of Dr. Robert H. Collyer and his somnambulist Frederick, who evinced no response to being stretched "upon the floor" or to the "firing [of] two large pistols near his head."[3]

Priscilla's feats as a "seeress and a prophetess" are also characteristic of the early days of mesmerism—chiefly a matter of answering questions from the audience about the future or the past. She is able to use her clairvoyance to travel in space, from "Arabia" to the "polar seas" or "East Indian forest" (*BR* 6, 202-3). Such travels were typical of the somnambulists of the early 1840s, who would take their audiences on guided tours of any domains they suggested. Furthermore, the "professor's" analysis of his powers, "in a strange, philosophical guise, with terms of art, as if it were a matter of chemical discovery," is also characteristic. He speaks of a "universally pervasive fluid," no doubt the "odic fluid" that most mesmerists postulated, the superfluity or undersupply of which determined one's potential as mesmerist or somnambulist (*BR* 200). Here, however, the distinction between mesmerism and spiritualism begins to blur, for Coverdale has already informed us (not quite accurately, it may be noted) that the latter had more of the affectation of science.

Also not quite in line with strict chronology is the emphasis on Priscilla's function as "medium"—a term used repeatedly in passages dealing with her, even in its nonspiritualist meanings. Westervelt claims that Priscilla is "in communion with the spiritual world" (*BR* 201). Depending on how we interpret this communion, it may be anachronistic to attribute such powers to a somnambulist of 1841. The mesmerists of the period did claim that their subjects could transcend time and space, and thus their services as seers were in demand, to plumb the depths of the future and even to examine the internal organs of diseased customers. Naturally enough, such limitless access to creation suggested still further unexplored territory to be tried, "the undiscovered country" of the dead. But professionals rarely exploited this side of their art before the "rapping" mania which Margaret and Katherine Fox started in 1848. A practitioner like Andrew Jackson Davis, for example, sometimes earned the $10 he charged for medical or prophetic interviews by calling in the spirit of Galen, as a sort of consultation with a specialist, or similarly raising the spirit of Swedenborg as an authority for his descriptions of the "seventh heaven"; but these were very different from the interviews with deceased friends and relatives that became the rule of the day after the first "Rochester knockings."[4] On the other hand, Georgiana Bruce, a member of Brook Farm not long after Hawthorne, says that her friend Cornelia Hall not only diagnosed and treated medical cases, but also attempted to mesmerize Georgiana, so that "I should see denizens of the other world; and . . . describe them so accurately that they would be recognized by their friends."[5]

This is very different from Davis's descriptions of the "Summer-Land," which are full of abstractions—powers, vortices, substance and quality, worlds and ultimates—but few personalities. He says "that spirits commune with one another while one is in the body and the other in the higher spheres," but up to the present the communication is "one-way," and the "person in the body is unconscious of the influx."[6] This is a strong hint of spiritual intercourse to come, but Davis did not yet claim its achievement. He was the first important somnambulist, however, to discard his "operator" and become a self-induced clairvoyant, that is, the first true "medium" whose "fluid" was acted on directly by his "spiritual guides" (Swedenborg and Galen) instead of a magnetizer. This (in 1844) was a significant step toward the uninvited appearance of spirits in the Fox household at Hydesville, New York, on March 31, 1848—"the rap heard round the world."

Although few if any popular mesmerists claimed full contact with the spirits before 1848, Georgiana Bruce Kirby's recollection is confirmed by Hawthorne's own letter to Sophia Peabody in 1841, in which he urges her to refuse to be mesmerized, and debunks her friends' accounts of the "seventh heaven," which only "degrade high Heaven and its inhabitants." Some of these marvels could not be disproved; but if they had to be accepted, it was as "physical" or "material" effects, not supernatural ones. Hawthorne does not believe in the spiritual origin of such "insight[s] into the mysteries of life beyond death," but attributes them rather to an "earthly effluence from Mrs. Park's corporeal system"—that is, mesmeric influences, which he considers as "chemical" as Westervelt himself. He compares the visions of the somnambulists with opium dreams, just as "bright" and "just as susceptible of proof." But whatever Hawthorne's skepticism, the phenomena described by Sophia must have been similar to those Georgy Bruce had hoped to experience at Brook Farm, and fully consonant with those exhibited by the Veiled Lady in *Blithedale.*

It is worth being rather precise about these details, since they bear directly on the problem of Westervelt's "goblin" nature. What, if any, credence did goblins and ghosts compel in Hawthorne and his readers? By 1852, his audience might be counted on to have become quite familiar with modern theories of the spirit world and its accessibility, and a great many people were full believers.[7] Moreover, as new converts to a system only a few years old, their interest might be assumed to run hot. Hawthorne, on the other hand, had not changed his opinion of 1841, and part of his desire to keep the mesmerism of that day separate from the spiritualism of the 1850s lay in his own theory of the phenomena. He still thought that the so-called spiritual visions were mere illusions produced by "earthly effluences." They could not possibly be genuine. "Do I believe in these wonders?" he asked himself in the *English Notebooks,* after hearing Garth Wilkinson's account of the spiritualist manifestations he had witnessed:

> Of course; for how is it possible to doubt either the solemn word or the sober observation of a learned and sensible man like Dr. Wilkinson. But, again, do I really believe it? Of course not; for I cannot consent to let Heaven and Earth, this world and the next, be beaten up together like the white and yolk of an egg, merely out of respect to Dr. Wilkinson's sanity and integrity. I would not believe my own sight or touch of the spiritual hands. (*EN* 617)

He was willing to believe in the *facts* of spiritualism, that is, the *reports* of visions, the *accounts* of poltergeists and apparitions, ghostly hands and spectral manifestations—but he preferred to attribute their causes to magnetic suggestion. This, of course, was quite close to the prevailing modern view of such matters. As he wrote in his journal a few years later, when his own family was subjected to a visitation of spirits through the writing-mediumship of his children's governess Ada Shepard, "They are facts to my understanding, which, it might have been anticipated, would have been the last to acknowledge them; but they seem not to be facts to my intuitions and deeper perceptions. My inner soul does not in the least admit them; there is a mistake somewhere. . . . In the communications between my wife and her mother, I cannot help thinking that (Miss [Shepard] being unconsciously in a mesmeric state) all the responses are conveyed to her fingers from my wife's mind" (X 394-95).

This interpretation is remarkable in two ways, First, Hawthorne shows himself still convinced that spiritualist effects are merely the products of mesmeric suggestion. Second, he seems to believe that such mesmeric influences can be transmitted unconsciously, apparently without the ordinary physical cues, mediated by the five senses. Just as magnetizers like Dr. Fiske or Dr. Collyer has asserted in the early 1840s, mesmeric suggestion might be entirely a matter of the will of the operator secretly exerted upon the susceptibilities of the subject.

The implications for *Blithedale* seems to be these: Westervelt does indeed have the power to "call" Priscilla over long distances, to throw her into a trance, to command her obedience, and to cause her to report visions of a spirit world. Her spiritualistic perceptions are not authentic however, merely induced. Priscilla is not a true seeress, but only the helpless tool of her enchanter. And as for Westervelt himself, he must not be a genuine goblin, but only a symbolic demon—in short, a mountebank.

If Hawthorne did not believe in spiritualism, why then did he bother to introduce the whole paraphernalia of "goblins" and "fiends" and "enchantments"? For one thing, the issue—more or less in abeyance since his antimesmeric letter to Sophia in 1841—had been revived for him in 1851, when he was just finishing up *The House of the Seven Gables* and preparing his materials for *The Blithedale Romance.* Mesmerism had already served his purposes well in *The Seven Gables*, where Holgrave's hereditary powers of enchantment (the "Maule eye") are explained as modern animal magnetism. It was a theme that fit perfectly into his generational plot, and there was even current authority for identifying old Salem witchcraft with present-day mesmerism. No doubt the material still seemed potent to Hawthorne when he began thinking about a new romance.

Moreover, several occurrences in his private life suggested the possibility of introducing mesmerism in its popular new guise as spiritualism into his next book. First of all, his old Salem friend William B. Pike, who had been plying Hawthorne with ghost stories since their days together in the Boston Customs House in 1839, had recently written to report, among other things, his latest experiences with "spiritual intercourse." Hawthorne replied, first mentioning his plan to treat Brook Farm in his next novel and then cautiously reacting to Pike's spiritualist enthusiasms: "I am very glad of your testimony in favor of spiritual intercourse," he wrote. "I have heard and read much on the subject, and it appears to me to be the strangest and most bewildering affair I ever heard of. I should be very glad to believe that these rappers are, in any one instance, the spirits of the persons whom they profess themselves to be; but though I have talked with those who have had the freest communication, there has always been something that makes me doubt. So you must allow me to withhold my full and entire belief, until I have heard some of the details of your spiritual intercourse."[8] As we know, later investigation did not alter Hawthorne's skeptical view of spiritual phenomena, which are the subject of a series of passages in the *English* and *Italian Notebooks,* culminating in the already-quoted notes on the spiritual communion between Sophia and her mother through Ada Shepard's mediumship.[9] Nonetheless, the very fact of such frequent encounters with believers must have tempted Hawthorne to give the subject more direct treatment than he had done in *The Seven Gables*.

Pike's testimony was not the first invasion of the spirits that Hawthorne had to cope with in 1851. Earlier in the year his sister-in-law Elizabeth Peabody—who, it will be remembered, was the first to introduce Sophia to the wonders of mesmerism in 1836—had written the Hawthornes to suggest that their six-year-old daughter Una would be an excellent spiritualistic medium and that she, Elizabeth, had friends who would be happy to join hands in the ghostly circle of a seance. Sophia wrote the following reply:

> My dear Lizzie, I do not know where you are but think you are probably in New York. Thank you for your most interesting letter, received last week through Mary Mann. Mr. Hawthorne says he never [underlined six times] will consent to Una's being made a medium of communication, & that he will defy all Hell rather, so that he will have to disprove the testimony of the spirits, if it comes

> to that. He says he cannot let you come here with Rappers in train—for he thinks it would injure Una physically & spiritually to be subjected to such influence. Thus he bids me say.[10]

This is a delicious glimpse into what must have been a recurring impasse of comic proportions—Hawthorne exasperated beyond words, Elizabeth perenially enthusiastic and proof against all insult, Sophia a bit dithered by her role as buffer between such formidable antagonists. Hawthorne might have expected Lizzie to suggest some such scheme; he had easily guessed her part in Sophia's experiments with mesmerism so many years earlier: "Thy sister Elizabeth would like nothing so much as to proclaim thy spiritual experiences, by sound of trumpet." Whatever Elizabeth involved herself in was likely to be full of the latest humbug.

Yet for purposes of fiction, and especially for a book that was to satirize the social sciences and philanthropies then raging in Boston and New York, perhaps Elizabeth might be the perfect weathervane of popular folly. When his good friend Pike also offered his testimony, Hawthorne must have begun to think seriously of bringing together several motifs of his earlier work—the ghosts and other conventional spirits of innumerable tales and sketches, the mesmerism of *The House of the Seven Gables,* and the theme of moral slavery that had long been building up pressure in his notebooks and had burst forth in "Ethan Brand" and *The Scarlet Letter.* Spiritualism provided the perfect means of amalgamating these materials into a single plot.

Westervelt is thus a goblin in the traditional sense, just as Dickon is Mother Rigby's "familiar" in "Feathertop," or as "The Gray Champion" serves as a spectral exemplar to the citizens of New England. At the same time, Westervelt is not a geniune goblin—that is, he is only a humbug, his spiritualist pretensions are fakery, and his ghostly quality is a mere symbol of the sham of his character. Then too, goblin or not, Westervelt exercises a certain mysterious but authentic magnetic power over Priscilla, which makes her his "bond slave" in effect, and which he uses to induce the spiritualistic trance that is the basis of his Veiled Lady act. Finally, all these conflicting versions of Westervelt also suggest the symbolic value of his role as a fantasy double or projected alter ego for Coverdale, apparently both a real person and a figment of Coverdale's imagination.

Of these aspects of his goblin nature, which is it that has "bartered his own soul for seven years' possession of a familiar fiend"? And who is the "fiend"? Why is the term "seven years"? And how do the other characters, also implicated in the seven years' contract, fit into the picture? Is Westervelt the only demon in the book? Is Priscilla the only bond slave?

Not all the answers are provided in *The Blithedale Romance*. Much is left a mystery there. Interestingly enough, some of the same motifs occur in *The Scarlet Letter,* and a glance at their earlier treatment will help sort out these issues. There too a sort of devil's pact is made, also seven years in duration, involving more than one bartered soul and more than one bond slave. In fact the parallels with *Blithedale* are so intricate as to suggest, if not conscious recapitulation and allusion (which seems unlikely), then a strong impulse to repeat certain symbolic patterns of deep psychic significance for Hawthorne.

In *The Scarlet Letter* Roger Chillingworth takes the Westervelt role. He too is a sort of necromancer, who has previously been married to the heroine and now relies on her secrecy to carry out his plots against another character. He too has somehow been transformed into a demon or devil feeding on the soul of another person; Chillingworth is presented as "a striking evidence of man's faculty of transforming himself into a devil"—a feat achieved "by devoting himself, for seven years, to the constant analysis of a heart full of torture" (*SL* 170). In some ways he is perhaps more like Ethan Brand than Westervelt, since the latter merely uses Priscilla's soul as a medium for his spiritualist reconnoitering, while Ethan Brand's inquiries are, if not quite torture, yet more directly focused on the evil in his subject's own heart. In any case, Reverend Dimmesdale "fancied himself given over to a fiend" (*SL* 171), while Chillingworth declares himself to have been a "mortal man, with once a human heart," now "become a fiend for his especial torment" (*SL* 172). The period of the torment is seven years, and just as in *Blithedale*, the chief action of the novel takes place as "the last year of the contract was wearing to its close." Further, Chillingworth's very method of working his evil on Dimmesdale is similar to Westervelt's deviltry: he intrudes on Dimmesdale's "magnetic sphere" (*SL* 193), thereby making him a sort of "somnambulist" (*SL* 147), whose spiritual powers are miraculously increased as his physical strength is sapped (*SL* 239).

All this emphasizes the symbolic nature of Westervelt's pact with the devil. Chillingworth is not really a devil so much as an "unhumanized mortal" (*SL* 260), just as Westervelt seems to be "altogether earthy, worldly, made for time and its gross objects, and incapable—except by a sort of dim reflection, caught from other minds—of so much as one spiritual idea" (*BR* 214).

The term of the pact—seven years—may be explained in several ways, but probably the most satisfactory is simply to point out the traditional mystic significance of the number, and the favor Hawthorne therefore showed it—in "Seven Tales of My Native Land," "The Seven Vagabonds," *The House of the Seven Gables, Septimius Felton,* and so on. Another explanation of the use of seven years, at least as the period of Dimmesdale's torment, points to the legal time of service required of an indentured servant or apprentice in colonial New England.[11] Thus when Hester goes to see Governor Bellingham, the door is opened "by one of the Governor's bond-servants; a free-born Englishman, but now a seven years' slave" (*SL* 104). Surely the connection was important to Hawthorne, for the theme of bondage and slavery, especially "moral slavery," is an essential part of the whole configuration: the seven years' pact with the devil, the control of another's soul, and the consequent loss of one's own.

From this point of view Dimmesdale must be regarded as more than Chillingworth's victim; like Priscilla in *Blithedale*, he is his bond slave as well. But the handling of this indenture is different in *The Scarlet Letter,* for Dimmesdale is not directly presented as Chillingworth's slave or "familiar fiend." Rather, as the witch Mistress Hibbins guesses and as Dimmesdale finally begins to suspect, he has become the servant of Satan: "Am I mad? or am I given over utterly to the fiend? Did I make a contract with him in the forest, and sign it with my blood?" (*SL* 220). To fill out the pattern Chillingworth must figure either as "Satan himself, or Satan's emissary" (*SL* 128). He too is a denizen of the forest and had been "in bonds" (*SL* 61) among the Indians, where he practised the "black art" with "savage priests" (*SL* 127). In all this he is akin to the "black man" of Hawthorne's tales, while Dimmesdale is another Young Goodman Brown, uncertain of the reality of his meeting or whether he has actually signed the devil's pact.

Again a parallel may be found in Westervelt, whom we first meet in the woods; he carries a cane carved with a serpent's head and wears "the devil's signet" (*BR* 121, 193). The paradigm is not followed in every detail in *Blithedale* however; Priscilla cannot be accused of having deserved her persecution, whereas Dimmesdale has sinned and therefore wears the devil's mark, the scarlet letter over his heart. Zenobia, on the other hand, is also in a sort of bondage to Westervelt, and she does carry an emblem—her flower—of a sinful past (no longer a bud, but a blossom). Indeed, many of the women in these novels seem to be subject to a special bondage, apparently by virtue of their sex. Hester is called "the people's victim and a life-long bond-slave" (*SL* 227), and in this she has a companion not only in the Veiled Lady of Zenobia's legend—"bond-slave, forever more" (*BR* 116)—but also in Zenobia, who refers to herself as "an hereditary bond-slave" in her final scene with Hollingsworth. Perhaps Hawthorne is thinking of marriage as woman's "hereditary," "life-long" bondage, for Hester has been Chillingworth's wife, as Zenobia has been Westervelt's. In both cases the slavery seems inescapable; eluded at one level, it returns at another. Hester, having violated her contract with Chillingworth, is now bound to keep the secret of his identity from her lover. Similarly, when Zenobia wishes to dishonor her vows to Westervelt, she is obliged to keep them hidden from her friends.

Nor is this the end of the duplications, for Hollingsworth also figures somehow as a party to these indentures, since "the fiend" has "made mirth" of him too, "these seven years past," and he like Westervelt is a "monster" and a "mechanism" (*BR* 218). In short, a whole set of ratios and equations would be needed to make an accurate accounting of the spiritual debits and credits of these characters. Westervelt torments and feeds on Priscilla's soul, as Chillingworth does on Dimmesdale's. To a lesser extent Hollingsworth has subjugated Zenobia's heart to his demonic ends. And just as Chillingworth and Dimmesdale are both sinners in the hands of Satan, so are Westervelt and Hollingsworth foils of soullessness. If Westervelt has acquired the services of a "familiar fiend" by selling his own soul, Hollingsworth has "conjured up" a "cold, spectral monster"—his "philanthropic theory"—to which he has ironically "grown to be the bond-slave" (*BR* 55). Of all these instances this last is perhaps the clearest example of Hawthorne's symbolic message—that the sick imagination brings to life spiritual goblins and monsters—"a spectrum . . . projected on the surrounding darkness"—which may then prey on guilt and innocence alike, but especially on the disturbed soul that gives rise to the "false deity" in the first place (*BR* 70-71).

It is worth noting briefly that the same motifs are just as full-blown in *The Marble Faun* as in *The Scarlet Letter* or *The Blithedale Romance:* (1) the heroine's bondage to a mysterious figure out of her past (the evil and insane Marchese, from another branch of her family, to whom Miriam had been betrothed in her youth), (2) the sense of guilt associated with this tormentor, whose own crime seems to consist largely in his disturbing the guilty secrets of his victim (Miriam's part in the murder of the Marchese is occasioned by his threatening to reveal her unknown secret), and (3) the supernatural setting for these acts and relationships (the Marchese appears out of the catacombs like a "spectre" to warn her: "You know the power that I have over you. Obey my bidding; or, within short time, it shall be exercised—nor will I cease to haunt you, till the moment comes" [*MF* 96-97]). Like Chillingworth and Westervelt, the Marchese is less than human; he is a "demon, or Man-Demon," who has lost his soul and is forever banished from grace (*MF* 32-33). The same patterns can be shown in still other works—for example, Alice Pyncheon in *The House of the Seven Gables* cannot marry because she is in spiritual bondage to Matthew Maule, who haunts her dreams in punishment for her defiance of his witchcraft.

What is the point of all these doublings, both across and within novels, and why are they so often combined with the spiritualist motifs of goblins and moral slavery? At one level this is nothing but Hawthorne's familiar method, the elaboration of his theme at every turning of plot, every touch of characterization, each trivial moment of description and digression—as when Coverdale, returning to Blithedale, "irrelevantly" remarks that the shadows of trees are "a kind of medium fit for spirits departed and revisitant, like myself" (*BR* 207). But more importantly spiritualism gave Hawthorne a profusion of opportunities to decry "the unpardonable sin," as Coverdale puts it, "That cold tendency, between instinct and intellect, which made me pry with a speculative interest into people's passions and impulses" (*BR* 154). The recurrence of the same motif in so many contexts shows how saturated Hawthorne's own consciousness was with the subject, even to the symbolic details of its presentation. All three—Westervelt, Hollingsworth, and Coverdale—turn out to be part of the seven years' enchantment, each a separate vision of the same diabolical propensity to feed off the souls of others.

Coverdale puts it very well, in terms that show the precise connection with "goblins" and similar manifestations, when he describes the failure of his attempt to remove himself from his friends and to conquer his obsession with their lives:

> After the effort which it cost me to fling them off—after consummating my escape, as I thought, from these goblins of flesh and blood, and pausing to revive myself with a breath or two of an atmosphere in which they should have no share—it was a positive despair, to find the same figures arraying themselves before me, and presenting their old problem in a shape that made it more insoluble than ever. (*BR* 157)

"More insoluble" to Coverdale perhaps, but not to the reader, who begins to see that everything converges and harmonizes until the prose resonates with the single multichorded theme.

The opening of "Zenobia's Legend" offers a nutshell theory of mimetic fiction that helps explain the peculiarity of Coverdale's (and Hawthorne's) art: the life of a character is compared to the "reality" of "the candlelight image of one's self, which peeps at us outside of a dark window-pane" (*BR* 108). On the one hand, there is the hallucinatory quality, bright as the visions of mesmerism or the illusions of optics and reflecting surfaces; on the other hand, there is the inner source of such a "shadowy phenomenon," the recognition that even the reflecting surface is merely "one's self."

In short, Coverdale is variously and repeatedly revealed as a fantast whose visions *are* the novel. Whenever he withdraws from communal life, the visionary nature of it all is accentuated, as in his hermitage or during his retreat to Boston: "Dreams had tormented me, throughout the night. The train of thoughts which, for months past, had worn a track through my mind, and to escape which was one of my chief objects in leaving Blithedale, kept treading remorselessly to-and-fro, in their old footsteps, while slumber left me impotent to regulate them. It was not till I had quitted my three friends that they first began to encroach upon my dreams" (*BR* 153). When close to his friends, his "dreams" have the feeling of reality; only at a distance do they seem visionary. Of course, the essence of this sort of fiction is that both the symbolic and the realistic interpretations are continuously available, just as Coverdale is always present both as narrator and as character, subject and object.

In Hawthorne's *Italian Notebooks* occurs a passage that might have served as a continuation of this theory of fictive illusion:

> The whole matter seems to me a sort of dreaming awake. It resembles a dream, in that the whole material is, from the first, in the dreamer's mind, though concealed at various depths below the surface; the dead appear alive, as they always do in dreams; unexpected combinations occur, as continually in dreams; the mind speaks through the various persons of the drama, and sometimes astonishes itself with its own wit, wisdom, and eloquence, as often in dreams; but in both cases, the intellectual manifestations are really of a very flimsy nature. (X 395-96)

This is not an explanation of literary effects at all, but of the spiritualist phenomena that had been occurring in Hawthorne's family during their Italian residence. He is attempting to account for Miss Shepard's belief in her own mediumship without having to call her a fraud. Yet his view of such illusions was closely related to his theory of fiction; especially in *The Blithedale Romance* the two—spiritualist susceptibility and the artistic imagination—had become one.

It was not a happy development in Hawthorne's estimate, leading as it did to the implication that fiction too was a rather "flimsy" affair. Hawthorne would not have admitted believing such a thing, except perhaps in his characteristic ironic tone—but nonetheless he was able to complete but one major work of fiction after *Blithedale,* and that quite labored and unspontaneous. We are seeing the breakdown of his art, as well as its most remarkable achievement, in the strange symbolic treatment of the artist in *Blithedale,* where all he had always despised and feared in the realm of the imagination seems to fragment and multiply and infect what he had most valued and tried to keep sane.

Eight

Feminism

One metaphor for power is sex. Sexuality was an especially useful theme for Hawthorne, since it resonated down his whole range of obsessions—the fantasies of dominance, the fear of commitment, the craving for community, the guilty clinging to secret sin. Moreover, just as there were social sciences that enshrined the vices of utopianism and solipsism, so too there was a social science that reduced sexuality to ideology. This was the women's rights movement, still in its infancy but already condemned as an ultraism by conservative pundits like Brownson.

Respectable as most feminists were, there were exceptions, real and imaginary, to lend color to insinuations that the women's rights movement encouraged free love. The rumors about Frances Wright and Robert Dale Owen were probably false, but the affair of Margaret Fuller and the Marchese d'Ossoli had produced more than gossip—a baby. There were less famous, and even less proper, examples for Hawthorne to draw on when he brought feminist issues into *Blithedale,* but everyone recognized Margaret Fuller in his characterization of Zenobia—though he denied any resemblance, as disingenuously as James denied using Hawthorne's sister-in-law Elizabeth Peabody for his Miss Birdseye in *The Bostonians* thirty years later. A faint but distinct innuendo played back and forth from Zenobia to Margaret, suggesting a failure of feminine delicacy somewhere. When Orestes Brownson made free love synonymous with feminism in *The Spirit-Rapper,* he was merely picking up where Hawthorne left off.

In *Blithedale* we are led to suspect that Zenobia had contracted a fatal liaison (marriage?—it is not clear) with Westervelt earlier in her career. She still seems oppressed when in his sphere, though apparently emancipated from his matrimonial embrace. Her sister Priscilla, never literally the mesmerist's sexual victim, is nonetheless in and out of his clutches throughout the novel. Ultimately she is rescued by the "true love" of Hollingsworth, who renounces his philanthropy in order to marry and thus save her permanently.

In *The Spirit-Rapper* Brownson merely condensed all of this. His heroine (also named Priscilla) is a combination of Hawthorne's Zenobia and Priscilla—first a seductive feminist, then a seduced somnambulist—while his protagonist first acts the part of a villainous mesmerist, then relents and gives up both his philanthropic designs and his already failing grip on his victim. Brownson thus offers a kind of analysis of the sexual philosophy of *The Blithedale Romance.* At its deepest level, Hawthorne's book is a study of mutual victimization—the complementary vices of spiritualism and feminism (both, in Brownson's view, offshoots of utopianism) spiralling into a single whirlpool of sin.

Mesmerist and somnambulist were stock figures of sexual domination and subjugation in novels of the period, from T. S. Arthur's *Agnes* to George Lippard's *Quaker City.* The interesting additions in Hawthorne and Brownson are the philanthropist and the feminist, new aspects of victimizer and victim. As the pattern developed, the philanthropist, already an egocentric dreamer, was imagined to degenerate still further when tempted by the sexy feminist, who prided herself on her freedom and unconventionality. Once the female figure has given up her place on the pedestal of chastity, the door is opened to her victimization by the mesmerist. He in turn becomes a compulsive fantast—Brownson's shrewd reading of the spiritualist-philanthropist's symbolic significance. Like a gothic hero possessed by demons, the philanthropist sinks into fantasies of universal potency, of which his magnetic power is more a pathetic example than a means of gratifying. The message seems to be that the follies of philanthropist and feminist are the first steps toward the sins of the mesmerist and his victim. Without a Hollingsworth, Brownson is saying, there could be no Westervelt; without a Zenobia, there could be no Priscilla. This is not a bad analysis of Hawthorne's plot: the self-seeking plans of Hollingsworth and

Zenobia are the causes of Priscilla's being turned over to Westervelt's control. If Hollingsworth had put love above his philanthropic schemes, he would not have agreed—as apparently he did—to Zenobia's betrayal of Priscilla. And Zenobia's sexual independence is what first led her into the liaison with Westervelt, which still constrains her, and now into the hopeless infatuation with Hollingsworth, which motivates her jealousy and so tempts her to dupe her sister.

It should be added that neither Brownson nor Hawthorne was willing to violate the literary convention of female chastity, though each hints that something more unseemly is taking place in the wings than anything on stage. Brownson's Priscilla, although she spends years completely in the protagonist's power, is never approached by him sexually. Yet the relationship certainly gives the impression of sexual slavery. Even her most chaste action—breaking her ties with the narrator and going back to her husband—seems a confirmation rather than a denial of the sexual bondage she has suffered. Similarly in *The Blithedale Romance* Zenobia is never quite accused of anything very depraved—perhaps she has been married, probably to Westervelt, and now she loves Hollingsworth to distraction, though still legally married. None of this is too spicy for print, but the reader is somehow led to feel, through pervasive innuendo, that Zenobia is much worse than she is. Coverdale is constantly undressing her in his imagination and inventing a juicy history of her frailties. Even the bloodless Priscilla serves as fantasy material as long as she is in unwilling servitude to Westervelt. Coverdale's insistence that she had kept "her virgin reserve and sanctity of soul throughout it all" (*BR* 203) reminds the reader of her indelicate position while pretending to guarantee her purity in spite of it.

Both Zenobia's supposed marriage with Westervelt and Priscilla's dangerous moments in the trance state are merely conjectured by Coverdale. Carefully examined, these sexual relationships turn out to be hypothetical indeed. Of course this is just what one expects when dealing with a tabooed subject—fantasy on the one side, gossip on the other. However it might originate in society, the function of sexual decorum in novels is precisely to protect and exploit these modes of vicarious experience. The romantic novel may almost be said to consist of fantasy and gossip occasioned by censored sexuality.

Not only that. It is also apparent that Hawthorne understands these mechanisms quite well and is intent on weaving them into his theme. He goes out of his way to remind the reader of the gossipy nature of his own story—for example, in suggesting that "there would have been rich food for scandal" in Westervelt's visits to Priscilla, had there not been something about her "that calumny could not meddle with" (*BR* 188), or in noting the "whispers of an attachment, and even a secret marriage," between Zenobia and an "unprincipled young man" (*BR* 189). All this is tied in with Coverdale's propensity for sexual fantasy: "sometimes, I strove to be ashamed of these conjectures. I acknowledged it as a masculine grossness—a sin of wicked interpretation, of which man is often guilty towards the other sex" (*BR* 47).

Thematically, this emphasis fits in neatly enough with the pattern to be seen in Coverdale's utopianism and Westervelt's spiritualism. Coverdale represents the utopian impulse of the writer, the passion for perfection and the instinct for control. He provides an ironic view of community as a conglomerate of self-seeking fanaticisms, each madly in pursuit of absolute power. Westervelt gives us that same utopian dream twisted to a parody of the artist's creative imagination—mesmeric access to the spiritualist's "seventh heaven," where every fantasy is instantly realized and desires better kept locked away in the unconscious are disastrously gratified. As we come now to Zenobia and her dallying with feminism and free love, the focus shifts from subject to object, from the fantast to the fantasy itself. Thus feminism, at least as Hawthorne seems to see it, is less a force than a condition of women, a betrayal of their weakness, a frailty. If a woman like Zenobia aspires to greater independence, she is in danger of becoming the object of gossip and fantasy, as indeed Zenobia is. And although her emancipation may endow her with a certain healthy animal vigor that seems attractive, when the chips are down it is not such a woman of the world that men desire, but rather the retiring, maidenly Priscillas, who end up with the husbands, the kids, and the cash, if *Blithedale* is any indication.

These are some of the underlying connections between utopianism, spiritualism, and feminism. Certain factors influenced the way these issues conjoined in *Blithedale.* Again Brownson had been one of the first to point out that these social sciences often flourished in the same garden of philanthropy. For purposes of public gossip and fantasy, the typical hotbed of such vices was the utopian community. As early as Frances Wright's Nashoba (1826-1829), there had been a popular notion that sexual irregularities inevitably occurred in communal life. Partly it was Fanny Wright's determination to speak her mind from public platforms that shocked conventional sensibilities, but partly it was what she had to say—certainly not so indiscreet as the free-love doctrines of Victoria Woodhull a generation later, but pretty heady for her time:

> The marriage law existing without the pale of the institution (Nashoba) is of no force within that pale. No woman can forfeit her individual rights or independent existence, and no man assert over her any rights or power whatsoever beyond what he may exercise over her free and voluntary affection. Nor on the other hand, may any woman assert claims to the society or peculiar protection of any individual of the other sex, beyond what mutual inclination dictates and sanctions; while to every individual member of either sex, is secured the protection and friendly aid of all.[1]

It was easy to read between lines like these, and for twenty years after the collapse of Nashoba Fanny Wright's name was good for a snigger in the sensationalist press. It was said that Brownson, who had worked for her on the *Free Enquirer,* used her as the model for his Priscilla, just as Hawthorne was supposed to have used her successor to such ambiguous fame, Margaret Fuller, for Zenobia.[2] In neither case was it the individual herself that tempted satire so much as the role she played—headstrong feminist toying with the radical utopianism of the day. Just as Fanny Wright had been the champion of Nashoba, so Margaret Fuller was associated in the public mind with the unconventional zealots at Brook Farm.

For the most part its leaders tried to ignore the slanders appearing in the New York and Boston papers, but Brook Farm was not immune to gossip about its sexual life. After the conversion of the community to Fourierism, the Brook Farmers seemed to feel they had a greater dignity to uphold, and since Fourier had produced some very radical pronouncements on marriage, the conservative press now had something it could get its teeth into. Defenses of the harmonic order began to appear in the *Harbinger.* As Ripley summed up one such attack, "the charge which this writer brings against the

Associative movement, is that it aims at universal licentiousness, seeks to abolish the institution of marriage, and free the relations of love from the restraints of order and propriety." His reply was blunt—"A more indecent calumny was never invented"—but much of it was rather beside the point, full of debater's points and rhetoric, so that by the time Ripley felt he had "said enough to explain our position to every honest and sincere inquirer," one could only wonder how all these denials and disclaimers added up to a position.[3]

The subject was discussed among the community's well-wishers. Emerson reports in his journal, with apparent relief, "Yesterday G[eorge] P. B[radford] . . . cleared up some of the mists which gossip had made; and expressed the conviction shared by himself & his friends there, that plain dealing was the best defence of manners & morals between the sexes."[4] Emerson thought of his friend Bradford and young Charles Newcomb as "sanitary" influences in the community. Much as he was interested in "the theory of impulse" that Brook Farm seemed to be testing, he worried because "this wish to obey impulse, is guarded by no old old Intellect—or that which knows metes & bounds."[5] To be sure, Emerson had more than mere "gossip" in mind when he spoke of the "theory of impulse," but sexual relations certainly came under that rubric.

When Hawthorne discussed the subject with Emerson, he agreed that Charles Newcomb's "presence" was felt "all the time."[6] It is not quite clear what Emerson and Hawthorne meant by "presence," but Marianne Dwight, a communitist, provides an illuminating illustration in one of her gossipy letters to her friend in Boston, Anna Parsons:

> [October 29, 1844] *Half past eleven.*
>
> The dance is over. —I have been a spectator for two hours. It was a beautiful dance. I was standing near Charles N[ewcomb], speaking with Amelia [Russell], when he went across the room, brought a seat and placed it beside him for me. From *him* I felt the kindness, and we all three sat there together the whole evening.—I wish you could have seen his heavenly smile when I left the room and he bade me good-night. Of course we sat together almost in silence.[7]

Marianne rather liked to imagine herself in close but not constricting relation to several gentlemen. Charles Newcomb was much too "mystical," not to say "sanitary," to become a serious romantic object even in fantasy, yet we see here how even his weighty presence could be turned to sentimental account. Other figures provoked different reactions—always good-humored, but of varying romantic intensity. The range, which provides some clue to sexual life at Brook Farm, can be suggested in a few passages from Marianne's further letters to Anna:

[December 30, 1844]

You ask how many flirtations I carry on now. Why, you saucy thing, I will box your ears when I see you. But I never "*evade.*" *One* with almost any body—no, one with Christopher List [decidedly not a favorite with Marianne],—two with J[ohn] Orvis [who at this point had not yet begun to court Marianne, his future wife], and Miss Russell says, "and *seven with Fred* [Cabot, with whom Marianne was indeed flirting, though not very seriously]." Now the fact is I *never flirt,*—the word is out of my dictionary.

[March 2, 1845]

I told you about the R. L. S. G. (or rejected lover's sympathising group), did I not? Well you can't think how amusing it was, a day or two ago, to hear Charles Dana announce gravely at table, a meeting of the R. L. S. G. to be held at half past ten that evening, in the nursery, a punctual attendance required from all the members.

[March 9, 1845]

I don't know how I feel about Fred [Cabot] and Mary [Lincoln—an intermittent communitist whose engagement to Cabot had just been announced],—glad and happy when I think of them, and yet not wholly confident. . . . I cannot think of Fred as married,—and *belonging* to any *one.* I don't like to think of myself in the matter at all, and I ought not, but this is human weakness—and I can't help fearing, that, for a while at least he must belong less to *me* than he has done. . . . Why do people foolishly want to marry? I am getting to think that Fourier is right, and in full harmony there will be no marriage—at least marriage will be a very different thing from what it now is.

[August 11, 1845]

To speak of another matter [her own feelings for John Orvis, who was actively courting her by this time],—I am glad you think me in a

> true and safe position. I feel that I am so, and that I ought not to have felt a doubt which I could not but feel. I don't ask nor care for advice,—knowing well that you can't give any thing definite, and that the fact of your giving it would not enable me to follow it. I keep calm and quiet, and wait the result.[8]

In this sequence, spanning but a few months, Marianne Dwight moves rapidly from humorous detachment, through a jealous (and somewhat threatened) renunciation of matrimony, to an infatuation of her own, soon to end in marriage. Fred Cabot had been a jolly companion for her—he appears in letter after letter until his engagement—and her chagrin at his loss is marked by more than Charles Dana's gentle banter. On the other hand, there is no hint that she viewed Fred as more than a *potential* lover. If she had, her references to him would have been more guarded, in the manner of the coy circumlocution she invented for John Orvis as their attachment developed. The overall impression is of a lively group of young people (Fred was about twenty, Marianne and John half a dozen years older) relatively free from parental supervision (Marianne's family was at Brook Farm, but in separate quarters) and thus living together in a kind of emotional hothouse. Accordingly, they had to find ways of protecting themselves from the pleasures and dangers of their situation.

As John Humphrey Noyes had pointed out in justification of the system of "complex marriage" he instituted at the Oneida Community, "Amalgamation of interests, frequency of interview, and companionship in labor, inevitably give activity and intensity to the social affections in which amativeness is the strongest element."[9] Noyes thought the only solution, aside from the communal marriage at Oneida, was the strict separation of the sexes as practiced among the Shakers.[10] A number of other utopian thinkers agreed. Even the flirtatious Marianne Dwight—how seriously it is hard to tell—was willing to consider Fourier's proposals for a new matrimonial dispensation in some perfected future phalanstery. And the ascetic Charles Lane, a member of Bronson Alcott's brief experiment in abnegation at Fruitlands, believed that the nuclear family and association were "incompatible." He doubted that "the affections" could be "bent with equal ardor on two objects, so opposed as universal and individual love."[11]

Lane noted on one visit to Brook Farm that very few married

couples lived in the community. He met with only four in a population of over seventy, not quite half of whom were school children. Lane's estimate was surely low, even for the summer of 1843; by August of the next year Marianne Dwight was recording the birth of three babies within a fortnight. Still, in the half dozen or so years of its existence, Brook Farm produced very few new alliances. Marianne Dwight and John Orvis formed one, Fred Cabot and Mary Lincoln another. Charles Dana and his sister Maria married siblings of the Macdaniel family, Eunice and Osborne, and there were at least two other marriages during the period of communal life. Another six or seven marriages solemnized after the breakup can be traced, more or less, to friendships formed in or through the association.[12] All in all historians have thought it a meager record. If one agrees, a possible conclusion is simply that associative life neither attracted married couples nor encouraged romantic attachments.

But this hypothesis is open to question. Marianne Dwight reports "some excitement" in September of 1844 "about the people who want to be married and have 'spoken for rooms' large enough for two, and are mad and vexed, because in our present crowded state, they can't have them."[13] It is probably time to abandon the old opinion, picked up from Lane by Lindsay Swift, that marriage was rare at Brook Farm, and to begin to concentrate on the ambience of sexuality that did exist.

One can sense a group ethic pervading the young people, not so ascetic as Shaker chastity, but relying on candor ("plain dealing") and youthful badinage (Dana's "R. L. S. G.") to keep the wounds of Cupid open to healing influences. Charles Dana, like Newcomb, was a community stalwart, and his clowning was one indication of the essential sanity which the young people displayed in dealing with sexual problems. A deeper force also tending to inhibit sexuality among such a band of eligible bachelors and maidens must have been the unconscious awareness of incest taboos. They thought of themselves as a brotherhood, and they treated one another as beloved siblings. Much of Marianne's feeling for Fred is sisterly, and part of her jealousy of Mary Lincoln may be ascribed to the violation of that familiar ground. Fred is taken out of the family as well as out of circulation. Such powerful feelings could work both ways, as the romance of the Danas and the Macdaniels proved. Taboos do not prohibit what no one desires, and the marriage of brother and sister to sister and brother may be regarded as the extreme solution to the ambivalence of sibling eros.

In that light too, it is perhaps a bit easier to understand the community's rather hostile attitude toward the Dana-Macdaniel liaisons. Marianne Dwight claimed that no one liked Osborne (a zealous nonmember in the New York circle of Brisbane followers), so that the attachment could only cause dissension,[14] and George Ripley hinted obliquely at the community's annoyance with Charles Dana's marriage by deploring "the mystery in which it has been kept." No one explains why it was "an injudicious step," or why "the influence of it will not be pleasant on his relation to the Association."[15] Outsiders like W. H. Channing did not see "any cause for our feeling as we do about it," Marianne Dwight noted, because they didn't know the whole story (whatever it was).[16] Gossip aside, what outsiders could not know was the intuitive sense that a taboo had been violated, and indeed, that any marriage within the community was likely to call up similar feelings.

Additional plausibility is lent to this theory by the fact that all of these marriages seem to have resulted in mutual alienation between the community and the happy pairs. The disastrous fire of March 1846, and the rapid dissolution of the community after that, were contributing factors to the hard feelings that developed in some cases. Charles Dana's marriage took place within a month of the fire and was a clear sign to others that he would "not stop here long, whatever arrangements we may make."[17] Marianne Dwight's marriage to Orvis was prudently postponed during the first months of confusion and indecision after the fire, but its announcement for Christmas Eve was tantamount to abandoning the communal experiment, though she and John stuck it out to the bitter end in the spring of 1847. How things might have gone had the fire not occurred is impossible to say, but it is worth noting that Fred Cabot became dissatisfied with the Association much earlier—soon after his betrothal in fact—and he quarreled with many of his old friends as he left to reenter the world. (Even Marianne was led to think "the less said to him the better," so "diseased" had his mind become.[18]) And one other couple of whom little else is known—Mary Donolly and R. G. Westacott—were married at the farm some months before the fire, and immediately moved to Boston.[19] It was as if the magnetism of love were a repelling force in the community.

Given this complex of pressures—the freedom from convention, the "fast living," as several called it,[20] the unconscious taboo, the official reluctance to take any radical stand on the marriage question—it is not surprising that the most prominent aspect of courtship at Brook Farm should turn out to be secrecy, with its usual attendant, gossip. We find Marianne Dwight chastizing her friend Anna for writing about her romance with "our friend" John Orvis too explicitly and then forgetting to seal the envelope. Further on in the same letter, she reports that "Gossip talks loud at Brook Farm about Charles Dana and Eunice," and she offers catty remarks of her own about Mary Lincoln, for whom her jealousy had reached a plateau by this time: "I can't help liking her, I believe her aims are high,—but . . . she is very childish—a mere baby in some of her ways; and to this I now attribute many of her odd actions. With much purity, she has, it seems to me, very little delicacy for a woman."[21] What a marvelous conglomeration of ambivalencies Marianne Dwight was! Her gossip, her jealousy, her own infatuation and the conflicting impulses to conceal and to reveal it—these perfectly sum up the relations of the sexes at Brook Farm.

The shadows of these affairs and romances fall across the pages of *The Blithedale Romance.* One can find an exact replica of Marianne Dwight's mixed feelings toward Mary Lincoln in Coverdale's assessment of Zenobia—extremely attractive but rather "coarse" after all, "deficient in softness and delicacy" (*BR* 15). The question of decorum was an issue in both communities. As at Brook Farm the ambience of Blithedale encouraged flirtation: "the footing, on which we all associated at Blithedale, was widely different from that of conventional society," so that "it seemed to authorize any individual, of either sex, to fall in love with any other, regardless of what would elsewhere be judged suitable and prudent. Accordingly, the tender passion was very rife among us, in various degrees of mildness or virulence, but mostly passing away with the state of things that had given it origin" (*BR 72).*

Nonetheless, for both Priscilla and Zenobia Blithedale is largely a refuge from sexuality, at least so far as Westervelt represents masculine aggressiveness and domination. The males on the farm are all quite sexless in comparison. Even Hollingsworth, whom we are supposed to accept as attractive to both Zenobia and Priscilla, is too absorbed in his dreams of penal reform to have any energy left over for sexual magnetism. (Perhaps that is what the sisters find appealing in him.) But all this is superficial. Underneath, everything is sexually charged. Every act, every accident, has sexual implications. If Hollingsworth pays attention to Priscilla, Zenobia becomes jealous; if he walks with Zenobia, Priscilla mopes; if Priscilla stops what she is doing to "listen" to an inaudible "call," it is Westervelt's sinister hold on her; if she romps with the children, it reveals her virginity; and if Zenobia looks Coverdale in the eye in a certain way, it shows she is no longer a virgin. All this is intensified by our secret knowledge that Zenobia and Priscilla are sisters—a disinfected version of the classic intrigue of the gothic novel, in which incest is always a prominent danger, unbeknownst to the victims, though apparent to the reader. The Brook Farm influence—if it can be agreed that incest taboos played a part there—perfectly matches Hawthorne's literary inheritance.

Of course the source of all this underground sexuality is the narrator himself. It is Coverdale whose imagination sees sexual implications in every glance and gesture. He is the one who registers his approval or disapproval of Priscilla's attire, who mentally undresses Zenobia, who decides that Priscilla needs a duenna, who wonders whether Zenobia is "a woman to whom wedlock had thrown wide the gates of mystery" (*BR* 47). And he is also the least involved, sexually, of all the characters. His merely platonic interest in Zenobia and her complete indifference to him are frequently reiterated, while his "secret" passion for Priscilla is so well hidden as to strike the reader as a pathetic joke when it finally surfaces at the end of the novel. In sexuality as in other areas, Coverdale's reality is pinched and narrowed so that his fantasy life may luxuriate unconfined.

We may ask how we are to take this pattern of repressed but active sexuality—as an attribute of Blithedale, or as a mere function of Coverdale's privileged position as its historian. The answer depends on one's point of view. As we have already seen, the community has little or no substance beyond Coverdale's own flimsy sense of it as a backdrop for the drama of the major characters. Yet at the same time, there was a prototypical Blithedale—Brook Farm—and other communities whose experience in social and sexual life Hawthorne could not have ignored. Furthermore, many of the elements of Coverdale's sexual nature are to be found in Hawthorne as well. Especially on the less unmentionable issues of feminism and female decorum, Hawthorne was clearly using the relationships among his characters as occasions for formulating his own opinions.

ii

There were really two quite different feminist camps in the early 1850s: the women's rights proponents and the free-love enthusiasts. Critics like Brownson tended to conflate the two, whether disingenuously or not, for purposes of invective: public life coarsened women, and sexual rights implied sexual license. One thesis of many antifeminist novels, from *Blithedale* to *The Bostonians,* was that the lack of domestic love and conventional sexual satisfaction was the source of most feminist agitation: a little male attention and the enthusiasts would shift their enthusiasm to hearth and nursery. As Horace Greeley said of Margaret Fuller, "a good husband and two or three bouncing babies would have emancipated her from a deal of cant and nonsense."[22] Zenobia is made to renounce all her feminist ideals the instant that she falls in love with Hollingsworth—much to the consternation of Coverdale, who fancies himself a fair-minded supporter of women's rights. This is just another version of the argument—also advanced in defense of slavery, by the way—that women are really better off as they are, under the protection and domination of men.

Mainstream feminists, the organizers of the Women's Rights Conventions of 1848 and succeeding years, were basically a conservative group, asking for equality in certain obvious areas of discrimination, but not really demanding basic changes in the social or domestic order. At this point they weren't even demanding the vote. Hawthorne's sister-in-law Elizabeth Peabody was a feminist of this stamp, at least so far as her public position went (her actual life was thoroughly independent), and Hawthorne's wife sympathized with the movement from a respectable distance. Thus it was well for Hawthorne to be circumspect in his criticism of the reformers. In particular, he had to make it clear that he did not consider all feminists potential free lovers, as Brownson seemed to. This was not so easy, since he did wish to bring the more radical philanthropy of free love into his sights, and its advocates in their turn did indeed believe that true women's liberation would mean sexual freedom for all.

The free lovers, interestingly enough, were chiefly utopianists; many were even Fourierists. In 1849, a pamphlet by a French disciple of Fourier himself, Victor Hennequin, was published in New York under the title *Love in the Phalanstery*. (The anonymous translator, who also wrote a brief prefatory endorsement, was none other than Henry James, Sr.; it is amusing to think of the son, three decades later, atoning for his father's vagaries of opinion in his antifeminist novel.) Hennequin's argument was utopian enough: in the achieved Fourierist society, there would be room for as many sexual practices and institutions as there were sexual natures, from *angelicate* and *vestalate* to *damoisellate* and *pivotate*—angels, virgins, matrons, free lovers, and so on. James of course had nothing to say on this score, beyond his opinion that it would be the "death-knell" of prostitution and licentiousness, but he did venture to suggest that marriage as legally constituted and enforced in the United States was oppressive to women. Not that he took any stand—the Fourierist auspices under which he spoke merely proffered one possibility, too often misrepresented in the press.

During the next few years—that is, the period just before Hawthorne began *The Blithedale Romance*—the free-love position sketched out in this pseudoscientific fantasy of Fourier and Hennequin was elaborated to a practical program in several utopian undertakings. Brook Farm of course had been abandoned in 1847, but the spirit of communal experiment was still alive. There was a new wave of colonies in the early 1850s—not nearly so numerous as in the associationist surge of the 1840s, but more extreme in repudiating established mores. Of these, the Modern Times community on Long Island was the most widely identified with the free-love movement. Founded in 1851 at what is now Brentwood, Modern Times was a totally anarchist community. Its guiding light was Josiah Warren, theorist of Individual Sovereignty, a complete economic, political, and social system of extreme laissez-faire, which was extended by Warren's followers into the realm of sexual life—rather to his discomfiture. Stephen Pearl Andrews in particular, Warren's chief disciple, promulgated the free-love doctrine, along with his hydropathic friends, Thomas L. and Mary S. Gove Nichols, who proposed to establish a "school of life" within the community, where every natural appetite would be fulfilled.

Although the Nicholses' school never got past the advertising stage, the practice of Individual Sovereignty was given fair trial in Modern Times during the next few years. Moncure Conway, the Unitarian man of letters who later wrote a biography of Hawthorne, visited the community in 1858 and found fifty to one hundred cottages whose inhabitants were bound to their spouses by "a red thread" worn upon the finger, signifying marriage only as long as it remained.[23] Conway talked to several "sovereigns" whose stories led him to believe that many of them were refugees from unhappy marriages elsewhere. "Marriage," one inhabitant put it, "is the suicide of love." "I should hate an angel if I were fettered to him."[24]

Several connections may be established between Brook Farm and Modern Times, not so much to demonstrate any development or influence as to make the point that the two experiments were part of a single phenomenon. Every experimental community had to deal with the sexual question in some way, and how it was dealt with reflected other aspects of communal bias. Modern Times exalted Individual Sovereignty whether in love or in labor, while Brook Farm chose to subject both to social control.

A young man named Marx Edgeworth Lazarus was the chief link between Brook Farm and Modern Times. Although never a member of either community, Lazarus was an active associationist in the 1840s and had contacts everywhere in the movement. He contributed over fifty articles and translations of Fourierist texts to journals like the *Harbinger* and its predecessor *The Phalanx.*[55] He was a frequent visitor not only in West Roxbury, but at Redbank, New Jersey, as well, where the North American Phanlanx was located. He was connected by marriage both to Brook Farm and to Modern Times, for his sister Ellen married one of the association's traveling lecturers, John Allen, after the death of his first wife; she in turn, after Allen's death, settled at Modern Times, where she was a member of Henry Edger's tiny Positivist flock.[26]

Lazarus was a rich young Jew from Wilmington, North Carolina, who had come to New York, one might almost say, to become a genius. He had a passion for pseudoscience, and in 1851-1852, the first years of Modern Times, he published no less than eight books on pseudoscientific subjects—*Homoeopathy, Involuntary Seminal Losses* (largely borrowed from Lallemand), *The Human Trinity, Passional Hygiene and Natural Medicine, Comparative Psychology and Universal Analogy,* and so on. With so many esoteric interests, it is not surprising that he was a great friend of all the reformers and system builders of the day.

Although he was certainly close to the communitists in West Roxbury, his chief cronies were New Yorkers—Albert Brisbane and the cadre he had been building up since 1840. He also knew the phrenologist Fowler brothers, who published everything he wrote, and he was friendly with their specialist in the water-cure department, Joel Shew, who edited the *Water-Cure Journal* for Fowler and Wells. It was through Shew, in the mid-1840s, that Lazarus met the redoubtable Mary S. Gove (later Nichols).

Best known today for her memoir of Edgar Allan Poe, Mary Gove was at that time a relatively obscure lecturer on female physiology, who had left her unsympathetic husband and come to find her fortune in New York City. Lazarus took to her as a fellow enthusiast, set her up as proprietress of a Grahamite boarding house, and moved in himself, along with a musician, a lady who translated George Sand, the adventurer-writer Charles W. Webber, and if one account is true, the famous Brisbane himself.[27] Through these contacts Lazarus first turned his mystic gaze on the question of sex.

About the time that *The Blithedale Romance* appeared, Lazarus brought out a sensational tract on the sexual question, *Love vs. Marriage,* which openly advocated free-love doctrines. Not only was the book notorious, it also was the occasion of a public debate on love, marriage, and divorce, between Henry James, Sr., Horace Greeley, and Stephen Pearl Andrews, in the columns of Greeley's *New York Tribune.* James reviewed Lazarus's book for the *Tribune* and was attacked as too soft on free love in a rival paper. Greeley gave him space for a reply, which was too conservative for Stephen Pearl Andrews, the Modern Times "sovereign," who entered the controversy as the champion of free love. He in turn was too radical for Greeley, who first answered his arguments and then refused to print Andrews's lengthy replies. Andrews retaliated by reprinting the whole exchange in a book, including still further last words in favor of free love.[28]

The next few years brought an avalanche of books on the question, all more or less set in motion by Lazarus's throwing the first rock at monogamy. Thomas and Mary Nichols brought out *Esoteric Anthropology*—a best-selling "medical" book—and then *Marriage,* even more explicitly a free-love argument. The phrenological Fowlers, never out of the running where there was money to be made on ideas, already had four or five books of their own on marriage and "amativeness"; they now published not only Lazarus's *Love vs. Marriage* but also James C. Jackson's *Hints on the Reproductive Organs,* John B. Newman's *Philosophy of Generation,* and Russell T. Trall's *Home-Treatment for Sexual Abuses,* all in 1853. These were anti-free-love tracts to counterbalance Lazarus; the fair-minded Fowlers, solid family men themselves, even claimed to have discovered that monogamy was a human instinct controlled by a phrenological organ, "Union for Life."[29] Henry C. Wright, the prominent abolitionist, took a middle ground in the controversy. His *Marriage and Parentage* celebrated the one grand passion, but allowed for divorce if it should turn out to be a mistake. Andrew Jackson Davis, the trance speaker, included *Physiological Vices and Virtues, and The Seven Phases of Marriage* as volume IV in his *Great Harmonia* series. (He had himself recently taken advantage of the law of affinities by taking up serially with two different married women, Katie Dodge and Mary Love, both of whom obtained divorces and married Davis.) All of these books appeared within three years of Lazarus's *Love vs. Marriage.*

Of course, if Hawthorne ever read any of these books, it could not have been before he finished *Blithedale.* Their relevance therefore lies in the ambience that they reflect. *The Blithedale Romance* may be considered one of the earliest attacks on a movement just beginning to pick up steam in 1852, and going strong by 1855. To understand precisely what Hawthorne was satirizing in Zenobia, it is important to know how the movement was developing and what issues were emerging.

Most of the free-love theorists from Lazarus on acknowledge Charles Fourier as an early pioneer in the work of sexual freedom. Their opponents were even more thoroughly convinced of this genealogy: "The championship of socialism, or of universal libertinism and adultery, which is but another name for the same thing, is carried forward under various disguises, and by many different agencies; but they all aim at the same thing,—the destruction of the marriage relation. . . . It is to Fourierism, therefore, and its introduction and promulgation, that we attribute the disgusting and detestable *free-love* system. . . ."[30]

John Humphrey Noyes, whose Oneida Community held that its own practice of "complex marriage" was not the same as free love, gave a slightly different account, tracing the ancestry back to Owen rather than Fourier: "Owen begat New Harmony; New Harmony (by reaction) begat Individual Sovereignty; Individual Sovereignty begat Modern Times; Modern Times was the mother of Free Love. . . ."[31] In any event, both the free-love enthusiasts and their most violent opponents identified the movement with utopian communism of one form or another. It is interesting therefore that Hawthorne does not go so far in *Blithedale,* but limits himself to the mild suggestion already quoted, that the unconventional "footing on which we all associated . . . seemed to authorize any individual, of either sex, to fall in love with any other, regardless of what would elsewhere be judged suitable and prudent." This was surely soft-pedaling the issue that Lane had identified in 1843 as *the* issue of association, and that Mary S. Gove formulated again in 1845 in a communique from the Columbian Phalanx she was visiting near Zanesville, Ohio: "The question of the relations of the sexes in Association is a momentous one; and though our friends may wish to evade or avoid it, fearing they shall be misunderstood, or that odium will attach to them if they speak out their thoughts—it must be met."[32]

Hawthorne's caution no doubt had something to do with his own reserve, especially when it came to using his old associates at Brook Farm, no matter how gingerly, as manikins for his fiction. Surely this is why Blithedale, qua community, is never allowed to come to life. We have already noted Hawthorne's denial of any similarity between Zenobia and Margaret Fuller, and indeed he begins the book with a general disclaimer: "It would, indeed, (considering how few amiable qualities he distributes among his imaginary progeny,) be a most grievous wrong to his former excellent associates, were the Author to allow it to be supposed that he has been sketching any of their likenesses" (*BR* 2). Whatever one may feel about the truth of such disavowals, two things are clear: first, that Hawthorne did not intend the usual identifications of *roman à clef* to be made, and second, he could not resist drawing attention to the possibility of such identifications. To understand the effect of this apparently ambivalent intent, and at the same time to sample further the free-love atmosphere in which *Blithedale* appeared, let us briefly consider one or two other *romans à clef* published about the same time.

iii

One of Marx Edgeworth Lazarus's fellow boarders at Mary Gove's Tenth Street water-cure and Grahamite spa was Charles Wilkins Webber, a young Kentuckian who was at that time associate editor of the *American (Whig) Review,* a monthly of politics and literature. Webber had already had a rather full life for someone in his mid-twenties—as a cowboy among the Texas Rangers, as a medical student, and even, for a brief period, as a student at the Princeton Theological Seminary. He had been through an alcoholic period and was now pulling himself together for a literary career. His sister, who also lived in the Tenth Street establishment, was intermittently insane.

Between 1845 and 1847 Webber became intimate with his landlady. He and Mrs. Gove were engaged together in several literary projects, including the publication of Edgar Allan Poe's "Ulalume" in the December 1847 issue of Webber's magazine. Webber was the "reviewer" who accompanied Mary Gove on her famous visit to Fordham and the "former hunter" who contested with Poe in "leaping," which led to Poe's breaking his gaiters.[33]

However cozy this may sound, by 1848 Webber and Mrs. Gove had quarreled. Mrs. Gove then met and soon married the worldly freelancer Thomas L. Nichols, and entered a new phase of her career as a lecturer on female physiology, water cure, free love, and spiritualism. Webber also married, a young artist from Boston who subsequently illustrated several of his books. But while Mrs. Gove's fortunes seemed to rise when she became Mrs. Nichols, Webber's fell when he left Tenth Street. He lost his job on the *American Review,* projected another magazine that failed before its first issue, and had to scramble for a living. There is some hint of another bout with alcoholism. His sister had to be committed to an asylum.

In response to all of these pressures—romantic, economic, and psychiatric—Webber published in 1853 a curious novel, *Spiritual Vampirism: The History of Etherial Softdown, and Her Friends of the "New Light."* Another in the series of antiphilanthropic *romans à clef* that began with *Blithedale* and included *The Spirit-Rapper* and ultimately James's *Bostonians,* Webber's book combined the earnestness of a *credo* with the jaded desperation of a potboiler. Just as Brownson was the protagonist of his own novel, so Webber is the hero of his, while the title role is a slanderous portrait of his former paramour Mary Gove.

According to Webber (whose name is Manton in the novel), it was Marx Edgeworth Lazarus (Dr. E. Willamot Weasel) who first introduced him to his siren landlady, at her importunity. Webber describes himself as almost comically reluctant to make her acquaintance. Before long his foreboding is justified in the following travesty of the usual masculine seduction scene:

> The lamp burnt low; there was not another sound to disturb the dimmed silence of that room, but the heavy breathings of Manton. But even that murky light was sufficient to disclose the figure of the woman stooping, as before, close to the face of the sleeper. Slowly her lips crept over, without touching it, lingering here and there, while her chest heaved with deep inspirations. You could not see, had you been a looker-on, the slight parting of the lips, nor could you have felt the heated furnace of her breath play along the helpless surface of those prostrate nerves. . . . But then, had you been patient, you would have seen, as the hours went by, a gradual twitching of the nerves possess that deathlike frame—a restless motion, a moan, an all-unconscious smile of ecstatic delight; and then, if your sense was not frightened and appalled by the fierce, swift blaze from those still eyes above, a fiend's triumph would be all familiar to you.[34]

The next morning Manton awakes, a fallen man. All this might be funny if Webber didn't take it so seriously. It is precisely the same mixture of burlesque and hell fire that we find in *The Spirit-Rapper.*

Etherial Softdown's skill in anatomy is no doubt based on Mary Gove's expertise in physiology and water cure, but Webber has added something vampiristic in his description of her at work on her victim's body. "Spiritual Vampirism" is a technical term; it does not refer to Etherial's knowledge of erotogenous zones so much as her abnormal craving for sexual activity. In a preface as pseudoscientific as any of the fanaticisms he attacks in his novel, Webber explains that mesmerism is a form of ancient vampirism. Whereas Brownson and others concentrated on the "demonic" powers of the mesmerist, Webber reverses the usual emphasis by focusing on the weaker and dependent constitution of the somnambulist. Everyone agreed that the mesmerist had an unnatural excess of "odic fluid" which gave him his power; the somnambulist was usually regarded as his passive opposite number. Webber asks us to think of such "negative poles" as not merely passive, but insatiably demanding the "spiritual fluid" they lack, not only from oversupplied mesmerists but even from ordinary persons. "They must have the Odic fluid restored and . . . in taking your 'enough,' they exhaust and undermine the holy purposes of your life to make up that deficit in their own. . . . These human vampires or sponges may be, therefore, as well absorbents of the spiritual as animal vitality. Their parasitical roots may strike into the very centres of life, and their hungry suckers remorselessly draw away the virility of manhood, or the spiritual strength."[35]

Mary Gove Nichols, alias Etherial Softdown, drained Webber's manhood by means of this mystic combination of mesmerism, vampirism, and sexuality. Etherial is clairvoyant, can go into complete cataleptic trance, and is able to mesmerize others by various manipulations and laying on of hands. According to Webber she can even simulate hemorrhage from the lungs, turning the "crimson flow" on and off like a spigot. These talents are convenient as a means of gaining sympathy and disguising her activities—as, for example, when she is caught by her husband kissing another man, or when her lover Manton threatens to leave her—for a bleeding consumptive is obviously unable to answer any embarrassing questions.

This plot is thickened with two more love affairs. First Manton falls in love with Etherial's seventeen-year-old daughter Elna, who is more or less her mother's "creature"—"a mere chip of the old block," Webber dares to say, and thus another vampire looking for a steady provider. Etherial makes the best of this reversal, immediately marrying the vulgar editorial hack "Narcissus." Meanwhile Manton realizes that his new sweetheart is almost as great a drain on his spirits as the old; he finally finds a girl with her own supply of odic fluid, a childhood friend of Elna, and their marriage allows him to escape from spiritual vampirism.

In all this wild tale, there is enough circumstantiality to tempt a reader to compare the facts, so far as they are known, of Webber's actual relations with Mary Gove. He did live in Mrs. Gove's boarding house; she was an amateur mesmerist as well as an expert in physiology. She did suffer from hemorrhages of the lung (which she claimed she cured with hydropathy). She did have a daughter, Elma, who was an artist, and who had a friend, also an artist, whom

Webber married in 1849. And she herself married Thomas L. Nichols, an opportunist reformer, in the preceding year. All this can be discovered in Mary Gove's own autobiographical writings. But of course her version is quite different from Webber's.

After *Spiritual Vampirism* came out, Mrs. Gove, now Mrs. Nichols, inserted the following defense in the September 1853 number of *Nichols' Journal of Health, Water-Cure, and Human Progress:*

> During the first two years that I kept this Water Cure [at 261 Tenth Street], a young man from the South, and his sister, were inmates of my house. Both had been insane, but both were persons of much interest. I did everything in my power for them, and had the satisfaction of seeing them greatly benefitted, especially the young man, who had been hopelessly under the influence of intoxicating liquors, before coming to my house.
>
> He appeared honestly intent upon a reformation of life, and the attainment of health and sanity. He became attached to my daughter, and finally engaged to her under a pledge of entire reformation.
>
> After a time, it became apparent to me, and my friends, that he could not be saved, that there was madness in the blood. I now did all in my power with the help of friends, to separate my child from this living death. She succeeded, by our aid, in emancipating herself from his influence.
>
> He tried all means in his power to take her from me, and to frighten me into giving my consent to their union. He threatened to take such vengeance as was never taken by man upon woman. For a time, I feared he would shed our blood, but he conceived a darker scheme than even murder, put his maniacal revenge in the form of a book, and found a publisher, who, it is to be hoped, knew nothing of the character of the work.
>
> Toward this man and his sister I ever lived as true and kindly a life as was possible to me. The sister has been in a mad-house for a long time. The wretched brother seems as hopelessly insane, though still at liberty. For both these persons, in a sane state, I had a tender friendship and I deeply deplore their present condition.[36]

To admit even this much of the story was to invite readers to believe the rest, or at least to buy a copy of Webber's book; Mrs. Nichols would have done better to ignore the attack altogether. A footnote to her defense hints that she thought so herself. She claims not to have read his book at all, the next best thing to denying its existence: "My husband read it, and asked me and my daughter to promise never to read it, or allow anyone to tell us what was in it. He characterized it as infernal."

But why even admit its existence then? The answer comes out in the same footnote. Apparently the book was being circulated at Dr. Russell Trall's rival water-cure establishment in New York City, with the names of the real persons written in. Some defense had to be made. Of course, the ultimate goal of the *roman à clef* author is to have his readers fill in the names of his actual models. It must have given Webber great satisfaction to read Mrs. Nichols's denials. His "darker scheme" had succeeded.

In the following year, Mrs. Nichols had her chance to take revenge when she published her own *roman à clef* in the pages of the *Nichols' Journal.* But by this time no doubt she had realized that any mention of the Webber episode cut two ways, since "her facts" corroborated so many of "his." Her autobiographical novel *Mary Lyndon* was already spicy enough to provoke a hostile response from reviewers; even her old associationist friends called it a "trashy" book.[37] There was no need to give her enemies a weapon by reminding them of *Spiritual Vampirism.* So what took up most of Webber's novel is condensed to a few cryptic paragraphs in *Mary Lyndon:*

> One young man was a musician; another was a poet and novelist, who had been insane and inebriate; but we had the faith to believe in his aspirations and resolve for a true life, and the enthusiasm to believe we could recover him from his maladies by a pure diet, water-cure, and a loving sympathy. . . . My simple faith in goodness had with these its lesson; and I learned by them that the manifested God may become a devil in the subversions and evils of this time-sphere. . . . The angelic demoniac, one who had found rest for a time from his insanity and amelioration from his evils, became the avowed lover of my daughter, and she was magnetized into a strong attachment to him. It did not seem a thing vital to her nature, but something imposed from his life and genius. I had watched him through two years, as he had risen to the light, again sunk in the darkness, and I saw that if he were doomed, like all, to rise to a harmonic life at last, he must, and would sink in the hell of discord and utter insanity first.
>
> I had two things to accomplish: to uncoil a serpent from my child,

> and save the loved one from the sting—the venom of the fallen one. He saw me as an all-conquering spirit, and he madly determined to destroy me. The child became her own and mine when separated from the bright, poetic spell of his presence, and she then saw plainly the blight of evil that was upon all his beauty, through drunkenness and an insane revenge.
>
> He saw his idol pass from his clasp, and he threatened me with the vengeance of a maniac fiend. He has since fulfilled his threat, and, like a scorpion, stung himself to death.[38]

In this account of course there is no hint of any liaison between Webber and Mrs. Nichols. But something in her tone—its self-righteousness—makes one believe Webber's version. Given her reputation, her opinions, her friends, and her history, the circumstantial likelihood is on Webber's side, though of course his use of the story was as venomous as she said it was. Mrs. Nichols's own revelations make Webber's version credible, for her recital varies from his only in emphasis and interpretation. What he takes for his main matter she condenses into a few paragraphs; conversely, her life story serves merely as a prelude to his exposure of life on Tenth Street.

iv

One thing immediately noticeable in these *romans à clef* is the crucial importance of their sources in actual persons and occurrences. Every turn of plot is engendered by some circumstance of the author's life, and the reader's interest, if excited at all, depends on the conviction that these people really lived and these events really happened. The outrage that *Mary Lyndon* provoked came from the reviewers' awareness that free love was not merely advocated in it, but literally waved under their noses. Whether or not the readers at Dr. Trall's Water-Cure believed Webber's accusations in *Spiritual Vampirism,* they passed the book from hand to hand to see whose names were written in the margins. But the appeal of scandal is never long-lived. Once these pleasures were exhausted, one might still take an interest in the more elevated debate over the issues of feminism—the legal rights of women, their proper sphere, and their duties as wives and mothers. These were lively questions in the early 1850s, with implications for the readers of books as well as the characters in them.

The Blithedale Romance shares these potencies and fascinations. Both novels appeared after *Blithedale,* so there is no question of influence, but along with *The Spirit-Rapper* they help fill in the literary scene. Nor is it so remarkable that four such novels came out in two years. The period favored mixed genres—what better examples than *Moby-Dick, Walden,* and *Leaves of Grass*?—and self-revelation was regular fare. Moreover, Brownson, Webber, and Mrs. Nichols are not such far-fetched companions-in-arms for Hawthorne. He was not quite in their circle of reformers and publicists, but neither was he insulated from it. Brownson had a son at Brook Farm, where his old friend George Ripley was in charge, and there was a period in the 1840s when he could be found frequently at Elizabeth Peabody's West Street Book Shop. Both Brownson and Webber reviewed Hawthorne's works as they appeared, though not always favorably. Hawthorne was acquainted with Webber and did him several favors, including a review of one of his books in the very month that he began writing *Blithedale.* In 1849 he sent him "Ethan Brand," then known as "The Unpardonable Sin," for publication in a new magazine Webber was starting.[39] During the same period Hawthorne, Brownson, and Webber were all contributors to O'Sullivan's *Democratic Review,* so the common audience is well established. Mary Nichols was also very widely known by reputation, but Hawthorne is unlikely to have met her. She too had visited Brook Farm, though after Hawthorne's residency, and she scribbled for the same popular audience as Brownson and Webber. Poe included her among his "literati," and Sophia Hawthorne no doubt read stories by "Mary Orne" in *Godey's Lady's Book,* where her husband was also publishing. Such connections, however, are less significant than the actual parallels among these four *romans à clef.*

Although there are a number of other minor analogues, the most important parallels have to do with the central female characters, their models in real life, and the feminist movement as they represent it. All four novels are stories of sexual dominance and victimization—a traditional theme of romantic fiction, but here thoroughly modernized by the introduction of mesmerism as a symbol of sexual power, and of feminism as an ideological backdrop for the old stories of monstrous lust and helpless innocence.

No single pattern of sexual oppression emerges, but certain issues come to the fore.

Webber takes the extreme position (found in later spoofs like *Lucy Boston* and *The Revolt of Man*) that feminism threatens to reverse the social order; his own victimization by Etherial Softdown illustrates the point, and a half-serious coda at the end of the novel alleges that feminism is a conspiracy. Brownson, though equally opposed to women's rights, is less disturbed by the movement; he believes that women, even feminists, dissolve into adoring servitude whenever the "right man" comes along—a formula found in many novels, from *Blithedale* to *The Bostonians*. Even Etherial briefly lapses into femininity when she loses Manton to her daughter—"O, woman! art thou woman, Etherial?" Webber gloats; and instead of another performance of hemorrhage and paroxysm, she quietly weeps for twenty-four hours.

Hawthorne, though he agrees with Brownson, is also aware that the patriarchy he prefers is easily abused by unscrupulous males like Westervelt; yet *Blithedale* offers women nothing but the hope that sooner or later some Prince Charming will come to the rescue of any heroine who manages to remain a virgin. Brownson, Webber, and Hawthorne are smugly secure in their masculinity, convinced that somewhere underneath layers of thick-skinned feminism or brazen sexuality lies a core of girlish devotion to some ideal man. Only Mary Nichols knows enough female psychology to avoid *that* cliché. Her story therefore has more than one love affair in it, and if she suffers by and for her man, it is never according to the old formula. An out-and-out feminist—though never accepted by her more respectable sisters in the movement—she too argues that women are easy prey in a male-dominated society. Her response is far from Hawthorne's stoic conservativism, or even the impatient call for reform heard among militants like Lucy Stone or Ernestine Rose; she boldly advocated civil and marital disobedience wherever necessary to obtain sexual rights.

In all four books these themes of oppression are handled as an aspect of modern marriage. The traditional "triangle" of romantic fiction is curiously transformed, so that adultery no longer seems a matter of secret longing and intrigue so much as an ideological struggle to escape the bondage of "cupid's yokes"—a shift in emphasis almost certainly attributable to the feminist and free-love agitation for more liberal laws of marriage and divorce. In each case the heroine is saddled with a husband who no longer appeals to her. In *The Spirit-Rapper* Priscilla's husband James (modelled after the nonentity spouses of the feminists—perhaps the pliable James Mott, or Fanny Wright's docile Phiquepal D'Arusmont) has all the virtues of a feminist's mate—that is, he is "meek, submissive, quiet." James is the ideal husband: "His love is not tyrannical, and it imposes no burden on me. He interferes with none of my plans, restrains none of my movements, and is satisfied with feeling that he is my husband and belongs to me, without once presuming to think of me as his wife and as belonging to him."[40]

Just how double-edged that irony was, Brownson refused to understand. In *Mary Lyndon* Mary Nichols described her flight from a brutal and greedy husband, to whom she legally owed all rights to her income, her body, and her child. She manages to escape only because her husband is in debt to her father, who threatens to demand payment unless Mary and her child are allowed to remain under his roof. Later, after her father's death, Mary's husband claims custody, and she is finally driven to abducting her own child and fleeing to another state. At long last Mary obtains her freedom when her husband decides he wants to remarry. He divorces her.

This dramatic tale is corroborated by Webber's involuted version of the facts. According to him, it was the husband who was mistreated—abandoned by his wife, who then stole away his child as well, and entered a life of sin and folly. Yet even in Webber's story, Hiram Gove's total legal power over his wife is assumed, and his failure to effect his wishes is ascribed to Mary's necromantic ability to feign illness.

The legal truth was just as these fictions had it: by marrying, a woman surrendered not only her property to her husband, but literally gave herself "into his custody." His right to her "person" included the right to reclaim her should she leave him, to "control and constrain her liberty" if she attempted to leave or was "guilty of improper conduct," and the "right to preserve the purity of her conduct," by force if necessary.[41]

In *The Blithedale Romance* Westervelt's relation to Priscilla is an example of this formula of sexual dominance, but her role is more the old-fashioned one of gothic heroines, the passive victim. Zenobia, a more modern heroine, has much in common with the heroines of the other novels. Not only is she an aggressively seductive feminist, like Etherial Softdown, or Priscilla in *The Spirit-*

Rapper, but she is also a matrimonial martyr in the manner of Mary Lyndon. This aspect of her story is somewhat veiled by Hawthorne's habitual reticence. Behind the bold appearance Zenobia makes in the early parts of the novel Hawthorne insinuates a private history very like that of Mary Lyndon. Many hints suggest that Zenobia had been married or otherwise sexually involved with Westervelt in her youth. Whatever the status of those ties at the time of her attachment to Hollingsworth, it is clear that Westervelt was attempting to hold her to them, no longer for conjugal purposes, but to force her cooperation in his intrigues against Priscilla. Since Zenobia already had a motive for betraying her sister—jealousy—Hawthorne need not have reiterated the clues to her former liaison unless he wanted its force felt as a hindrance to her love for Hollingsworth.

At the end of the novel, when all is lost, Zenobia accuses Hollingsworth of having taken her into his plan only "as long as there was hope of my being available" (*BR* 218); probably she is referring to the availability of her fortune, now reverted to Priscilla, but she may also have in mind some revelation about her former life with Westervelt, since that too has come out into the open by this point. "And what subjects had been discussed here?" Coverdale asks himself, having come upon his friends in the midst of their final scene. "Zenobia's whole character and history; the true nature of her mysterious connection with Westervelt. . ." (*BR* 215). The legal and moral chains that bind a woman once she has married, a central theme of the other three novels, are surely in Hawthorne's mind when he has Zenobia repine at the end: "What had I to offer him [Hollingsworth]? A miserable, bruised, and battered heart, spoilt long before he met me! A life, too, hopelessly entangled with a villain's ! He did well to cast me off." She hints that her situation was so irretrievable that she had intended suicide even before her final reversal—"had he trusted me, and borne with me a little longer, I would have saved him all this trouble" (*BR* 225).

Zenobia's acceptance of her fate—"woman's doom"—is expressed in a way that suggests that she regards herself as a deserving victim for having "swerve[d] one hair's breadth out of the beaten track"—that is, for having hoped for Hollingsworth while already married to Westervelt (*BR* 224). Hawthorne's view is that there is no reprieve from the sentence of marriage, even when "a woman's evil fate has yoked her with a man like [Westervelt] . . . with hardly any sensibilities except what pertain to us as animals" (*BR* 103).

Except for his refusal to accept any solution, Hawthorne's statement of "woman's doom" almost sounds like the complaint of Mary Nichols and other free lovers, who believed "that marriage without love was legalized adultery."[42] "It is nonsense," he said, "and a miserable wrong—the result, like so many others, of masculine egotism—that the success or failure of a woman's existence should be made to depend wholly on the affections, and on one species of affection; while man has such a multitude of other chances, that this seems but an incident." Yet Hawthorne has but one vague recommendation for a cure—that "the world should throw open all its avenues to the passport of a woman's bleeding heart" (*BR* 241).

In words very similar to Hawthorne's, Mary Nichols spoke of the "scorpion whip of public opinion," always ready "if woman leaves the tow-path of custom, or, in vulgar parlance, goes out of her sphere."[43] But Hawthorne believed that "with that one hair's breadth, she goes all astray, and never sees the world in its true aspect, afterwards" (*BR* 224), whereas Mary Nichols thought that only after braving this censure could woman begin to see her condition truly. Both Zenobia and Mary Lyndon call themselves "bond slaves."[44] The facts were largely agreed upon; the ethics differed.

Both Brownson and Hawthorne thought of the feminists as merely frustrated in their natural inclinations toward domesticity. Brownson blamed "unhappiness, discontent, uneasiness, want, at home,"[45] and Hawthorne remarked that women "seldom disquiet themselves about the rights or wrongs of their sex, unless their own individual affections chance to lie in idleness, or to be ill at ease" (*BR* 120-21). Both writers thought the result quite as lamentable as its cause. Again Mary Nichols held a different view: she too condemned the bad husband who forced his wife into defiance, but applauded the heroine who emancipated herself from matrimonial servitude. Mary Lyndon's husband spurred her feminism, provoking her to deny his rights to her person and property, to find ways of earning her own living, to kidnap her child, and finally even to become an advocate of liberalized divorce and free love.

Mary Nichols relied on her own experience in sketching out this evolution of a feminist. She was able to supply so many details of her persecution and conversion that no reader could doubt the authenticity of her story. The accusation that feminists were merely frustrated malcontents melted before her circumstantial tale of suffering and resolution. None of her male opposition could manage so believable an account, though all three also based their heroines on actual persons. Prejudice being what it is, however, her defense of the radical feminist—that is, the free-love—position had little chance of getting a fair hearing, while the masculine point of view, which satisfied every reader's sense of the proprieties, easily secured the judgment against Fanny Wright, Margaret Fuller, and Mary Nichols herself, the actual defendants whose cases were presented in that biased court.

V

Of the three male novelists, Hawthorne's picture of feminism is the fullest and fairest, and his treatment of Margaret Fuller is more temperate than the portraits Brownson and Webber painted from their models. Part of this relative impartiality stems from the fact that Zenobia is not wholly based on Margaret Fuller, and further, that the representation, insofar as it is of Margaret, does not merely reproduce her character, trait for trait.

In his novels Hawthorne regularly inserts some living figures—his colleagues at the Custom House, his political enemy Charles W. Upham as Judge Pyncheon, various persons he had known in Italy as characters in *The Marble Faun.* He just as regularly insists that no such identifications are to be made and typically disguises his portraiture so that no one can accuse him of open caricature. Upham was "perfectly recognizable to all who knew his real character," Julian Hawthorne recollected, "but so modified as to outward guise that no one who had met him merely as an acquaintance would ever suspect his identity."[46] Hawthorne's use of Margaret Fuller had similar ambiguities. Critics have usually said, as if it were a final proof, that she was too notoriously ugly to have provided the model for Zenobia—who would fix on her for a sexual fantasy? But in fact this very argument can be turned around to show how Zenobia *was* based on Margaret Fuller and what that choice meant.

First of all, was Margaret Fuller indeed as homely as people said?

"She certainly had not beauty," admitted William Henry Channing in the *Memoirs* her friends put together after her death, "yet the high arched dome of the head, the changeful expressiveness of every feature, and her whole air of mingled dignity and impulse, gave her a commanding charm."[47] Much as she was disliked by some, including Hawthorne, she also held a powerful attraction for others. Emerson's intense feeling for her, chaste as it was, certainly had sexual elements in it. Her magnetism in conversation—especially *tête à tête* but also in groups—was legendary. "Mingled dignity and impulse" and "commanding charm" are certainly found in Zenobia as well, though mixed with a beauty that Margaret Fuller never possessed.

On the score of Zenobia's beauty, it is well to look closely at the text, for Coverdale's description of her is rather carefully hedged: she had "features which it is safe to call remarkably beautiful, even if some fastidious persons might pronounce them a little deficient in softness and delicacy" (*BR* 15). In short, there was a certain coarseness to Zenobia. In later years Hawthorne said of Margaret Fuller, "she had a strong and coarse nature, too, which she had done her utmost to refine, with infinite pains, but which of course could only be superficially changed."[48] How far is this from Coverdale's secret opinion of Zenobia, formed in her drawing room in the city: "passionate, luxurious, lacking simplicity, not deeply refined, incapable of pure and perfect taste" (*BR* 165)?

It is interesting to consider Fuller's physical attributes in still more precise detail. Channing reports two that seemed characteristic and unusual to him: "The first was a contraction of the eyelids almost to a point,—a trick caught from near-sightedness,—and then a sudden dilation, till the iris seemed to emit flashes; an effect, no doubt, dependent on her highly-magnetized condition. The second was a singular pliancy of the vertebrae and muscles of the neck, enabling her by a mere movement to denote each varying emotion; in moments of tenderness, or pensive feeling, its curves were swan-like in grace, but when she was scornful or indignant it contracted, and made swift turns like that of a bird of prey."[49] Neither of these traits match anything in Hawthorne's description of Zenobia, but they are coincidentally similar to the salient physical features of Mary Nichols, at least in Webber's malicious portrait of her as Etherial Softdown, where she is said to have a "squint eye and stooping shoulders."[50] The parallel is worth mentioning not because of any possible connection in life or in fiction, but simply because of the perspective that Webber's bias affords. Channing's friendly description of "contraction" and "dilation" could also have been reduced to a "squint," had his picture demanded it; Margaret Fuller's graceful neck was termed "curvature of the spine" by other observers. Moreover, just as Etherial Softdown's slump is improved by "Odic irradiation and absorption"—that is, by vampiristic draining of her husband's sexuality—so too Margaret Fuller was miraculously cured of her spinal curvature in a surprisingly similar manner. This anecdote is relevant to *Blithedale* and must be treated in full.

Margaret Fuller's twisted spine appeared in 1835, along with chronic headaches, when she was in her mid-twenties—the aftermath of Asiatic cholera. Her father—always a stern pedagogue to his daughter—surprised her by the tenderness he showed during her fever, when her life was in danger. Upon her recovery he himself was stricken and died in a few days. No doubt the headaches and the painful spinal contortion were somehow connected with her feelings for her father as well as with her own illness. She suffered both for a decade, and then suddenly discovered a cure, much as Etherial Softdown had found a treatment for her "harsh angularities" in *Spiritual Vampirism*.[51]

In 1844 Margaret Fuller began to take an interest in mesmerism. Her investigations probably started at Brook Farm, where she was a popular visitor. Marianne Dwight and her friends were adept at "reading" sealed letters—not the messages but the characters of the senders. Fred Cabot treated headaches with magnetic passes, and Amelia Russell put Maria E____ into a trance to diagnose diseases.[52] Anna Parsons, Marianne Dwight's epistolary friend in Boston, was a well-known clairvoyant reader, or "psychometrist" as it was termed then, and in January 1844 Margaret Fuller was attending Miss Parsons's demonstrations and urging Emerson to lay aside his prejudice and join her at a session.[53]

These occasions must have been significant, but Fuller had yet to submit her own will to the mesmeric influence. Though not so recalcitrant as Emerson and Hawthorne, she was slow to accept the authenticity of the new science. Some years earlier, she had had an experience with a somnambulist that still haunted her:

> . . . I went, unexpectedly, into a house where a blind girl, thought at that time to have attained an extraordinary degree of clairvoyance,

> lay in a trance of somnambulism. I was not invited there, nor known to the party, but accompanied a gentleman who was.
>
> The somnambulist was in a very happy state. On her lips was the satisfied smile, and her features expressed the gentle elevation incident to the state. At that time I had never seen any one in it, and had formed no image or opinion on the subject. I was agreeably impressed by the somnambulist, but on listening to the details of her observations on a distant place, I thought she had really no vision, but was merely led or impressed by the mind of the person who held her hand.
>
> After a while I was beckoned forward, and my hand given to the blind girl. The latter instantly dropped it with an expression of pain, and complained that she should have been brought in contact with a person so sick, and suffering at that moment under violent nervous headache. This really was the case, but no one present could have been aware of it.
>
> After a while the somnambulist seemed penitent and troubled. She asked again for my hand which she had rejected, and, while holding it, attempted to magnetize the sufferer. She seemed touched by profound pity, spoke most intelligently of the disorder of health and its causes, and gave advice, which, if followed at that time, I have every reason to believe would have remedied the ill.[54]

Although no names appear in this account, it was probably one of the demonstrations given in the late 1830s by George Capron and his blind somnambulist Lurena Brackett, because a few years later Fuller visited the Perkins Institute for the Blind, where Lurena Brackett had retired after her clairvoyant powers receded, and found "this same girl seated there":

> "Do you not know me?" She answered, "No." "Do you not remember ever to have met me?" She tried to recollect, but still said, "No." I then addressed a few remarks to her about her situation there, but she seemed preoccupied, and, while I turned to speak with some one else, wrote with a pencil these words, which she gave me at parting:—
>
> "The ills that Heaven decrees
> The brave with courage bear."
>
> Others may explain this as they will; to me it was a token that the same affinity that had acted before, gave the same knowledge; for

> the writer was at the time ill in the same way as before. . . . The blind girl perhaps never knew who I was, but saw my true state more clearly than any other person did, and I have kept those pencilled lines, written in the stiff, round character proper to the blind, as a talisman. . . .[55]

Margaret Fuller tells this anecdote in a review she wrote for the *New York Tribune* of pseudoscientist J. Stanley Grimes's *Etherology*. The dip into personal revelation was typical of her writing, but by this time (February 17, 1845) she could have told an even more intimate story if she had wished. She was herself seeing a mesmerist regularly, who was curing her headaches and her twisted spine.

On April 9, 1844, before Margaret Fuller had come to write for it regularly, the *Tribune* published a letter from "F. G. B." reporting the magnetic wonders being performed by Dr. Théodore Léger, a New York mesmerist (or "psycodunamist" as he preferred to call himself), who had cured numbers of patients, including a "Miss B____P____, the sister of one of our best writers of the day, [who] was under a malady of the spine for the last ten years." "F. G. B." was probably Charles Poyen's friend, Mons. F. Bugard, a Boston teacher of French who sometimes helped Poyen in his magnetic demonstrations. Who "Miss B____P____" was I do not know, but if Margaret Fuller saw this item—as I suspect she did—she may have guessed its dramatis personae.[56] In any case, she not only looked further into Dr. Léger's claims, but soon submitted herself for "dunamising," with apparent success.

Her Brook Farm friend Georgiana Bruce gave details: "Her garments were made to open so as to leave the spine bare. She was seated on a convenient stool and the doctor held his right hand horizontally, close against the vertebral column, the fingers pointing towards but never touching it. Slowly he moved his hand from the very end of the spine to the base of the brain, charging it with his vigorous magnetism. There was a slight trembling of his arm as he *willed* that power should flow from him to the patient. She described the sensation as like having a rod of iron worked into her poor spine."[57] In two months she was able to throw away the horsehair padding she had worn "over one shoulderblade to make it correspond with the other." Measured before and after, she had grown three inches in height.

In the spring of 1845 Fuller was seeing her mesmerist regularly—

every Saturday morning, the evidence suggests[58]—and for a time the treatments worked beautifully, according to Georgiana Bruce. But mesmerism was not the only medicine she was taking at this time. Margaret Fuller had fallen in love during the winter and was using Dr. Léger's office as a convenient rendezvous with her sweetheart James Nathan. Her *Love-Letters* provide a fascinating case history of the reciprocal effects of love and pseudoscience upon her health. All went well until Nathan announced that he would leave for Europe soon and that he considered their affair platonic. Now it became apparent, as Hawthorne told Sophia, that love is the stronger magnetism, for the patient's headaches returned with a vengeance. "My head has ached ever since you were here, and needed you to take away its pain—but you come not."[59] Nathan left in early June, and mesmeric treatments seemed useless against this new calamity. Indeed the headaches acted as a sort of electrical static to Dr. Léger, who now advised Fuller to break off the weekly visits and try a change of "scene and air" instead.[60] Whether her spine suffered too is not recorded, but the headaches contined through the following year, and ultimately she took Dr. Léger's advice, leaving for Europe on August 1, 1846, with some faint hope of seeing Nathan.

This story must have been known by others besides Georgy Bruce. Margaret Fuller was in constant contact with her friends in Boston and Concord, and it is unlikely that she kept her own counsel on such a discovery. What must Hawthorne's reaction have been to a cure so similar to his own wife's mesmeric treatments for chronic headache a few years earlier?

The connection between Margaret Fuller and Zenobia is thus reinforced by the association of both (though in quite different ways) with mesmerism. Nor is it beside the point that in three cases—Margaret Fuller's, Etherial Softdown's, and Sophia Peabody's—the recovery from illness was apparently related to sexuality as well as mesmerism. Etherial's example is too obvious to need analysis; her peculiar vampiristic variety of "reverse magnetism" is almost literally equated with sexual gratification. Sophia's headaches yielded temporarily to Dr. Fiske's and Mrs. Park's mesmeric applications, but love turned out to be the "true magnetism," and after her marriage no more treatments were necessary. The Fuller case is more complex, but the facts suggest that her recovery was also tied to her love life.

After her abortive affair with Nathan, Fuller seems to have found a more permanent cure in her liaison with the Marchese Giovanni Angelo Ossoli. She met Ossoli in Italy. He was remarkably handsome—Hawthorne noted in his journal, years later, "the handsomest man whom Mr. Mozier [his informant] ever saw"[61]—but literally unschooled. Though titled, he was a patriot during the revolution and was penniless. Altogether it was a very romantic affair: Fuller fell in love, had a child, married clandestinely, and transformed her life. Her friend Mrs. William Wetmore Story reports: "she seemed so unlike what I had thought her to be in America, that I continually said, 'How have I misjudged you,—you are not at all such a person as I took you to be.' To this she replied, 'I am not the same person.'"[62] Her drowning in the wreck of the ship on which she and her family were returning to America in 1850 prevented any further test. One may guess that her headaches would not have returned, though the social ordeal she faced with her new values and encumbrances might have proved more painful than any migraine.

Mary Nichols, whether or not she experienced the "odic" lift that Webber claimed sex gave her, quickly regretted her marriage to Hiram Gove, a man who used to burn her books and even her letters. Unequal marriage, when the woman was the more cultured of the pair, was a standard argument for divorce among the feminists and free lovers. Margaret Fuller is a particularly poignant example. So far as we know she did not live long enough to regret her marriage, but all her friends were sure that she would have, had death not intervened. They might have pointed with irony to a passage in *Woman in the Nineteenth Century,* where she had herself predicted the fate they saw for her:

> The electrical, the magnetic element in Woman has not been fairly brought out at any period. Everything might be expected from it; she has far more of it than Man. This is commonly expressed by saying that her intuitions are more rapid and more correct. You will often see men of high intellect absolutely stupid in regard to the atmospheric changes, the fine invisible links which connect the forms of life around them, while women, if pure and modest, so that a vulgar self do not overshadow the mental eye, will seize and delineate these with unerring discrimination.
>
> Women who combine this organization with creative genius are

> very commonly unhappy at present. They see too much to act in conformity with those around them, and their quick impulses seem folly to those who do not discern the motives. This is an usual effect of the apparition of genius, whether in Man or Woman, but is more frequent with regard to the latter, because a harmony, an obvious order and self-restraining decorum, is most expected from her. . . .
>
> Those who seem overladen with electricity frighten those around them. "When she merely enters the room, I am what the French call *herissé,*" said a man of petty feelings and worldly character of such a woman, whose depth of eye and powerful motion announced the conductor of the mysterious fluid.
>
> Woe to such a woman who finds herself linked to such a man in bonds too close! It is the cruelest of errors. He will detest her with all the bitterness of wounded self-love. He will take the whole prejudice of manhood upon himself, and, to the utmost of his power, imprison and torture her by its imperious rigors.
>
> Yet, allow room enough, and the electric fluid will be found to invigorate and embellish, not destroy life. Such women are the great actresses, the songsters. Such traits we read in a late searching, though too French, analysis of the character of Mademoiselle Rachel, by a modern La Rochefoucault. . . .
>
> Sickness is the frequent result of this overcharged existence. To this region, however misunderstood, or interpreted with presumptuous carelessness, belong the phenomena of magnetism, or mesmerism, as it is now called, where the trance of the Ecstatica purports to be produced by the agency of one human being on another, instead of, as in her case, direct from the spirit.[63]

This passage marvelously brings together threads from all the actual and fictional lives that we have been tracing, and knots them firmly in Margaret Fuller's own conception of herself. Here is Mary Lyndon's disastrous marriage to a handsome but ignorant Quaker; here is Etherial Softdown's undercharge of odic fluid, inverted to an overcharge as dangerous to its possessor as Etherial's lack was to her lover's supply; here is the illness that accompanied magnetic imbalance, either too much, as in Margaret Fuller's case, or too little, as in Etherial Softdown's (and perhaps even in Sophia Peabody's); here is the unconventionality, the swerving out of the "beaten track" or "tow-path" that calls down society's censure; and here is Fuller's own destiny, almost clairvoyantly predicted—

her marriage to a man who, as Hawthorne said later, "could not possibly have had the least appreciation of Margaret, and the wonder is, what attraction she found in this boor, this man without the intellectual spark—she that had always shown such a cruel and bitter scorn of intellectual delinquency."[64]

From all these separate but overlapping cases, one can begin to piece together an almost paradigmatic pattern that lies behind the portrayal of Zenobia in *Blithedale.* This is not to say that Hawthorne was directly influenced by such cases in constructing his plot, for even the example of Margaret Fuller was only partially known to him, and that part ignored or transformed in his use of it. But the pattern did exist, and Zenobia did fit it closely enough to seem its most complete exemplar, Hawthorne's mythic personification of the feminist *par excellence.*

Zenobia's basic feminity and flamboyant sexuality were derived from the extremists of the women's movement—free lovers like Mary Nichols, especially in her incarnation as Etherial Softdown. But Margaret Fuller too was a daughter of Eve, and as Hawthorne triumphantly pointed out in his musing on her marriage to Ossoli, "by and by, this rude old potency bestirred itself . . . she proved herself a very woman, after all, and fell as the weakest of her sisters might."[65] In any case, a lavish endowment of sexuality is at the heart of Zenobia's attractiveness, just as a magnetism deeper and more fiery than mere surface beauty flashed in Margaret Fuller's eyes and flickered in her impulsiveness. Abnormalities in a woman's eyes—squints and "obliquities" like Mary Nichols and Etherial Softdown's—have always been thought lascivious signs.

Thus enlivened with sexual desire—whether from an excess of magnetism, as Margaret Fuller supposed, or an undersupply, as Webber theorized—the feminist-to-be is next put in a situation where her feminity is frustrated or oppressed. In Zenobia's case, like Mary Nichols's, the obstacle was a husband whose own development, especially on the spiritual plane, lagged behind that of his wife. Margaret Fuller's case was slightly different. She had no husband to repine, only a father who withheld affection and treated her like a son to be educated and disciplined. Yet the result was not unlike "Zenobia's inward trouble," which Coverdale claimed could be measured "by the animosity with which she now took up the general quarrel of woman against man" (*BR* 121).

Sophia Hawthorne had read "Queen Margaret's" *Woman in the Nineteenth Century* when it first appeared in 1845; she must have discussed it with her husband, for Coverdale's analysis of Zenobia sounds exactly like Sophia Hawthorne's view of Margaret Fuller: "It seems to me," Sophia wrote her mother, "that if she were married truly, she would no longer be puzzled about the rights of woman. This is the revelation of woman's true destiny and place, which never can be *imagined* by those who do not experience the relation. In perfect, high union there is no question of supremacy. Souls are equal in love and intelligent communion, and all things take their proper places as inevitably as the stars their orbits. Had there never been false and profane marriages, there would not only be no commotion about woman's right, but it would be Heaven here at once."[66] Here is half of Zenobia's story in embryo, six years before *Blithedale*.

The frustration of the highly magnetized but unfulfilled woman leads her into feminism. In Mary Lyndon's first speech from the lyceum platform, on "The Sphere and Condition of Woman," she spoke of "marriage as the annihilation of woman, as often the grave of her heart and the destruction of her health and usefulness." Shortly thereafter she "repudiated" her own marriage and took up with another man. Zenobia intended, if she lived another year, to "lift up my voice in behalf of woman's wider liberty" (*BR* 120), soon after she had fallen in love with Hollingsworth. These opinions grow out of the cramp of an obsolete marriage on a blossoming new relationship.

If no man appears to siphon off the excess of sexuality, the result is likely to be physical illness, an imbalance of magnetism that can be corrected, at least temporarily, by mesmeric treatment, but is permanently repaired only by Sophia Hawthorne's "perfect, high union." Zenobia manages to commandeer enough masculine attention to protect her from developing any of the characteristic symptoms, but her half-sister Priscilla, a typical somnambulist, exhibits the full syndrome: lack of male relationship, general neurasthenic debility, and clairvoyance. Once Priscilla begins to fall in love with Hollingsworth, her health and spirits improve so much that Coverdale notes with surprise her "great exuberance of gesture, as is the custom of young girls, when their electricity overcharges them" (*BR* 60). Immediately afterward, however, she pauses, "as if she heard some one calling her name," and we are encouraged to suppose that Westervelt's evil magnetism is still in control, pulling her back to him.

Even Coverdale rather comically illustrates this hydraulic theory of psychic compensation for physical deprivation: during his illness he becomes clairvoyant, a male Etherial Softdown, absorbing energy from "Zenobia's sphere" (*BR* 46) and using it to divine "psychometrically" that the letter Priscilla brings him in his sick-chamber is from (what could be more appropriate?) Margaret Fuller! Priscilla even seems to *look* like Margaret Fuller, as long as she holds the letter. The features she acquires are just those that Fuller shared with Etherial Softdown, "a certain curve of the shoulders, and a partial closing of the eyes, which seemed to look more penetratingly into my own eyes, through the narrowed apertures, than if they had been open at full width" (*BR* 51-52). Thus Priscilla thriftily manifests those traits of Margaret Fuller that would not fit into Hawthorne's conception of Zenobia.

Although the sexual/magnetic imbalance is primarily a handicap, it can also provide the motivation and energy for a feminist career. As Margaret Fuller hinted, "allow room enough, and the electric fluid will be found to invigorate and embellish, not destroy life." She cites Rachel, and of course has her own fame as a conversationalist in the back of her mind. Horace Greeley thought she "had marvelous powers of personation and mimicry, and, had she condescended to appear before the foot-lights, would soon have been recognized as the first actress of the Nineteenth Century."[68] It was almost a cliché that women of such endowments belonged on the stage, thereby accounting for their extraordinary platform eloquence. One thinks of Etherial's use of her mesmeric talents to simulate illness—the ultimate in realistic acting. Zenobia is repeatedly described as acting a part (*BR* 165), or as "made for a stump-oratress" (*BR* 44). "The stage would have been her proper sphere" (*BR* 44). It was "an intolerable wrong to the world, that she did not at once go upon the stage" (*BR* 106). Just as everyone said of Margaret Fuller, she "had the gift of telling a fanciful little story, off hand, in a way that made it greatly more effective, than it was usually found to be, when she afterwards elaborated the same production with her pen" (*BR* 107). In short, her overcharge of magnetism gave powers of eloquence that could be put to feminist use, like those of Verena Tarrant in *The Bostonians* a generation later. But given their source, these powers tended to evaporate with their stimulus. Hollingsworth has only to exert his own magnetism—and point out that feminists "dream of such things because they have missed woman's peculiar happiness" (*BR* 123)—to reduce Zenobia to inarticulate tears. "'Well; be it so,' was all she said" (*BR* 124). Similarly Margaret Fuller wrote her lover James Nathan in the heady spring of 1845, "I like to be quite still and have you the actor and the voice."[69]

Once imbued with feminist principles, the woman on the rebound from an unequal match is not likely to make the same mistake again. Her second attachment is characteristically to a fellow idealist, a "philanthropist" in Brownson's broad sense of the term. Examples abound. Priscilla in *The Spirit-Rapper,* Mary Nichols and her fictional shadow Mary Lyndon, Margaret Fuller and Zenobia all find that a reformer is the best lover, whether a mesmerist/revolutionary like the protagonist of Brownson's novel, or merely a handsome rebel like the hero of Margaret Fuller's own life story.

It is significant that none of the reformers for whom feminists conceive these passions are really communitarians. When Mary Nichols finds her final mate, Thomas L. Nichols, he turns out to be an "Individual Sovereign" in the school of Warren and Andrews—that is, an anarchist. The protagonist of *The Spirit-Rapper* is a "loner" of more gothic proportions, and therefore even more inalterably anindividualist, à la Byron. Hollingsworth too, whether pursuing his pet scheme or doing penance for his sins, is always an individualist, paying the merest lip service to the common good: "It is all self!" Zenobia insisted in her anger, "Nothing else; nothing but self, self, self!" (*BR* 218). This is the negative side, but the more acceptable Hollingsworth of the last pages is no less devoted to his own ends; indeed, having given up the attempt to "redeem his brother," he now is entirely focused on reforming his own soul.

Thus the literary paradigm of the feminist career required an affair with a reformer whose bias was anticommunitarian. In strictly realistic terms, this made sense if, as Charles Lane claimed, marriage and community were mutually exclusive institutions. Lane's theory speaks directly to the archetype of the feminist as we have seen it unfold. The sexual energy that mesmerism might temporarily discharge, and that feminism could channel and sublimate in political activities, could only be naturally burned up in "woman's peculiar happiness," which the "universal love" of community seemed to preclude. Of course this is a preeminently male view of feminism, though shared by Sophia Hawthorne, Mary Nichols, and Margaret Fuller. The archetypal feminist was herself a male-dominated conception, rooted more deeply in the culture than ideology. That was why it appeared so consistently in so many places and so many lives, real or imaginary, in the movement and outside it.

What proper ending could there be to a feminist career? Like the fever that accompanies disease, the agitation would abate once women found their rightful place in society, whether that meant achieving their rights or merely attracting suitable mates and bearing children. Margaret Fuller and her fictional sister Zenobia are absolved from any final choice by death, yet they had already chosen matrimony. For the feminist, one might almost say, marriage was a form of suicide. Both Margaret Fuller and Zenobia landed in limbo. Fuller married so unconventionally that her future was in jeopardy, and Zenobia, though ready to give up her feminism for love, was without a bridegroom. Perhaps this too is part of the paradigm, for no satisfying conclusion can be made out of mere survival—outliving one's *raison d'être*—and that is what success as a feminist would entail.

Nine

Prison Reform

AFTER COMPLETING THE MANUSCRIPT of *The Blithedale Romance,* Hawthorne sent it to his friend and critic E.P. Whipple for a first reaction. The book was really finished; though Hawthorne was doubtful about its effect, he was more uncertain about its title, as if he were not quite willing to call it done and give a name to his imaginings. In his letter to Whipple he mentioned half a dozen possible titles but the one he had finally written on the title page was "Hollingsworth."[1] He had rejected "The Veiled Lady," he said, because he did not wish to emphasize that aspect of the plot: presumably his later cancellation of "Hollingsworth" was similarly motivated. The question remains, how did he come to settle even temporarily on Hollingsworth as his titular hero? In what sense is it really Hollingsworth's story?

Even more than the other major characters in this very schematic book, Hollingsworth is identified with his philanthropic mania, prison reform. One might argue that he is the model of such identifications in the novel, so totally has he submerged himself in his crusade. Insofar as *Blithedale* is an attack on philanthropy, it is fitting that Hollingsworth should be its protagonist. Although Hawthorne finally decided to muffle this theme of the novel also and call it simply *The Blithedale Romance,* his tentative willingness to single out Hollingsworth's significance gives us an insight into his intentions.

There were plenty of social sciences to choose from; why did

Hawthorne cast Hollingsworth as a penal reformer? He might have been a hydropathist like Thomas and Mary Nichols, saving humanity through water. There had been a hydropathic movement at Brook Farm, and several communitists had built a shower at a nearby spring, where devotees could be battered into health by volleys of icy water.[2] Or he could have been an "Individual Sovereign" like Stephen Pearl Andrews and his friends at Modern Times, self-confessed egoists whose extreme form of individualism made Brook Farm and other Fourierist communities look like collectivist experiments. This would have given another sort of philosophical grounding to Hollingsworth's betrayal of the Blithedale communitists—but Hawthorne might have rejected the notion for that very reason.

Or he could have made Hollingsworth a temperance man—a Washingtonian who had gone on the wagon or a total abstainer imposing his purity on the world. There is evidence in the treatment of Old Moodie, a toper with a relatively serious habit, that Hawthorne had strong opinions on temperance—probably stronger, in fact, than his notions of prison reform. Hawthorne does not begrudge Moodie his alcoholic "warmth." "What else could possibly be done for him?" Coverdale asks (*BR* 180). And surely it is Hawthorne who generalizes further, on the question of alcoholics: "But the true purpose of their drinking—and one that will induce men to drink, or do something equivalent, as long as this weary world shall endure—was the renewed youth and vigor, the brisk, cheerful sense of things present and to come, with which, for about a quarter-of-an-hour, the dram permeated their systems. And when such quarters-of-an-hour can be obtained in some mode less baneful to the great sum of a man's life—but, nevertheless, with a little spice of impropriety, to give it a wild flavor—we temperance-people may ring out our bells for victory!" (*BR* 178).

Of course neither Hawthorne nor his narrator was a temperance man, except for rhetorical purposes. In fact Coverdale thinks of his bottle rather frequently, and Hawthorne is known to have been fond of both wine and brandy—he especially liked to drink with Herman Melville—despite Mrs. Hawthorne's silent disapproval. If nothing else, Sophia's sensibilities would have kept temperance out of the limelight in *Blithedale,* for much as Hawthorne took a mischievous pleasure in inserting Old Moodie and his tippling into the novel, he would not have injured her feelings by airing his antitemperance opinions any more freely. Perhaps she showed similar restraint in not complaining about his own moderate indulgence, though after his death her zeal was strong enough to obliterate all traces of it from his notebooks and journals.

A decade earlier abolition would have been the most obvious target for Hawthorne's debunking conservatism, but by the early 1850s no writer with a northern audience could afford to satirize the antislavery movement, whatever his private opinion of such enthusiasms might be. Given the importance of the theme of moral slavery in *Blithedale,* abolition would certainly have been an apt choice, but the slightest mention of it would have been enough to throw every other aspect of the novel into comparative eclipse. The subject was simply too hot to handle in the period of the Fugitive Slave Law.[3]

What Hawthorne needed for Hollingsworth was some ultimate philanthropy, a summation of all the do-good projects and salvation sciences of the times. The point was not that any one of the "great manifestations of love to man" (*BR* 55) was more misguided or corrupt than the rest, but that every reform tended to shut out all but its own blinding light. This might be exemplified through any of them. Some readers have thought that Orestes Brownson was Hawthorne's model, since his conversion to Catholicism made him a well-known one-idea man; but of course he also developed a reputation for despising philanthropy and "ultraism" much more vehemently than Hawthorne. Moreover, Brownson showed little interest in Hollingsworth's pet project. A likelier candidate would be Charles Spear, who was famous in his day as a one-man prisoners' aid society in the Boston area. Spear was rightly known as "the prisoner's friend"; he not only published a magazine by that name, but also acted as free-lance advocate, counselor, and emergency relief agency for all those accused or convicted of crimes who lacked the means to defend themselves. His brother John Murray Spear was for many years his partner in prison philanthropy. Like their even more famous counterpart in Philadelphia, Isaac Hopper, the Spear brothers haunted the courtrooms and jails and saved hundreds from unnecessary suffering and injustice.[4]

Other potential models for Hollingsworth might have been Judge John W. Edmonds, President of the Board of Inspectors at Sing Sing and founder in 1844 of the New York Prison Association;

or the Reverend William Henry Channing, one of the Prison Association's most active members and a dedicated enemy of "Legalized Murder" and "Cruelty to Criminals." Either would have been a good example of the typical philanthropist interested in penal reform, though only Charles Spear was as unswervingly devoted to his one career as Hollingsworth. The others spread their virtues over many fields, including several under attack in *Blithedale.* Judge Edmonds was becoming a major figure in the spiritualist movement while Hawthorne was writing *Blithedale* (his first contact with the spirits was in January 1851), and Channing, a leading apologist for Fourierism, had been a nonresident member of Brook Farm, and a friend to all reform in his radical journals *The Present* (1843-1844) and *The Spirit of the Age* (1849-1850). Even John Murray Spear became both a spiritualist and a communitist, receiving his first *Messages from the Superior State* on March 31, 1852, and a few years later attempting to found a spiritualist (and, said some, a free-love) colony near Jamestown, New York.[5]

But obviously none of these figures stands behind Hollingsworth in the way that Margaret Fuller does Zenobia. If there is a trace of any actual person in Hollingsworth, it is probably of the famous Elihu Burritt, "the learned blacksmith," who in the years just preceding *Blithedale* had become famous for his campaign to gather "peace pledges" (on the temperance model) from individuals all over the United States and Great Britain. But aside from the borrowing of Burritt's trade and his background as a self-educated reformer, Hollingsworth has little in common with the founder of the League of Universal Brotherhood. Although Burritt was closely identified with the international pacifist movement during the late 1840s, he was not a one-idea man like Hollingsworth and interested himself in many other philanthropies.[6]

Indeed, Hawthorne's picture of the single-minded reformer unable to appreciate any but his own patented scheme is perhaps a bit overdrawn. Although many "mad scientists" claimed to have discovered the key to the golden age—J. A. Etzler and his "satellite" or "iron slave," Edward Palmer and his crusade against money, Samuel Bower and his nudism—there were far more eclectics, who advocated as many causes as they found flaws in the universe. Most had a word to say about prison reform. Samuel May, a long-time abolitionist, was also a correspondent of the Prison Association of New York, and contributed his analysis of the social origins of crime: "In most instances, we, as members of society, owe to our criminal brethren all the assistance we can give them to reform, because they have been misled by the false education, corrupted by the vicious examples society has given them, if not forced into crime by the pressure of the unrighteous institutions which society upholds."[7] *The American Phrenological Journal* published an article in 1845 entitled "The Law of Love a Far More Effectual Preventive of Crime than Punitive Measures, Capital Punishment Included." Samuel Gridley Howe, the famous teacher of Laura Bridgman, was active in asylum reform with Dorothea Dix, sided with Hawthorne's brother-in-law Horace Mann in the struggle for common schools in Massachusetts, and also lent his voice to the chorus of prison reformers. So did Theodore Parker. So did Thomas C. Upham, the professor of mental and moral philosophy at Hawthorne's alma mater, to whom Charles Spear dedicated his *Essays on the Punishment of Death.*[8] Abolitionists, phrenologists, and reformers of education and the treatment of the insane all joined in expressing their support for prison reform during the half dozen years preceding *The Blithedale Romance.* Hawthorne needed no particular person to serve as the model for Hollingsworth.

More interesting perhaps than any individual prison reformer is the ambience in which such philanthropies were attempted. Connections with spiritualism and associationism have already been mentioned, but these were accidental. Several other movements of the period—feminism, phrenology, and asylum reform—had closer ties with the developing "science" of penology, at least as it might have appeared to Hawthorne.

Feminism had little or nothing to say about penal reform directly, yet several feminists were deeply involved in prison work, in a manner likely to have come to Hawthorne's attention. In 1844 Judge Edmonds had used his influence as president of the Board of Inspectors to get Mrs. Eliza W. Farnham, a vigorous and talented young woman only twenty-eight years old, appointed head of Mountain Pleasant Prison, the female department of Sing Sing. Of course any woman who worked in a prison in the 1840s was automatically a radical, but Eliza Farnham was more than that. She later became a celebrated feminist, first when she attempted to recruit a "bride-ship" for the womanless gold rush towns of California in 1849 (a venture that might not be considered so liberated today), and later in 1864 when she published her remarkable argument for the biological superiority of the female, *Woman and her Era*.

Before any of this, Eliza Farnham was a force to be reckoned with in penological circles of the mid-1840s. She edited M. B. Sampson's phrenological *Rationale of Crime* for Fowler and Wells in 1846, and added an introduction and notes that made other prison reformers pay attention. Charles Sumner, a leader in the Boston Prison Discipline Society, praised her work, and Horace Greeley published reports on her progress in the *Tribune*. The Fowlers took her under their wing as one of their promising young social scientists, along with Stephen Pearl Andrews and Marx Edgeworth Lazarus.[9] Her annual reports to the Prison Association were outspoken—so much so that she finally became the center of a struggle between phrenological reformers and traditionalist prison officials for power at Sing Sing. The officials finally succeeded in having her dismissed, accusing her of Fourierism, among other things.[10]

Eliza Farnham had been in office only a short time when she appointed as one of her four assistants Georgiana Bruce, lately of Brook Farm. In her autobiography Georgiana Bruce told the story of reforms instituted by her friend at Mountain Pleasant—kind treatment, better food (at least on holidays), less capricious punishment, and reading and writing privileges, including improved lighting in the cells and the substitution of books like *Oliver Twist* and Combe's *Constitution of Man* for the seventy-five copies of *Baxter's Call to the Unconverted Sinner* that had previously constituted the prison library. A friend of Mrs. Farnham sent "dozens of papier-mache slates, with the necessary pencils," and during the noon hour those who were not reading "would push their slates under the locked doors . . . to have the spelling of what they had written corrected. Two, at my request, agreed to write sketches of their lives for me."[11]

Other activities followed until, as Georgiana Bruce put it, the "prison was turned into a school."[12] Most interesting of all is the possibility that Hawthorne had a detailed account of all this as it was going forth. Although he left Brook Farm before Georgiana Bruce arrived there, he had probably heard of her through friends, most likely through Margaret Fuller, whom Georgiana Bruce had chosen as her idol during one of Fuller's visits to West Roxbury.

Margaret Fuller helped her get the job at Sing Sing by suggesting that Mrs. Horace Greeley introduce her young friend to Mrs. Farnham. Once she had begun work, Georgiana Bruce wrote her patroness a series of letters reporting her experiences. In addition to her own account, she sent several journals and autobiographies of the inmates to Fuller, who urged her friend to continue "to note for me the salient traits of every day."[13] Georgiana Bruce's letters are lost, but a few of Margaret Fuller's replies are quoted in Bruce's autobiography, including one dated from Concord in July 1844, which mentions that she is staying with the Hawthornes. It seems likely that Margaret Fuller would have shown Hawthorne her friend's letters, and perhaps even some journals of the prisoners.[14]

It is not crucial to establish a link between Hawthorne and the reformers at Sing Sing. Prison reform was popular enough that most magazine readers would have been somewhat informed on the issues that penologists debated. Margaret Fuller herself wrote several articles on "Prison Discipline" and "Asylum for Discharged Female Convicts," and if Hawthorne missed those, he is still likely to have read an article on "Prison Discipline" published in his friend O'Sullivan's *Democratic Review* for August 1846, since it immediately preceded a work to which his own name was attached as editor, an installment of the "Papers of an Old Dartmoor Prisoner."[15] Surely curiosity alone would lead him into an article so conspicuously placed to provide a context for a work that bore his name, and that also treated the subject of prisons and prisoners.

Hawthorne had not actually done much with the "Papers of an Old Dartmoor Prisoner"; he merely touched up the work of a Salem political crony, Benjamin F. Browne, to whom Hawthorne was indebted for financial and perhaps other favors. Browne had been a prisoner at Dartmoor during the War of 1812 and his reminiscences had a certain realistic verve, much as did the *Journal of an African Cruiser* which Hawthorne edited for his friend Horatio Bridge the preceding year. Nothing can be affirmed on the basis of Hawthorne's editing, except that he must have known Browne's story well by the time he had finished with it, and was therefore familiar with some of the classic cruelties of prison life.

The installment published in the August *Democratic Review* begins with a description of the "black hole" at Dartmoor, in which prisoners were punished for escape attempts and other misdemeanors by solitary confinement on bread and water, sometimes for months. If Hawthorne read "Prison Discipline" in the same number, he would have been especially interested in the figures which compared the increase of the crime rate in the British Empire—"where the old systems of prison government have prevailed, with all the accompaniments of the scaffold and penal colonies, loathsome dungeons, and personal suffering"—to the decreasing crime rate in the United States, where "the great agent . . . at work to produce these results has been the mild, the humane, and the just spirit which has been infused into the penitentiary systems of this country."[16]

"Prison Discipline" was essentially a review of the *Reports* of the Prison Association of New York for 1844 and 1845. It praised the work of well-known philanthropists like Judge Edmonds, Isaac Hopper, and Eliza Farnham. Here too Hawthorne could have found instruction regarding the most debated issue in prison reform circles of the day, the "separate" vs. the "congregate" systems of penal organization.

The congregate system was an attempt to reform the traditional pattern of prison organization and discipline, which might be observed in older institutions such as Dartmoor. There the prisoners had lived a barracks life, much on the order of a modern concentration camp. Within the limits of certain established routines and regulations, the inmates were thrown upon themselves to patch together a semblance of ordinary existence. Society only asked that its enemies be locked away for a term; what they did in captivity was of little concern. As humanitarians and reformers began to examine the prisons, however, it became clear that such a system was neither reformatory nor humane. Convicts infected one another with vice; prisons were schools of crime. The inmates suffered under the ad hoc regimen of their fellow-prisoners, the worst of whom organized themselves into gangs—called "rough allies" at Dartmoor—which terrorized the rest of the community into subservience and tribute.

To correct these abuses, the congregate system was designed. Prisoners were no longer left to their own devices. They were divided into groups, put to work at useful industry, and continually monitored by guards and superintendents. Most important of all, to eliminate the evil influence of prisoners upon one another, they were forbidden to speak—thus the system got its other name, "silent."

The anonymous author of "Prison Discipline" pointed out the crucial problem with the congregate or silent system: apparently it could "only be carried on effectively by placing in the hands of perhaps an uneducated and violent keeper the discretionary power of inflicting the most degrading corporal punishment."[17] Some theorists, among them Eliza Farnham, maintained that the system could be administered without recourse to flogging; she reported that in her first six months at Mountain Pleasant no female prisoner had been whipped, and at the same time there had been "not a single instance of violence between the prisoners, or towards their officers."[18] The Boston House of Corrections also reported success in the abandonment of the "cat" a dozen years previously.

Other experts, however, presented counterevidence. The most famous of female prison reformers, Dorothea Dix, opposed the congregate system because she had decided that it necessitated the resort to violence. "I am forced, with unspeakable reluctance," she said of the "lash," "to concede, that I believe it may be sometimes *the only* mode by which an insurrectionary spirit can be conquered."[19] In her excellent study, *Remarks on Prisons and Prison Discipline* (1845), she quoted reports that thoroughly established the actual (if not the necessary) interdependence of the congregate system and flogging. At Sing Sing in October 1844, twenty-five convicts out of 868 received a total of 255 lashes, eight or ten at a time: "for destroying property and leaving his work," "for talking and leaving the shop without leave," "for having prohibited articles in his cell," "for making a noise in his cell," "for noise and talking in his cell," "for not doing his work—*and not well,*" "for singing in his cell," and so on. This record was a "great diminution since April, May, and June."[20]

These facts—and he must have been aware of some of them—cannot have left Hawthorne sanguine about the condition of prisoners in his nation's penitentiaries. Even granting Dorothea Dix's unsentimental view of the tractability of convicts, what obstinacy or insolence could warrant such cruelty? Melville had canvassed the question thoroughly in *White Jacket,* a book Hawthorne had surely read by the time he came to write *Blithedale.* There it was admitted as a possible argument in justification of flogging that the crews of British warships were often hardened criminals impressed from Bridewell or Newgate. Yet the point was conceded only to be withdrawn, when Melville reminds us that an officer like Collingwood, "for years together, governed 'such seamen' without inflicting the lash."[21] It was not a subject on which Melville and Hawthorne were likely to disagree, at least so far as it was a matter of seamen in their country's service.

In prison reform, the alternative to the congregate system with its silence and its punishments was the "separate" system. It came also to be known as the "Pennsylvania" system, since one of the few institutions designed and financed adequately for its trial was the Eastern State Penitentiary at Philadelphia. Dorothea Dix regarded this as a model prison and devoted much of her book to its description and praise. She quotes a letter from a convict there to show the excellence of its facilities. Every prisoner had his own heated cell, with running water, "a good bed . . . , a clean sheet every Sat. and blankets enough to keep me warm the cold winter nights." Each cell had both a window and a grated door opening onto a small yard in which the prisoner cultivated some of his food for an hour each day—"I have right fine corn and beans and cucumbers and various sorts of flowers growing in it."[22] Inmates worked in their cells at shoemaking and other solitary occupations. They saw none but guards and official visitors, and were thus in a kind of solitary confinement for their entire term. The theory here was to provide them an occasion for self-examination and reform, insulated from the bad examples of fellow prisoners and the distractions of a complex and difficult social life.

It was this prison that Dickens had visited in 1842 and attacked in his *American Notes* as inhumane in its perpetual isolation. A few years earlier the famous phrenologist George Combe had examined the same prison and come to a similar conclusion, "that the system of entire solitude, even when combined with labor, and the use of books, with an occasional visit from a religious instructor, leaves the moral faculties in a passive state."[23] Combe's disciple in America, Eliza Farnham, agreed that the separate method was "directly at war with natural law," and pointed out "cases reported and commented on in all physiological works, of individuals who have suffered irreparable injury to the mind and nervous system from only partial seclusion, or from spending considerable periods in situations in which the mental faculties have been deprived of their proper and requisite stimulus!"[24] Mrs. Farnham estimated that the average prisoner spent about seven minutes each day in any sort of converse with guards or official visitors. That seemed to her a terrible deprivation, not a promising therapy. In her own institution the most severe punishment meted out to women was just such confinement in a "solitary cell."[25]

An effect of the separate system that George Combe drew attention to was that "convicts here, after long confinement in solitude, shudder to encounter the turmoil of the world, they become excited as the day of liberty approaches, and feel bewildered when set at liberty."[26] Miss Dix suggested that *all* convicts were likely to have similar emotions at their release, but Combe's observation had literary appeal, and both Dickens and Hawthorne, though they spoke against prison reform generally, made novelistic use of the pathetic circumstances of the prisoner released after long years of solitary confinement, in *A Tale of Two Cities* and *The House of the Seven Gables.*

Actually, although it is clear that old Doctor Manette had been making shoes all by himself for a generation, it is not quite certain whether Clifford Pyncheon had also been separated from all human contact for the thirty years of his imprisonment; but he displays all the symptoms that phrenologists warned would follow such treatment. His very footstep hesitates and falters, not from any physical impairment, but from long psychic habituation to confinement. "It was the spirit of the man, that could not walk" (*HSG* 104). His former character had been "high-wrought and delicately refined" (*HSG* 107), yet the years without stimulus had coarsened his sensiblities, perhaps brutalized his moral nature (which had never been ascendant even in his youth). His look is full of "effort and unrest," uncertain of his new surroundings, afraid that they may fade, that they are mere illusion. He is accustomed to speak softly, in a "self-communing voice" (*HSG* 111), and in moments of excitement—like his wild train ride with Hepzibah—he seems quite mad to casual observers (*HSG* 262). All in all, it is apparent in every move he makes that Clifford's soul "must have suffered some miserable wrong from its earthly experience" (*HSG* 106.) Of course this wrong is partly his suffering unjustly for a crime he did not commit; but surely it is also the bare suffering itself, the cruelty of the punishment, deserved or not.

Here again, as in the alternative congregate system with its discipline and lashes, Hawthorne cannot be imagined to approve of the method of solitary confinement practiced in the newest and most enlightened American prisons. What then shall we say of

Hollingsworth's ambitions to reform such institutions and reclaim criminals' moral natures by appeal to their "higher instincts"? What did Hawthorne find to complain of in these hopes?

Hollingworth's plan was "to obtain funds for the construction of an edifice, with a sort of collegiate endowment. On this foundation, he purposed to devote himself and a few disciples to the reform and mental culture of our criminal brethren" (*BR* 56). The emphasis placed on an "edifice" in Hollingworth's philanthropic scheme is true to penal reform, and not merely another aspect of his idiosyncrasy. In spite of Coverdale's ridicule, it is quite reasonable that Hollingsworth spend much of his leisure time drafting and redrafting designs for his model prison, for both the separate and the congregate methods of correction were essentially "architectural"—that is, in large part they were functions of the physical facilities available. The separate system was very expensive, both because it required more elaborate individual accommodations and because no existing structure was adaptable to its requirements. But even the congregate system, to work properly, demanded more space than most institutions had. The greatest difficulty with the congregate method occurred when there was overcrowding, as at Sing Sing, which made it impossible to police the workshops and other common rooms adequately.

But precisely what sort of an edifice does Hollingsworth plan? Can it be a typical penitentiary on either the separate or the congregate model? More to the point, what exactly will be the official status of his undertaking? Nothing is ever mentioned to suggest how he imagines he will acquire inmates for his institution. He apparently has no government backing. One must assume that it is not so much a prison he plans as a sort of "half-way house," where exconvicts may come voluntarily for further rehabilitation, should their terms in prison have proved insufficiently reformatory. Put this way, his hopes may seem absurd, but a case could be made out for some such scheme in the 1840s—perhaps not entirely on a voluntary basis, but according to some probationary schedule.

A surprising number of reformers thought that prison terms were too uncertain—as often not long enough as too long—and too easily commuted by official pardons. Several experts called for indefinite sentences for all offenders, to be terminated not by legal limits, judicial discretion, or political favor, but only, as Eliza Farnham put it, "by competent persons, who shall be cognizant of the conduct of the criminal in prison; of his progress in improvement; of his efforts at reformation"—in short, by professionals, preferably phrenologists, whose roles would be rather like that which Hollingsworth imagines for himself.[27] Samuel May agreed: "You ask *for how long a time* he should be sentenced to such confinement? Obviously, it seems to me, until the evil disposition is removed from his heart." Until then he should "be subjected to such discipline, such treatment only as shall be intended and adapted to remove the evil disposition from his heart; to reform him, and restore him to a free intercourse with his fellow-beings."[28]

How would Hollingsworth's "half-way house" fit into this scheme? George Combe, who took the lead in proposing the principle of the indefinite sentence, also supplied a detailed plan for its application, in a chapter "On the Treatment of Criminals" in his *Moral Philosophy.* He envisioned boards of inspectors with the power to free reformed prisoners, to retain the unregenerate, and to parole still others "whose dispositions appeared favourable to reformation," provided that "responsible relatives or friends" should undertake "the discharge of the same duties towards them in private which the officers of the penitentiary would discharge in public."[29] It was but a short step from this suggestion to a system of private reformatories, on the model of private asylums for those with infirmities other than moral. The only necessity was that "the public authorities should carefully ascertain that the natural qualities of the offender admitted of adequate improvement by private treatment; and, secondly, that private discipline was actually administered."[30] Here then is a basis for Hollingsworth's "edifice, with a sort of collegiate endowment." It was a typical philanthropic idea, on the model of the Perkins Institute for the Blind, or McLean's Asylum for the Insane.

The stimulus behind these proposals for indefinite sentences was a recognition that many released convicts quickly found their way back to prison again. Dorothea Dix cited the figures at Sing Sing for 1845: "of 848 convicts discharged since the spring of 1840, 43 were recommitted; 94 were pardoned; and of these last, 4 were recommitted; and the chaplain reports that '100, when last seen and heard from, were doing well.' "[31] Her own opinion is that "no endeavor on the part of the teacher, however assiduous, will secure radical reform in the majority of convicts. Against these results we have the almost insurmountable antagonisms of debased habits, low views, lives formed on bad and corrupting influences, a vicious parentage, and an evil neighborhood, naturally weak understandings with many, and ignorance with a yet larger number."[32] Although in favor of better treatment, she placed her faith not in the "thousand projects and theories of the day" but in the gradual introduction of "*moral education* in the scale of instruction" of the young in society at large, before they could begin on criminal paths.[33] Yet others hoped for more success than the old retributive system of punishment could boast.

If proposals like Combe's indefinite sentences were ignored, there was another flank on which to attack the problem. A growing number of penologists favored some kind of assistance to the newly released convict if he or she were not to return to the habits and associations that had originally led to crime. This was the danger that men like Isaac Hopper or the Spear brothers were daily combatting in their work with prisoners and discharged convicts, whose struggles to adjust to society they aided by lending them money, finding them jobs, and even taking them into their own homes. Public agencies were beginning to appear for similar functions. The Prison Association of New York was founded by Judge Edmonds largely to ameliorate "the destitute condition of discharged convicts,"[34] and prisoners' aid offices were soon established, where they might be "sustained" until they found jobs. Hawthorne could have read in the *Democratic Review* a report on the first year's work of two such "houses" in New York, where "229 discharged prisoners have been relieved."

Part of the emphasis of such prisoners' aid activities was purely practical, having to do with the necessities of life and livelihood, but a very large part was moral and religious. No reformer ignored this side of his obligation to the convict, and many regarded the rehabilitation of the conscience as their only goal. So far as one can see, this comprised most of Hollingsworth's philanthropic purpose in *Blithedale.* One can probably get an accurate notion of Hollingsworth's principles in the manifesto of Samuel Gridley Howe, who, by the way, had been "a prisoner myself," in a Prussian jail, "for the offence of aiding the Poles in their struggle for liberty":

> The doctrine of retributive justice is rapidly passing away, and with it will pass away, I hope, every kind of punishment that has not the

> reformation of the criminal in view. One of the first effects of this will be, I am sure, the decrease in the length of sentence and the adoption of some means by which the duration and severity of imprisonment may in all cases be modified by the conduct and character of the prisoners. What we want now—what no system I know of offers—is the means of training the prisoner's moral sentiments and his power of self-government by actual exercise.[35]

The very expectation that reform might be accomplished by means other than mere punishment was relatively new in the 1840s, at least as a popular belief. Just as the treatment of lunatics had long been merely to lock them up—often in the same cells with thieves and murderers, though sometimes only in almshouses, with the poor, aged, and infirm—so the whole reformatory effort with criminals often consisted of merely seeing to it that they served out their full sentences. Recently a more enlightened view of all social misfits had begun to supplant the theories of incurability and incorrigibility. The scientific arguments that supported the new attitudes and practices came primarily from the phrenologists.

The "discovery" of the organs of the brain and their functions had occurred in the first place as an extrapolation from the observation of cases of local brain damage; the phrenologists had been quick to move into the field of psychiatry, explaining all types of mania and lunacy as diseases of specific phrenological organs. Several leading superintendents of asylums—including Hawthorne's fellow students at Bowdoin, Drs. Luther V. Bell and Isaac Ray—were phrenologists or sympathizers. The new "moral treatment"—moral because not merely physical—with kindness, conversation, occupational therapy, and home-like surroundings, instead of chains and straitjackets, was being developed at institutions like McLean's and Butler's, where Bell and Ray presided. With proper care, Bell thought in 1840, 90 percent of his patients could be cured.[36]

The analogy between the lunatic and the criminal was soon recognized by phrenologists. Isaac Ray had published his famous *Treatise on the Medical Jurisprudence of Insanity* in 1838, the first systematic discussion of the legal rights and responsibilities of the insane, including the still-agitated questions of "irresistible impulse" and "temporary insanity." Soon the line between insanity and criminality began to be blurred. Eliza Farnham argued that most felons, endowed at birth with excessive phrenological propensities toward vice, could not be held responsible for their acts unless society made an effort to strengthen their poorly developed moral and intellectual faculties. "It is in this sense that persons addicted to crime may be pronounced insane," she said, essentially distinguishing a class of what might be called "sociopaths" today.[37] The legal problem was to distinguish the diseased from the merely depraved mind, but obviously the new science led ultimately to a denial of such distinctions. All depraved minds were diseased.

The formulation was identical to that of the conservatives, though its implications were totally different. Hawthorne, for example, would have agreed that every depraved mind was diseased, but this made no differences in the attribution of guilt or the deserving of punishment. The notion of "a physician for the cure of moral diseases" strikes him as curious enough to be worth setting down in his notebook as an idea for a story. "Disease" in that context was symbolic; what was meant was something different from ordinary diseases of the body. A moral disease was repulsive and unnatural like many bodily ailments. Was there a way of treating sin as cholera? It was a kind of pun, a new play on the old metaphor of sickness in the soul, with many resonances in Hawthorne's imagination; that was what intrigued him about the formulation, not its practical truth as the phrenologists would have seen it.

The implications of the enlightened views of criminal insanity were far-reaching. Capital punishment was the ultimate barbarism, retaliation instead of rehabilitation, and prison reformers like Charles Spear campaigned against the death penalty. "We believe," Spear wrote in 1844, "that a murderer is as much an object of commiseration as a man afflicted with a loathsome bodily disorder, and that it is as much our duty to heal the moral maladies of the former, as the physical infirmities of the latter."[38] This was the literal reading of Hawthorne's metaphor, and Reverend Spear took his calling as "the soul's physician" seriously.

Hawthorne viewed such practices, even when undertaken according to the older religious sanctions, as dangerous and suspect. His own position on capital punishment had certain similarities with that of Spear. "The best of us being unfit to die," he wrote in his journal just before beginning *Blithedale*, "what an inexpressible absurdity to put the worst to death!" (*AN* 310). Yet Hawthorne had in mind no rehabilitation program of exploration and catechism of the depraved soul by self-appointed "physicians" of its "disease."

One thinks of Chillingworth in *The Scarlet Letter* as Hawthorne's typical "healer" of sin; "Leech" was the pun that Hawthorne thought appropriate to such cases. In a crucial confrontation, Chillingworth tells his patient, "a sickness, a sore place, if we may so call it, in your spirit, hath immediately its appropriate manifestation in your bodily frame. Would you, therefore, that your physician heal the bodily evil? How may this be, unless you first lay open to him the wound or trouble in your soul?" "Not to thee!" Dimmesdale replies, "if it be the soul's disease, then do I commit myself to the one Physician of the soul! . . . who art thou, that meddlest in this matter?—that dares thrust himself between the sufferer and his God?" (*SL* 136-37). It might be that a sinner would sooner or later repent his sins and reform his life, and Dimmesdale himself reports the relief that others have felt in confessing their sins to him—"not only on the death bed"—but Hawthorne obviously sympathizes with those more reticent consciences that "shrink from displaying themselves black and filthy in the view of men" (*SL* 132). What mere man had the right to know such things? What could be the motive that would lead a man to inquire after them?

Even the most spotless soul, like Hilda's in *The Marble Faun,* properly guards its sanctuary from the prying of other eyes. Her adventure in the confessional at St. Peter's is a good example. When burdened with a secret that is not even her own—knowledge of Miriam's wish and Donatello's act of murder—Hilda is caught in a spiritual dilemma. The secret is an undeserved weight on her conscience; she cannot throw it off without confessing it to some other person. But she feels, with Hawthorne, that such a confession is in itself almost a violation of her soul: "If I had been a wiser girl, a stronger, and a more sensible, very likely I might not have gone to the Confessional at all. It was the sin of others that drove me thither; not my own, though it almost seemed so" (*MF* 367). The problem, as Hilda further suggests, is not in the confession itself, for that is a true impulse of the guilty (even vicariously guilty) sinner; but there is no human being pure enough to hear the sins of others, to receive the guilty knowledge: "If its ministers were but a little more than human, above all errour, pure from all iniquity," Hilda reasons, then Catholicism might be the true religion and the confessional its central sacrament (*MF* 368). But no earthly physician, spiritual, physical, or psychological, had the right to enter the individual's "holy of holies." Again the path of philanthropy and social science led to the unpardonable sin, prying into the conscience of another person.

The "inexpressible absurdity" of putting "the worst to death" was therefore not a matter of saving them for conversion to useful citizens, out of bondage and into the bonds of the social order. Rather, Hawthorne wished to draw attention to the irony that judges and executioners are hardly less deserving of death than the convicted and condemned. It was the same mordant sense of fitting the punishment to the crime that led to his grim musings on the Tarpeian Rock in Rome: "it was a good idea of the stern old Romans, to fling political criminals down from the very height of that Capitoline hill on which stood the temples and public edifices, symbols of the institutions which they sought to violate" (*MF* xxxvi-xxxvii). He thought well enough of these sentiments to insert them in *The Marble Faun,* giving them to his spokesman Kenyon to repeat. There the simple point, at first saying more about the Roman sense of decorum than of justice, is rendered ambiguous when Donatello hurls Miriam's persecutor over the precipice. Provoked though it is, the act is neither "irresistible impulse" nor "justifiable homicide," as the rest of the novel goes to show; and the smug irony of Kenyon's earlier remark is undercut by the terrible reality of Miriam's arrogation of judicial power, and Donatello's acceptance of the duties of hangman. Again it is not that the model does not deserve to die, but only that no one has the right to sentence or execute him.

The emphasis is shifted when Donatello in his turn is presented as deserving of his punishment, for taking the law into his own hands. The agents of his judgment and sentencing are carefully preserved behind a veil of total anonymity—the most impersonal workings of social, or perhaps eternal, justice. That complication avoided, Hawthorne can concentrate on his own puritan conception of crime and punishment, not a matter of laws and their sanctions, but of sin, guilt, and penitence. Donatello is rightly punished, as he admits even before giving himself up to the authorities; he is also expected to profit by his incarceration, just as he has already grown spiritually through his plunge into remorse. There is no question here of society avenging itself on a malefactor, but neither is the reformation of the criminal imagined to be accomplished by "treatment" or "moral instruction" of any kind—only by private suffering and penance.

A philanthropic mind would have been uncertain of Donatello's guilt. His "faunlike" nature, lacking as it was in "moral severity" or "any high and heroic ingredient" (*MF* 9), might be exculpated on the grounds of "moral insanity." Though apparently normal, and even rather charming in other respects, the morally insane person—or psychopathic personality, to use a modern term—was devoid of moral sensibility and so should not be held responsible for trangressing laws of which he could have no conception. "They certainly have not that mental soundness," argued Eliza Farnham, "which enables them to perceive and adhere to the highest standard of rectitude which society requires and judges its delinquents by."[39]

Hawthorne's view was subtler than any such legalistic or pseudoscientific pigeonholes could accommodate. "Moral obliquity" was never an excuse in Hawthorne's eyes, but the direst accusation. It was "the besetting sin" of Hollingsworth and of philanthropists as a class, rather than a failing of their patients or charges (*BR* 132). Nor was this the only instance of Hawthorne's turning the "scientific" analysis of guilt and punishment upside down. Again the example of *The Marble Faun* is apposite: granting the moral vacuum in Donatello, Hawthorne assumes that the immoral act, the murder itself, begins the education of his moral sense, humanizing Donatello by introducing him to guilt, remorse, and penance. Where the reformer located the excuse, Hawthorne saw the crime; where the law saw the crime, Hawthorne saw the beginning of rehabilitation. The loss of Donatello's innocence coincides with the germination of his conscience. He has eaten of the Tree in the Garden and gained the forbidden knowledge—*felix culpa.* This was not a conception available to the philanthropic theorists of expediency in the social order.

This same pattern of moral obliquity, sin, remorse, and spiritual growth through penance is enacted in the career of Hollingsworth. His passionate commitment to his own philanthropic idea was at the expense of "his sense of honor"—"persuading himself that the importance of his public ends renders it allowable to throw aside his private conscience" (*BR* 132). There is even a further hint, dropped by Coverdale, that his devotion to the cause had begun to tell on his sanity, and "Hollingsworth was fast going mad" (*BR* 56).

His is the special variety of moral insanity peculiar to social scientists and other philanthropists.

Hollingsworth's first deliquency is his all-consuming ambition to reform criminals "through an appeal to their higher instincts." Coverdale facetiously suggests that he "ought to have commenced his investigation of the subject by perpetrating some huge sin, in his proper person, and examining the condition of his higher instincts afterwards" (*BR* 36). In truth, this is more or less the story of Hollingsworth's career, for until he sins in earnest he achieves little progress toward his goal, but after his betrayal of Priscilla and his "murder" of Zenobia, he is presented with his first guilty conscience to work on. "Ever since we parted," he tells Coverdale in their final interview, "I have been busy with a single murderer" (*BR* 243). His "grand edifice for the reformation of criminals" has never been built, for, as he says, "A very small one answers all my purposes." Like Donatello, who betook himself to a lonely cell-like room in a tower after his crime, Hollingsworth has withdrawn from society, and except for Priscilla's constant attendance as a sort of "guardian"—perhaps a "warder"?—"his way of life was exceedingly retired" (*BR* 242). Hawthorne clearly wishes to suggest that his philanthropist is confined to a self-inflicted solitude much as a convicted murderer might be immured in his cell. The motif appealed to Hawthorne. There is a self-imprisoned "murderer" in *Doctor Grimshawe's Secret,* too (*DGS* 194). In his final appearance Hollingsworth displays the same hesitancy and loss of confidence that thirty years of prison produced in Clifford, and in old Sir Edward Brathwaite. As if he too were the victim of many years of solitary confinement, Hollingsworth had "a depressed and melancholy look, that seemed habitual; the powerfully built man showed a self-distrustful weakness," and his eyes were forever "fixed on the ground" (*BR* 242-243).

In short, it is not stretching matters too much to suppose that Hollingsworth has finally discovered the method of reforming criminals that he undertook to teach the world at the outset. His original intentions were quite in keeping with the most enlightened penology of his day—to reform "by methods moral, intellectual, and industrial, by the sympathy of pure, humble, and yet exalted minds, and by opening to his pupils the possibility of a worthier life than that which had become their fate" (*BR* 131). But these benificent aims lacked the essential ingredient—one which the reader will find singularly lacking in most of the philanthropic writing on prison reform in the 1840s, not to mention later periods—namely, any feeling for what it must be like to be a sinner, any awareness of one's own guilt. It is precisely this lesson that Hollingsworth must learn before he can go to work on his first case; for every reformer's first case must be himself.

Even Charles Spear, perhaps the most selfless of all the philanthropists, seems not to have understood this basic principle. He is close to some such recognition when he asks, "May we not live to see converted thieves and murderers bringing back the degraded and the forsaken of their own cast[e] to truth and virtue?"[40] But this is not an insight arrived at through self-examination; it is what Spear called an "encouragement"—in short, a hopeful idea, conceived more as a sociological technique than a moral necessity. Spear borrowed the notion from William Ellery Channing, who had cleverly thought of it on the model of the Washingtonians (the Alcoholics Anonymous of the day) and had passed it along to "the prisoner's friend." Neither of them ever expressed any sense of the deeper implication of the suggestion.

One can scarcely complain of any such blind spots in Hawthorne, whose compassion for sinners, especially doubting and despairing sinners, is extraordinarily full; but it is worth noting that Hollingsworth remains a somewhat distant figure in the novel, rather under the microscope than at one's elbow. Hawthorne's sympathies and anxieties center on Coverdale, whose sins are more congenial, and whose moral diseases are chronic among authors. Of course Hollingsworth shares most of his sins with the other characters. They are all extremely egoistic, private beings, secret "plotters," covert enemies of the communal virtues Blithedale supposedly represents. It is appropriate for Coverdale to suggest, jokingly, that each of them should "systematically commit at least one crime apiece," to satisfy Hollingsworth's hunger for philanthropic objects (*BR* 22). When Zenobia answers with "a strange kind of a glance," Coverdale does not know what to make of it, but by the end of the novel, it has become clear that she thinks of herself as a criminal, "on trial for my life." She only requests that Hollingsworth join her as one of the accused, rather than sit as "judge, jury, and accuser . . . in one man" (*BR* 214).

In many ways Hollingsworth's ambitions and sins reflect those of the Blithedale community as a whole, which is not so virtuous an endeavor as it might seem. The communitists are also very much concerned with finding the funds to erect an edifice—a Phalanstery rather than a reformatory (*BR* 128)—and that is one reason why Hollingsworth is so tempted to take over the Blithedale foundations and convert them to his own ends. Just as Hollingsworth betrays the narrowness of his vision by refusing to countenance any reform other than his own, so too Blithedale is finally accused of merely "playing at philanthropy, . . . in our effort to establish the one true system" (*BR* 227). Finally, Hollingsworth himself points out that the Fourierist "has committed the Unpardonable Sin" in appealing to man's "passional organization"—to put it bluntly, his selfishness—as the motive force of utopia (*BR* 52). This is still another example of meddling in the private consciences of men for the sake of some "scientific" scheme for their salvation, precisely the means and end of Hollingsworth's own philanthropy.

Hawthorne might have selected associationism or spiritualism or feminism as the paradigmatic philanthropy, but Hollingsworth's ruling passion is most inclusive, an emblem for all the others, for it demonstrates most explicitly that man's depraved nature cannot be redeemed by mere man. As always in Hawthorne's fiction, we are in the Garden after the Fall, observing the results of sin rather than its temptations—the altered consciousness, the new awareness of self and others, the sexual guilt, the remorse and despair. Most of all, especially in this reckless novel of self-deception and fatal illusions, Hawthorne raises the problem of the loss of faith that accompanies the knowledge of evil. On the one hand we see the cynical materialism of a psychopathic personality like Westervelt, or the milder but no less faithless skepticism of Coverdale, whose artistic habits of mind teach him to doubt the reality of his own perceptions. On the other hand, we are confronted with Hollingsworth, the man whose faith is a function of his "tremendous concentrativeness," his own "indomitable will" (*BR* 135). The "solemn murmur" of his morning prayers echoes in Coverdale's chamber, where the poet lies in bed, saying his prayers backwards, "cursing my day as bitterly as patient Job himself" (*BR* 39-40). Hollingsworth illustrates the problem of faith better than Coverdale or Westervelt, for in him we see the price of believing, measured in the shriveling of human sympathies, the refusal to bend to the different needs and views of other men. Hollingsworth cannot accept Coverdale as a friend unless he is also willing to be his coadjutor in his philanthropic schemes, and it is implied if not quite stated that he is willing to contemplate love with Zenobia or Priscilla only under conditions still more mercenary. Hollingsworth sacrifices everything to his faith, a "spectral monster." At one point Zenobia attempts to defend his monomania: "Blind enthusiasm, absorption in one idea, I grant, is generally ridiculous, and must be fatal to the respectability of an ordinary man; it requires a very high and powerful character, to make it otherwise. But a great man—as, perhaps you do not know—attains his normal condition only through the inspiration of one great idea. As a friend of Mr. Hollingsworth, and, at the same time, a calm observer, I must tell you that he seems to me such a man" (*BR* 166). But Zenobia's words ring false; it is special pleading for her lover. In this novel as elsewhere in Hawthorne, faith is bestowed only on the innocent and pure, the Priscillas and Hildas and Phoebes whom sin has never even tempted.

Hawthorne might well have imagined a tragic hero such as Zenobia half describes—perhaps Ethan Brand was to have been such a character—but his suspicion of inspiration and enthusiasm was too complete to allow him to portray an Ahab or a Pierre Glendinning, Melville's classic fools of faith. The Coverdale in him is quick to mark the flaws in the heroic character, the egotism behind the absorption, the cold intolerance for any piety other than his own, the "awful truth in Bunyan's book of such;—from the very gate of Heaven, there is a by-way to the pit!" (*BR* 243). And the overriding truth in Coverdale's whole arsenal of dismal facts—one that Hawthorne often seems to believe himself—is that "little as we know of our life to come, we may be very sure, for one thing, that the good we aim at will not be attained" (*BR* 75).

This worldly wisdom accounts for the theme and tone of much in Hawthorne, and especially for the not-quite-embarrassed self-mockery of *Blithedale.* Oh, sighs Coverdale, I too was a believer once, like Hollingsworth, but look where it gets you, look at the reformer pining away in his cottage! It is in the context of such pathetic tonalities that we must read Coverdale's final confession that he too was in love with Priscilla—that is, that he too would have settled for as much flesh and blood as her meager constitution promised, in a world where realities were scarce indeed. Yet if he *would* have, he *did* not. Abandoned schemes, abandoned hopes, this is the elegaic mood that Hawthorne always sinks into, mourning possibilities that were strangled at birth for the sake of keeping them eternally alive in the imagination, in art. This is the crime of the author, "to live in other lives" (*BR* 160), "making my prey of people's individualities" (*BR* 84), tampering "with earnest human passions," "a monstrous scepticism" (*BR* 170).

III

Ten

The Mad Scientist

THE MYTH OF THE "mad scientist" existed before Hawthorne, in more than one classic version, and since the advent of Rappaccini and Chillingworth, Maule and Westervelt, its development has been even more lively and multifarious. Partly because he lived when he did, partly as a result of an almost instinctive feel for its nuances, Hawthorne's brilliant use of the myth lights up the whole gallery of mad scientists, from the zany philosophers of Laputa to the disembodied "brain" that throbs sinisterly in so many science-fiction films.

There are two main strands of the myth, easily distinguished both before and after Hawthorne. In his fiction they meet and intertwine. The older tradition is that of the crackpot scientist—balmy alchemist, virtuoso, projector—used by Swift as a satiric metaphor for the utopianism of the Royal Society in the third book of *Gulliver's Travels.* This is the strand elaborated in the treatment of social science in *The Blithedale Romance.* It goes back beyond Swift of course, to Sir Thomas More, and still further to Plato, and it may be traced in utopian and anti-utopian novels all the way to Orwell's *1984* and Huxley's *Island.*

The divergence of utopian and anti-utopian bias does not represent any major discrepancy in structure; whether sane or mad, hero or villain, the utopian scientist is conceived as a mastermind, and mind over matter provides the premise of motivation and event in both branches of the genre. On the other hand, the satiric treatment of the utopian mentality may be undertaken, as in *Blithedale,* without the introduction of any realized utopian institutions. This is a more significant difference. Like the utopia, this correlative form has its history too, in books like Orestes Brownson's *The Spirit-Rapper,* William Dean Howells's *The Undiscovered Country,* and Henry James's *The Bostonians,* to name three that were directly indebted to Hawthorne. Especially after the Civil War, the mad scientist appears only in absurd guises in this tradition, and is never taken seriously enough to warrant the imagining of his accomplished vision, whether utopia or dystopia. The subject matter is reform and reformers rather than an ideal society; the aim is primarily comic rather than polemic. Of course these distinctions must be adjusted to individual works: *The Undiscovered Country,* for instance, does briefly treat utopian institutions, but its description of Shaker life is certainly not so detailed an account of paradise as Howells presents in his officially utopian novel, *Through the Eye of the Needle,* or as his contemporary Anna Bowman Dodd spelled out in her equally orthodox dystopia, *The Republic of the Future.*

The other main tradition of mad scientists seems to begin with the gothic novel, and its most famous example is *Frankenstein.* Of course *Frankenstein* is a relatively late example of the gothic, and Mary Shelley is usually credited with being the first to introduce science as a vehicle of horror, in a tradition that went back half a century. No doubt the prize should go to her, if any single author, for the invention of the mad scientist; but earlier gothic protagonists may usefully be regarded as scientists too, *sans* laboratory, for they share with Victor Frankenstein his passion for esoteric knowledge and his monstrous interference with the course of nature. That their mechanisms are supernatural rather than scientific is less of a difference than the hindsight of twentieth-century readers may suppose. In a period when the word "pseudoscience" had not been coined, it was not so crucial to distinguish the elixirs of a St. Leon or a Medardus from those of a Jekyll, or the wish fulfillments of the monastic cell, like Ambrosio's phantom Matilda, from the laboratory spectre born of Frankenstein's sibling rivalry and incestuous desires.

More significant is the difference between the utopian and the gothic versions of the mad scientist. While the utopian scientist may be either a model of self-sacrificing idealism or a self-deluded figure of fun, the gothic scientist is almost invariably a Faustian experimenter, sacrilegiously meddling with the souls of his victims and thereby forfeiting his own innocence. *Blithedale* offers an example in the diabolic Westervelt, and the number of similar characters in Hawthorne's fiction—Rappaccini, Aylmer, Heidegger, Chillingworth, Grimshawe, and others—reveals his fascination with this archetype. It was an increasingly popular conception in his day. The evil mesmerist was perhaps the mad scientist *par excellence,* and Edgar Allan Poe, George Lippard, T. S. Arthur, Charles W. Webber, and Orestes Brownson all took advantage of the developing myth, perpetuated in later times by a few vastly successful classics like Du Maurier's *Trilby* and Weine's *Cabinet of Dr. Caligari.*

Although both of these traditions existed before Hawthorne, by the time of *The House of the Seven Gables* the gothic novel was approaching the end of its remarkable efflorescence, while the utopian novel, with the appearance of *Blithedale,* was just entering what was to be an extraordinary renaissance. The two traditions thus meet both structurally and historically in Hawthorne as in no other writer. Moreover, the two "sciences" with which we have been dealing, pseudoscience and social science, also come together in Hawthorne's work, providing a cultural context for the transformation of the mad scientist from his gothic to his utopian incarnation. One might go further and say that the mad scientist, especially as he appears in Hawthorne's fiction, is the *medium* of the shift from the gothic novel to the utopian, a metamorphosis that—if it could be proved—ought to be of considerable interest to literary historians and theorists.

As we have seen, Hawthorne's only attempt to graft the social scientist and the pseudoscientist in a single character—Holgrave—failed to come to life; the reformist qualities of his nature are easily abandoned at the end of the novel because they are so unconvincing to begin with. In a period when many utopians and philanthropists were also dabblers in pseudoscience, it should have been easy for a novelist to combine the two in a protagonist, yet aside from Brownson's *Spirit-Rapper* only one rather limping utopia attempted to exploit the connection. Before going on to consider Hawthorne's place at the crossroads of these traditions, it will be well to look briefly at this book and a few other cases where the pseudoscientist and the social scientist seem almost to join as a single mad scientist.

In 1846 an anonymous novel entitled *Henry Russell: or, The Year of Our Lord Two Thousand* made use of mesmerism as an instrument of reform. The plot is just a conventional love story, scarcely enlivened by the fact that it is set in the future. At one point there is a brief utopian episode, when one of the characters—not even the hero—dreams that he is back in the nineteenth century, where his ancestors still labor under the curses of class structure, unequal distribution of wealth, intemperance, war, and slavery. Calling on his mesmeric powers, strangely enhanced in his new surroundings, he influences the warhawks in Congress to declare peace, then goes to the Senate and abolishes slavery; he persuades the liquor manufacturers to enlist in the temperance movement, sets up departments of public instruction, and establishes Fourierism everywhere. He is on a boat to Europe where he plans to duplicate these feats, but finds his magnetic powers ineffectual against storms; he is "dashed against a rock in the ocean" and awakens in the year 2000 again.[1]

The two traditions—wild-eyed reformer and evil-eyed mesmerist—are not really joined in *Henry Russell.* There is no mad scientist here, and mesmerism is a mere tool of philanthropy in the hands of a benign dreamer. Orestes Brownson's attempt to fuse the two figures in the "autobiographical" hero of *The Spirit-Rapper* was more thoroughgoing. Brownson's narrator begins as a gothic experimenter. Once he has discovered his mesmeric powers, he quickly "somnambulizes" the feminist Priscilla, and partly as a result of her influence he then moves into a "social science" phase, during which he mesmerically organizes rebellions in a dozen European countries. To some degree this plot manages to weld the utopian and gothic impulses together in a convincing symbolic action, albeit rather surrealistic.

Brownson based his combination of mesmerism and utopianism on a reading of the contemporary scene. The connection, he thought, was historical before it was literary. Many prominent communitists were also believers in mesmerism and its offspring spiritualism, including Adin Ballou of Hopedale, the Nicholses of Modern Times, John Murray Spear of Kiantone, Warren Chase of Ceresco, Thomas Lake Harris of Brocton—not to mention the Shakers, who, as Howells pointed out, claimed to be the original spiritualists. Still others, such as Robert Owen and his son Robert Dale Owen, of New Harmony, were converted after their communities had expired. Albert Brisbane had been interested in animal magnetism even before Fourierism, and he became a spiritualist in the 1850s, as did Marianne Dwight's John Orvis, a veteran of both Skaneateles and Brook Farm. George Ripley himself attended seances, though only in the capacity of a reporter. Even at Oneida studies in spiritualism were sanctioned in the last days of the community, as a means of combating "materialism."[2]

In the light of such historical precedents, it is curious that Brownson's narrator is not more convincing and that no other novelist attempted a similar amalgam of mesmerist and utopian archetypes. The fact is, the two sides of the spirit-rapper's character seem a bad fit and continually interfere with one another. Having subjugated Priscilla, for instance, the narrator never follows up his advantage sexually, as a good gothic villain should, but merely puts her to work in his insurrectionary intrigue, helping set up his "batteries" for the galvanic eruption of 1848. At the same time, the narrator is too much a gothic solipsist to enter into his revolutionary activity with communitarian zeal. Priscilla is his only comrade, and she is merely his slave. As in *Henry Russell,* the political ends of *The Spirit-Rapper* are achieved without any meeting of minds, except for the sniper fire of the mesmerist's will at his unsuspecting victims. The hero is no more a charismatic utopian than he is a sinister Svengali; he is a secret plotter, an arm-chair general, a terrorist. Perhaps this may help account for the curiously mixed tone of Brownson's book, half in earnest, half burlesque. In combining the two traditions, he created self-contradictory hybrids—the selfless solipsist and the solitary socialist.

Such incongruities were also built into the historical models Brownson had to work with. The individualist and the communitist might come together in the person of a prophet like John Humphrey Noyes ("Father" Noyes as he was called) or an eccentric like Bronson Alcott (whose community, said Emerson, "has only room for one"[3]); but these were complex cases, not easily imitated in fiction. A mythic imagination automatically tended to polarize the impulses toward selfhood and community. Hawthorne found it more convenient to present his mesmerist Westervelt in opposition to the communitists of Blithedale than as their leader. This does not mean that the two figures were invariably pitted against one another, in fiction or in life, but only that certain conceptions of their roles were incompatible. So long as the utopian hero and his colony were taken seriously as a paradigm of the social order, gothic elements were crowded out. Alternatively, if the gothic side were allowed to dominate, then it was at the expense of any treatment of the ideal society. The more attention paid the protagonist, the less concern with a social world. Ultimately the utopian hero would either dwindle to a mere point of view for describing social mechanisms, or he would become a crypto-gothic hero, not really a communitarian at all, but just another mad scientist.

There is a brief hint of this second possibility in George Lippard's *Quaker City,* where we are fleetingly introduced to the "Brotherhood of Ravoni," a collection of male worshippers the mesmerist has gathered to further his political ends just as his entranced harem ministers to his sexual desires. The harem is by far the dominant fantasy, however, so that Ravoni never for a moment displays a utopian imagination. Still, it was an available framework for utopian fiction, with a historical foundation in a number of "religiotopias" that arose from the claims of prophets to divine inspiration in the trance state. Ann Lee and Jeminia Wilkinson, Joseph Smith, Thomas Lake Harris, and John Murray Spear all imposed on their followers in this way. Yet novelists were somehow unable to bring off such a combination of gothic and utopian figures. Lippard and Brownson seemed to glimpse the possibilities, but it remained for a modern novelist, in a book published in 1967, to take full advantage of this tempting combination; Alison Lurie's *Imaginary Friends* is not so much an example as it is a witty critique of the genre, a demonstration of what novelists like Hawthorne and James might have done with today's spiritualists and social scientists. Only a few "insider novels," like Rosa Emerson's *Among the Chosen* or the fictionalized exposés of the Mormons, even come close—certainly not very close—to the sort of anatomy of enthusiasm we might expect.

As it happens, one class of novels did exploit the mesmerist-utopian figure, though not so much in his mad scientist incarnation as in his stoop to charlatan and humbug. These novels are neither gothic nor utopian, but rather satires on philanthropy, in the tradition of *Blithedale* and *The Spirit-Rapper,* though with some significant differences and developments. Here the mesmerist-reformer was stripped of any genuine powers, political or occult, and relegated to the seedy outskirts of the plot, where he could be ridiculed for his incongruous pretensions—his vulgar boarding-house brotherhood on the one hand, his bogus Svengali-ism on the other. Henry James's *Bostonians* is the best known of these debunking satires. Its heroine is a women's rights orator who, in the first stage of her career, seems to derive some of her eloquence from her father's mesmeric applications. But it quickly becomes clear that Verena Tarrant's powers arise less from her father's magnetism than from her own displaced sexual energy. In James's view she needs a man, not a magnetist. Her father can scarcely be taken seriously, even as a sharper; at best he is a pathetic dupe of his own misunderstood feats.

In such deflations the gothic bogeyman was likely to be associated with utopian visions, but these too were introduced only to be made light of. James's Selah Tarrant had been a member of the "celebrated" colony at "Cayuga" (read "Oneida"), and in *The Undiscovered Country* Howells's Dr. Boynton, who also practises mesmerism on his daughter, joins a Shaker community to harness its traditional spiritualism to his own murky investigations. A still earlier novel, Bayard Taylor's *Hannah Thurston,* which Hawthorne himself read and admired in the last year of his life[4], chides women's rights, spiritualism, and utopian communities. Taylor's fly-by-night villain, who advocates all three reforms, is caught attempting to run off with a married lady to a colony where everybody is married to everybody else—Oneida again. Even John Hay's sleazy medium in *The Bread-Winners,* although a very minor character, has communal loyalties to the "Brotherhood of Bread-Winners," Hay's travesty of a labor union. All these figures are has-beens and failures. Their fates are paltry and degraded. Taylor's Dyce is told to be "on the midnight train." Professor Bott of *The Bread-Winners* addresses the courtroom—"I appeal from this outrage to the power of the people and the judgment of history"—and ends his career "making shoes in the State penitentiary."[5] The last epithet bestowed on Selah Tarrant is "jackass," and Dr. Boynton admits on his deathbed that the spirit messages are merely "electricity," not evidence of an afterlife. In short, the utopian-cum-mesmerist had become a laughingstock.

All of these novels owe something to *The Blithedale Romance.* James's indebtedness is easily traced and well known. Howells tips his hat more than once in Hawthorne's direction, not only in his plot (Dr. Boynton seeks to bend the Shaker community to his own ends much as Hollingsworth wished to trim Blithedale to his), but also in incidental detail, as when one of his characters, having suggested that Boynton's somnambulist daughter might be "innocent in the midst of fraud," goes on to defend his conjecture as "worthy of Hawthorne"—an explicit reference to Coverdale's staunch belief in Priscilla's innocence after her escape from Westervelt.[6] But *Blithedale* takes seriously what these later fictions sneer at: the supernatural powers of the mesmerist and the precarious idealism of the utopian adventurer. Although *The Blithedale Romance* was certainly one source of this satiric tradition, Hawthorne had models of his own to look to, and other bequests to pass on.

If the two versions of the scientist are only falteringly combined in Hawthorne's characterization of Holgrave, yet the two nineteenth-century genres they normally inhabit, the gothic and the utopian novel, seem to meet and merge in his work more successfully. Indeed, he offers the literary historian an extremely rare and instructive opportunity to study how one genre gives way to another, a sort of literary mutation that reveals much about the nature of genres and their relation to cultural context and individual genius. *The House of the Seven Gables* is one of the last great gothic novels, along with *Wuthering Heights, Jane Eyre, A Tale of Two Cities,* and *Pierre,* the classics of the genre's high period. At the same time, Hawthorne is among the first of a new wave of utopian novelists in a genre that would not crest until the 1880s but was already beginning to swell in the 1840s and 1850s, in books like Melville's *Typee* and Cooper's *The Crater. The Blithedale Romance* is not really a utopian novel (nor is *Typee*), but it contains many of the elements that would constitute the genre when it came to fruition. What one can see in Hawthorne so vividly, as if under glass, is the way in which the one genre seems almost to "become" the other; feature after feature appears in its gothic costume in *The Seven Gables,* and in utopian guise in *Blithedale.*

Of course the two genres may be regarded as "sister" forms rather than source and product. As we have already noticed, the "child" of the two, the utopia, is much older than the "parent" gothic. Yet it makes a good deal of sense to consider them as a single developing genre, sloughing off its antiquated cloak of supernaturalism and emerging in the new white lab coat of science. Not that all of the relevant shifts and congruities are apparent in Hawthorne's own work, but if we take him as a pivotal figure and compare the genres with his example continually before us, the metamorphosis may be glimpsed. The archetype of the mad scientist will be seen to play a central role in mediating the transformation.

The House of the Seven Gables exhibits most of the classic traits of the gothic: usurpation, witchcraft, a family curse, a haunted castle, confusions of appearance and reality, willful villains and helpless maidens, a magic portrait, an episodic plot, interpolated tale, long-lost will, and so on. These are not mere decorations, but cohere as a system of interrelated elements that define the genre.

As in *The Castle of Otranto* and so many of its progeny, the usurpation forms the basis of the Pyncheon family curse. The symbol of its continuing force is the castle, in this case the "house of the seven gables"—the stolen property still in the usurper's hands. The plot is episodic, and is interrupted by the "flashback" tale of "Alice Pyncheon," because the curse must be provided with a structural embodiment, the circling return to the source of evil. In the gothic novel the plot is not "what happens" but what prevents anything from happening—the secret sin that is committed by every generation, in a compulsive repetition that cannot be escaped until some symbolic act of renunciation, atonement, and rebirth.

Characteristically the hero is an author surrogate, Holgrave, whose ambivalence and confusion suggest that Hawthorne had something at stake in the story of the lost birthright and the long-awaited revenge. In any case the blame for the perpetuation of the curse has now begun to spread from the Pyncheons to the Maules. Perhaps the original Matthew Maule deserved his punishment as a witch after all, if his descendants are such literary spellbinders as Holgrave, whose story of Alice almost hypnotizes Phoebe. It is not clear who is guiltiest, the usurper or the usurped. All that is settled at the end is that it is sinful to indulge the imagination; the only innocence seems to reside in renouncing imaginative powers and joining the society of ordinary men, the "magnetic chain of humanity."

These patterns can be traced in most gothic fiction, as any reader familiar with Hawthorne's literary models—Matthew Lewis, William Godwin, Charles Brockden Brown, Mary Shelley, Charles Maturin, James Hogg, and others of that school—must know. What is much less apparent is how these same motifs inform the utopian novel as well, the genre of *Looking Backward* and all its companion pieces and descendants.

Take the theme of love and sexuality for example. Most utopian novels provided a romantic entanglement to lend some color to the monotony of life in Shangri-la, but as the social side of the genre became more prominent, the sexual themes were correspondingly diminished. Nonetheless, the motifs bear a striking resemblance to certain aspects of gothic sexuality. In more than one novel of the Bellamy school the "romantic interest" is entirely based on the difficulties of a courtship stretched across the centuries. Typically the hero must accept the loss of his sweetheart in the nineteenth century and learn to love a twentieth-century substitute—always with the threat, sometimes fulfilled, of a sudden irrevocable return to his earlier existence. This transfer of affections can be effected smoothly, but more often there is a crisis of feeling—"romantic culture shock"—brought on by the intimacy with an alien being. Twain's Connecticut Yankee may finally get used to his sixth-century girlfriend, as Julian West learns to love Edith Leete in *Looking Backward,* but neither Edith Bartlett nor Puss Flanagan ("Hello Central") is forgotten.

Antecedents in gothic fiction included blighted love affairs across cultural, temporal, and even species lines—Ambrosio and Matilda in *The Monk,* Melmoth and Immalee in *Melmoth the Wanderer,* and Giovanni and Beatrice in "Rappaccini's Daughter," to name only the most obvious examples. Even the more mundane "beyond the pale" hindrances of Zenobia's situation in *Blithedale* or Isabel's more serious disability in Melville's *Pierre* are probably related to the vague uneasiness felt by a utopian time traveler wooing his first sweetheart's great-grandchild. No doubt all of these impossible gulfs have incest taboos lurking somewhere in the darkness; the classic case is *Frankenstein,* where the monster—a "flesh and blood" creature of the hero's imagination—serves as both symbolic and literal obstacle to Frankenstein's marriage with the sister-like companion of his childhood. The utopian novel has nothing to compare with so blatant an exhibit, but the typical father-daughter-lover triangle is probably just as frequent in one genre as the other, though fathers in utopia seem to look on the brighter side ot it—not losing a daughter but gaining a son.

Hawthorne's treatment of these themes is characteristically transitional, halfway between a gothic and a utopian rendering. In both *The House of the Seven Gables* and *The Blithedale Romance* the plots include interpolated tales (both a gothic and a utopian technique) in which the story of an earlier event is told in a way that suggests that it lies near the source of the ongoing action. In *The Seven Gables* it is the mesmeric mastery of Alice Pyncheon, a symbolic seduction that takes place under the very nose of her father; in *Blithedale* it is the similar mesmeric influence exercised on Priscilla by Westervelt while she is still a girl living under the ineffectual protection of her father, Fauntleroy *alias* Moodie. Both of these Oedipal premises to the fictive action are later followed up when Holgrave refuses to repeat the sin of his ancestor Matthew Maule and when Hollingsworth rescues Priscilla from Westervelt's magnetic clutches. The theme as Hawthorne presents it seems to be basically antisexual: it is a sin to steal away the affections of a daughter from her father, and the sin can be expiated only by the hero's renunciation of his youthful ambitions (both Holgrave and Hollingsworth give up careers as reformers), which somehow neutralizes the mesmeric force (here, as frequently in gothic texts, a metaphor for sexual magnetism).

In the later utopian handling of these materials, the "reform interest" is no longer perceived as the same threat to the "romantic interest," because the former has completely won out. The utopian scene usurps the stage, and the hero's lovelife is cut short both by his sudden departure for a tour of future civilization and by the author's inability to find room for a romantic plot in the midst of a narrative of social progress.

The plot structures of the two genres are similar in other ways as well. The episodic gothic narrative reappears in the repetitive slide show of the utopia. On the one hand, there are the "wanderers" of the gothic tradition—St.Leon, Melmoth, Dolliver—whose plots are eternal picaresques; on the other, there are the time travelers of the utopias, equally doomed to a treadmill existence, though they pass through more cheerful landscapes, the streamlined cities of the future. Generational conflicts appear in this context in both genres. Where the gothic plot tends to be based on a family curse, provoked by some family sin recommitted by each generation, the utopian adventurer has to deal with the fact that he is, so to speak, "his own grandfather," still saturated with the outmoded vices and ignorance of a past epoch. The stock episode in which the utopian hero falls ill and suffers hallucinations is an externalizing of this "culture shock"—sweating out the "old Adam" upon entering the new Eden. Examples range from Coverdale to Julian West, or, to go back to some the proto-utopias, from *Robinson Crusoe* to *Typee* and *The Crater.*

Any book that deals with societies more primitive as well as more advanced than that of its readers tends to utopian (or anti-utopian) themes, since the implicit comparison of institutions can hardly be avoided. The desert-island narrative is an interesting precursor of the utopia, which shows some further connections with the gothic tradition. For instance, in the usual Robinsonade the hero is a disobedient son gone to sea despite his father's wishes (*Crusoe*), engaged to be married in defiance of parental advice (*The Crater*), jumping ship to escape from the authority of an unreasonable captain (*Typee*). These elements of plot are related to the usurpation motif of the gothic. Whether the upshot of filial disobedience is total solitude or immersion in an alien culture (the difference between being sent to one's room and being turned from the door), the effect is the gothic loss of patrimony and brotherhood with other men. Further, if one is marooned on an island, the classic picaresque structure is forced inward, into another dimension; the landscape immediately becomes symbolic, a mirror of consciousness much like gothic solipsism. Here the difference is that the desert-island narrative, from *Robinson Crusoe* to *Walden,* tends to become an inverted utopia rather than a psychomachia: the very absence of civilization serves to reflect the nature of social life, and a vision of rational existence can be presented as the castaway or hermit recapitulates the discovery of human necessities and reinvents a technology to satisfy them.

Timothy Savage's *The Amazonian Republic,* a curious novel of 1842, is a useful example here because it combines the castaway format with an out-and-out utopian purpose. Savage's hero finds himself among an ancient race of Amazons hidden in the jungles of South America, and his description of their society functions as a critique of both the follies of women (though Savage is not antifeminist so much as misogynist) and the absurdities of United States civilization in general. Like Melville's Tommo and Cooper's Mark, once isolated from "his own kind" the hero immediately begins to think in utopian terms, to assess every fashion and taboo as a possible hint for the good life. At bottom the old question, "What would you take with you to a desert island?" is a utopian invitation.

The Blithedale Romance is obviously neither a desert-island narrative nor a utopia, but it shares enough features with both and with the gothic novel to make it a landmark in the transition of genres. When Coverdale leaves the habits and vices of ordinary society to enter on his communal adventure, he too finds himself in an unfamiliar culture, where the old expectations and rules do not necessarily apply. He has given up his life of leisure at the expense of others, his coal fire, his decanter of old wine. Everything must be reconsidered: "Have we our various parts assigned?" someone asks, and Zenobia announces that the women will take care of culinary matters, but warns that "perhaps, when our individual adaptations begin to develop themselves it may be that some of us, who wear the petticoat, will go afield, and leave the weaker brethren to take our places in the kitchen!" (*BR* 16).

Part of the result of being thrown into new circumstances is Coverdale's illness: "What, in the name of common-sense, had I to do with any better society than I had always lived in!" he groans from his pillow, and beseeches Hollingsworth "to send me back to town, in a close carriage" (*BR* 40-41). This is also the beginning of Coverdale's morbid isolation from his Blithedale brethren. Alone in his sickroom he begins to have fantasies about his friends as well as second thoughts about his experiment in communal life. Later a symbolic landscape springs up—the "wood-path," the "hermitage" arbor in the pine tree—representing his isolation in both of its aspects, as critical contemplation of his comrades and as a withdrawal into the self, where fantasies fill the consciousness. In these patterns of alienation, isolation, and projection, one may see how the utopian and the gothic imagination differ and yet remain congruent. Coverdale starts as a utopian, asking what the good life must consist in, and ends as a gothic fantast, projecting his desires on the reality that he is no longer in touch with.

The point is that once the protagonist loses contact with ordinary reality, he has but two choices: to remake the social order he has lost or to go mad. (Of course the anti-utopian novelists had a different formulation: the desire to remake the social order implied the loss of contact with reality—madness.)

If the choice is to reestablish the social order, the new pattern will probably be little more than a refurbishing of the status quo, projecting the internalized mores of one's civilization onto the screen of an imagined future. Thus Robinson Crusoe recreates England on his island, and Bellamy fantasizes a perfected version of his own nineteenth-century America. The city of the future represents a certain dissatisfaction with the present, it is true, but just under the surface of that alienation is the desire to embrace things as they are, to rediscover the way to be happy with one's life. More cynically, Coverdale points out that the moment the communitists have separated themselves "from the greedy, struggling, self-seeking world," they begin to imitate it (*BR* 20).

If, on the other hand, the choice is to "go mad," that is, to abandon the social order entirely, then the symbolic landscape that fills the scene will be the gothic world of fantasy. Sometimes, as in the "Immalee" sequence of *Melmoth the Wanderer,* there may appear a sort of hybrid vision—an idyllic Eden of the imagination from which the solipsistic hero and his Eve view at a distance the sins and follies of civilization. More often it is the protagonist alone who is on the "outside," gazing enviously at the ordinary domestic happiness of a human family "within." The cottage scene in *Frankenstein,* with the monster skulking piteously in the woodshed, is a particularly memorable example of a very common motif. Ambrosio's magic mirror in *The Monk,* in which he sees Antonia disrobing, is a still more typical gothic vista, a fantasy of sexual desire that, unbeknownst to the fantast, is also a longing for his family, since Antonia is his long-lost sister.

In the utopian novel these symbolic landscapes tend to be made up of anthropological and sociological content. Glimpses of life in the new society fill the eye of the alien visitor, while in the gothic the inward gaze is usually focused on images of primal desire. The difference may be indicated by comparing Holgrave's view of the Pyncheons—his spying on Clifford, his study of Alice, his daguerreotype of Jaffrey—with Coverdale's various peephole vantage points—the hermitage in the woods, his hotel window in town. Both visions are combinations of fantasy and fact—not quite gothic and not quite utopian—but Coverdale's appears more objective and more social, though of course *we* know that it isn't.

Both gothic solipsism and utopian renovation of the social order place an extraordinary emphasis on the nature of human consciousness, on questions of perception, memory, desire, and will. Suspense in these plots revolves around not what will happen next, but what is real. Accordingly the narrative movement is necessarily episodic, cyclic, repetitive.

Coverdale is Hawthorne's purest case of the alienated artist who cannot trust either reality or his own imagination. If characters and events really are what they appear to be, then he must resign himself to being an outsider, a voyeur living a vicarious life through his friends. Or, supposing that his part in the plot is more central—that he can actually determine his experience and control his fate—then he must accept the premise of such power, that his friends and their entanglements are nothing but figments of his imagination, and that all reality is only a fiction. It is not hard to see how this dilemma, near which all of Hawthorne's work hovers, could serve as a paradigm for the transformation occurring in the gothic novel as it reached the 1850s. What had begun as an interest in the agonized conscience of the gothic villain (probably an inheritance from the fascination with the suffering heroine in epistolary novels like *Pamela*), had become, by the time of *The House of the Seven Gables* and *The Blithedale Romance,* an all-encompassing concern with the nature of consciousness, especially as it was manifested in the literary imagination.

After a self-reflexive novel like *Pierre,* there was really nowhere for this interest to go. It may seem perverse to say that an obsession which reappears in Kafka and Genet had reached a dead end by the early 1850s, but something of the sort was occurring in the final stages of the gothic during Hawthorne's novel-writing period. Obviously there are other factors involved—shifting attitudes toward science and the supernatural, industrialization and urbanization, the Civil War and its aftermath—but whatever the concomitant causes, there seems to have been a formal limit reached in the symbolic representation of consciousness, beyond which novelists were unable to imagine any new possibilities.

One might say that the narrative manner of *Blithedale* could be carried only one step further, to the extreme of the utopian novel, where the basis of the entire adventure is brought into question at the outset, with the mesmeric trance, the dream, or some other framing device implying an altered state of consciousness. This doubt whether the whole story is mere hallucination could be exploited "within" a work like *Blithedale* to raise the question of consciousness and the themes of appearance and reality, but once invoked as the very premise of everything that follows, the subject is taken "outside" the range of thematic treatment and becomes almost completely merged with the ordinary assumptions of all fictions—the willing suspension of disbelief, the prerogative of the author to introduce his "givens" without apology or justification.

Thus the theme of consciousness, even as it appears in *Blithedale,* is curiously subversive of the narrative unity—surely a source of the confusion that prevails at the end, when Coverdale "confesses" his own surprising sense of the meaning of his story, that *he* was in love with Priscilla. By the time of *Looking Backward* the ambiguities have developed beyond thematic considerations to characteristics of the genre itself. "Fantasy literature" is a name that the utopian novel sometimes goes by, and this is accurate insofar as it suggests the sort of authorial self-indulgence that Hawthorne struggled with—say in *Doctor Grimshawe's Secret* or *Septimius Felton*—but that Bellamy and others merely take as the privilege of the "historian of the future."

The wandering figure in the gothic—St. Leon, Melmoth, Ethan Brand—is licensed to roam unrestricted in the realms of the imagination, as his literal wayfaring symbolizes. These wanderings may be distinguished from the somewhat similar travels of utopian heroes chiefly because the latter's explorations are treated as entirely guiltless. The gothic wanderer is punished for his Faustian sin by being condemned to commit it eternally. In the utopian novel the same fantasies of omnipotence are neutralized by their banal content—the electric trains and TV sets—and most of all by the attribution of their source to an uninvited alteration in consciousness, for which the hero cannot be held responsible. But it is the same mechanism of psychic projection. Although scarcely anyone took mesmerism seriously in fiction after Hawthorne, still the utopian novelists of the 1880s made extensive use of its phenomena as a framing device. Macnie's *The Diothas,* Bellamy's *Looking Backward,* and even Twain's *Connecticut Yankee* depend on a mesmeric trance as the means of entry into the ideal society of the future. (Actually Hank Morgan enters the sixth century via a crack on the skull, and *exits* by mesmerism.) From the outset, then, these novels raise the problem of appearance and reality—not in the gothic manner, as a question of the hero's sanity, but rather as a political fantasy, the representation of a desired but not yet achieved society.

Moreover, some of the utopias inherit the more immediate concern of the gothic with consciousness itself and its illusions and susceptibilities. In *Looking Backward,* for instance, Julian West is continually noticing the disorientation that his 113-year sleep has imposed upon him. "The past was dead, crushed beneath a century's weight, and from the present I was shut out."[7] Like the wanderer in the gothic, West is thrown back on his own consciousness by the loss of a social reality. He begins to doubt his "personal identity": "I lay there and fought for my sanity. In my mind, all had broken loose, habits of feeling, associations of thought, ideas of persons and things, all had dissolved and lost coherence and were seething together in apparently irretrievable chaos. There were no rallying points, nothing was left stable. There only remained the will, and was any human will strong enough to say to such a weltering sea, 'Peace, be still'?"[8] Like E. T. A. Hoffmann's Medardus in *The Devil's Elixirs,* West solves the problem of split consciousness by assuming that he is not one but "two persons, that my identity was double,"[9] a literal rendering of the common gothic theme of the Doppelgänger.

For a utopian novelist, Bellamy is perhaps unusually interested in varieties of mental states and the problem of personal identity. In another novel, *Miss Ludington's Sister,* he explores a theory of spiritualism based on the notion that as one changes and matures the spirits of one's outgrown selves survive in heaven. But other utopian novelists also treated the subject, though in more conventional terms. *Young West,* Solomon Schindler's sequel to *Looking Backward,* contains a long passage explaining the nature of "mind," its inherence in all matter, and its continued existence after "death."[10] Schindler, however, makes no attempt to represent these qualities of consciousness from within. Even Bellamy typically handles the theme "objectively" rather than "subjectively." In most utopian fiction, instead of a report by the narrator of what it feels like to be "two people," there is likely to be a sequence during which the hero must pretend to be someone else. He wears a disguise, and his true identity recedes and becomes more and more illusory the longer he goes incognito.

This device of the secret identity—milked for its gothic effects in novels like *Caleb Williams* or, more dizzyingly, in *The Devil's Elixirs*—became a trademark of a certain subgenre of the utopia—the so-called "cataclysmic novel." The same cultural facts that gave rise to the gothic obsession with selfhood also produced novels in which the problem of alienation was located in the social order rather than in the consciousness of the protagonist. In such a world often the only safety was in disguise, pretending to blend in with the rest of the brainwashed population. Works like Mark Twain's

Connecticut Yankee, Ignatius Donnelly's *Caesar's Column,* and Jack London's *Iron Heel,* which are focused on the social order in its breakdown (cataclysm) rather than its perfection (utopia), reflect a shift in the actual extent and intensity of alienation, and the failure of the romantic vision to deal with the individual's relation to society in terms that matched the public's sense of the social reality.

This progressive alienation may be suggested by one more brief comparison of the uses of mesmerism in gothic and utopian novels. George Lippard's mesmerist is still imagined as a demonic figure, exerting his will over the will of his victim; Hawthorne's Matthew Maule is also presented as strangely endowed with mysterious powers, but their effects are somewhat domesticated when the same powers appear in Holgrave, now explained as pseudo-scientific rather than supernatural phenomena. By the time of *Young West* mesmerism has undergone a more dramatic change, though along thoroughly predictable lines. In Schindler's utopia, mesmerism has become hypnotism, the trance is employed not to seduce or dominate, nor to explore the unknown, but to accomplish a carefully defined and circumscribed psychotherapeutic purpose: in the nursery school in which Young West is raised, a new incarnation of the mad scientist makes periodic visits, during which he takes "difficult" children on his lap, and puts them "to sleep":

> The Doctor then began to talk to him softly: "Bobby will not wake until I count three; Bobby does not want to pinch and scratch other children, Bobby will never throw stones again, do you hear me, Bobby?" Though his eyes were closed, Bobby said: "Yes sir."[11]

Schindler betrays no sense of ambivalence about such techniques—that was for a later subgenre of the utopia, dystopias like *Brave New World* and *1984,* to initiate. Before such inversions could be written, there was first a period of transition, during which, alongside of the orthodox utopia (*Looking Backward*) and the equally traditional satire on philanthropy (*The Bostonians*), there developed a curiously mixed genre, half utopia, half anti-utopia. These were the cataclysmic novels.

The Crater is the earliest of this subgenre. Remarkably, it is an example of a desert-island narrative, a utopia, and a cataclysmic novel successively, which almost makes it a miniature history of the genres it belongs to. Cast away on a desert island, Mark Woolston first rehearses the Robinson Crusoe story, building a technology that will support his basic human needs. Then he adds other colonists to his society, establishing a utopian community. But this collection of men and women is no better than any other, and they soon fall into the errors of modern civilization. Bad goes to worse, and finally the entire island—a thriving but rotten imitation of the United States in 1847—is punished for its innate wickedness by a volcanic eruption that leaves no survivors (except the hero and his intimates, fortunately away on a voyage at the time). If we take the utopianism and the ensuing disaster as causally linked, as he did, we may say that Cooper invented the cataclysmic novel.

Obviously such a model could prove extremely popular with a generation of novelists who had, in Henry James's phrase, "the imagination of disaster" forced upon them by numerous incidents of terrorist and insurrectionary violence in both Europe and America. Where Cooper's 1847 catastrophe is a direct result of the Creator's (God's *and* Cooper's) displeasure with the sins of civilization, later novelists attributed the upheaval to class struggle, and that in turn was traced to the failure of industrial society to work out institutions that would protect the workingman from enslavement to the very technology that, in more utopian visions, was supposed to free man from hunger and drudgery. The cataclysmic novel also begins with typical utopian descriptions of miraculous gadgetry, but moves quickly into intrigue and counterintrigue, and ends with the corpses piled so high that they constitute a health hazard to the few survivors of the class slaughter. ("Caesar's column" is a stack of such cannon fodder, coated with cement and commemorated with a plaque.)

There is something especially ominous about the wonders of technology presented in these books, for they invariably have as their chief scientific miracle some new and monstrous weapon—the dirigible warships that are called "demons" in *Caesar's Column,* the gatling guns and electrified barbed wire of *A Connecticut Yankee.* These authors are not simply pastoralists decrying the rise of industrialism; they are truly ambivalent about the technology they describe, Twain most of all. His fantasy of Arthurian times combines a journey into the barbarous past in the manner of *Henry Russell* with a recapitulation of the history of technology à la Cooper. Hank Morgan's well-intentioned introduction of modern industrialism (and weaponry) into a primitive society is supposed to be comic, but the reader soon realizes that the plot is working toward a disaster that Twain himself is reluctant to face, and only slowly comes to see as inevitable. This ambivalence no longer appears in a dystopia like *1984:* the sense of suspense gives way to the sense of doom.

Although this fatality is not so obviously at work in the more orthodox utopian novels, one can feel it in *Looking Backward,* for example, where continual reminders of West's uneasiness in his new surroundings create a nameless dread, finally justified in his brief "return" to the horrors of the nineteenth century. This anxiety is another inheritance from the gothic novel, which dwells on questions of free will and fate in both its themes and its plots. The cyclic narratives, returning obsessively to the same scene, seem to be saying that there is no escape from character, no avoiding the inherited family curse. Utopian novels sometimes seem to offer an opposite message, at least in their explicit themes, which celebrate the power of reason to choose the right and facilitate the march of progress. But the utopian plot, like the gothic, is merely a series of tableaux, window shopping for a future that cannot be altered because both the past *and* the present have been abandoned. This is the source of the slightly catatonic quality that typically permeates the euphoria of utopian fiction.

The cataclysmic novel tells the other side of the story, for it preserves the gothic horror in the face of a totally determined world; the symbolic family curse is supplanted by a literal representation of humanity's propensity to sin. "What this folk needed," says Hank Morgan, "was a Reign of Terror and a guillotine."[12] Perhaps Rabbi Schindler did not quite know what he was talking about when he imagined twenty-first-century pediatricians combing the snarls out of their patients' characters with mesmerism, but Twain seems to know every inch of the way to 1984, and though he cannot give up his belief in the vote and the machine, neither can he quite lie to himself about their successes. Just this ambivalence was the first sign of the next subgenre to follow the cataclysmic novel—the dystopia with which modern readers are only too familiar. From *Caesar's Column* and *A Connecticut Yankee* it is but a step to *Brave New World,* in which prediction of future disaster is merely a disguise for an attack on things as they are (just as the optimistic utopias of Bellamy and his imitators were no more than complacent fantasies of a sugar-coated status quo).

These developments parallel the relative fates of the social sciences and pseudosciences on which Hawthorne and others in his period drew for the materials of their fictions. The shifts in literary emphasis reflected a cultural change, though it is difficult to isolate all the factors involved. Hawthorne's *American Magazine of Useful and Entertaining Knowledge* had been part of a general surge of interest in adult education and self-improvement during the second quarter of the century. The American Lyceum, a network of popular programs—libraries, study groups, and lectures—was the heart of a movement that swept the country not long after Hawthorne's graduation from college. Scientific subjects were the lyceum favorites up until about 1840, when they began to be superseded by topics drawn from the new social sciences. The transition period from about 1840 to 1850 was the heyday of the pseudoscience hybrids.

This is not to say that interest in science and technology lapsed at mid-century, but only that the appeal of such subjects to the popular imagination was undergoing a profound change. For example, during most of this period the inventions of "practical scientists" like Joseph Fiske and Robert H. Collyer were reported in the *Franklin Institute Journal,* the *Popular Mechanics* of its day; it was the end of an epoch when the federal government finally took over the responsibility for annual publication of patents granted. The transformation had to do with the recognition that there was money and power in science. During the Civil War the Smithsonian Institution tested materials and armaments for the North. Government and industry were beginning to sponsor and control research, and both pure and applied science became specialist pursuits, still admired by the public, but no longer followed with the same sort of participant devotion.

Earlier, "technology" had meant something more accessible to the average man. *Elements of Technology,* a book published in 1829 by Harvard professor Jacob Bigelow, was essentially a recipe book, more like the "do-it-yourself" manuals of modern counterculture than an MIT textbook. By most accounts, Bigelow, whose job at Harvard was to bridge the gap between Yankee inventors and collegiate research scientists, was the first to use "technology" in its modern sense; but *was* that its modern sense? After *The Elements of Technology* the next landmark might be Brisbane's *Social Destiny of Man* in 1840, and in the 1880s Bellamy's *Looking Backward*—the how-to-do-it books of the century. One might argue that this progressive alienation of the ordinary man from science and technology created the modern image of the mad scientist; the whole history of increasing dependence on and dwindling access to scientific knowledge is contained in the transition from the monomaniacal Westervelt or Grimshawe to the schizophrenic Dr. Strangelove.

At the same time the figure of the social scientist was developing its own split personality. The philanthropists of *The Blithedale Romance* and *The Spirit-Rapper* gave way not only to the enlightened human engineers of the Bellamy school, but also, in the industrial 1880s and 1890s, to radical and revolutionary figures in a wave of political and labor novels. Often the evolving archetypes, scientist and reformer, have done battle, the "good" version of one pitted against the "bad" version of the other—scientific genius vs. terrorist, or insane doctor vs. true leader of the people. However the roles are designated, it is evident that all the avatars are really the same mad scientist confronting his alter ego on the field of the popular imagination. In a world where technology has abolished much of the essential ground for community while fostering the mass production of ritual fantasy, it is not surprising that such figures should usurp our imaginations.

In some ways Hawthorne appears to have been the first to understand this "mirror" phenomenon in the popular conception of the mad scientist; more than any other novelist of his time, he was tempted to sympathize with his villains and find fault with his heroes. Characters like Holgrave and Coverdale, Hollingsworth and Grimshawe, are typical examples of pseudoscientists and social scientists whose initally good intentions take them to the brink of sin. The terms of the ambivalence are different—science has not yet become technocracy, and utopianism has only begun its metamorphosis into human engineering—but there is no doubt that scientists and utopian reformers are already dubious figures for Hawthorne.

The gothic monster, whether conjured up by the hero's imagination as Matilda is in *The Monk,* or scientifically fabricated as Frankenstein's creation, is essentially recognized as an emanation of repressed desire or fear. In the utopian novel the repression seems more successful, at least until one looks at the cataclysmic versions of the genre, in which the same energies that created the monster now produce the mob violence of the proles—and, more symbolically, the displaced and unacknowledged spectre from the unconscious, represented by the "demons" in *Caesar's Column* and by the half-comic, half-mythic figure of Merlin in *A Connecticut Yankee.* When we look for the equivalent manifestation in the dystopia, it appears to have vanished again, but in fact the energy has merely been spread out over the entire society, which has already all but engulfed and assimilated the hero, much as the earlier forms of monsters or demons usurped the field of his consciousness. In short, the cataclysmic novels, taken in conjunction with the utopia proper, seem to fall neatly into place as part of an evolving chain of fictive genres that flourished from the late eighteenth century to the present. The pattern of development is from a more or less openly symbolic representation of a divided consciousness to a flat, schematic naturalism that pretends to be a literal account, all the while smuggling in the same symbolic meanings in the larger, structural elements of plot, setting, and narrative stance.

Again Hawthorne is at the center of this transition. The divided consciousness that manifests itself in hallucination and monsters in the gothic has, by the time of *Blithedale*, been domesticated in the symbolic treatment of Coverdale, Westervelt, and Hollingsworth as alter egos expressing different aspects of what might be called the mad-scientist mentality. Or, to take a slightly later example that shows the very genesis of a similar symbolic coupling, Doctor Grimshawe and his opposite number in England, the old pensioner, if traced through successive drafts of that romance, will be seen to begin as a kindly old chemist and a disgraced man of the world, and slowly to trade places, until Grimshawe has become the evil genius and the pensioner a fountain of benignity modeled on Bronson Alcott. The examples could be multiplied—Chillingworth and Dimmesdale, Maule and Holgrave, and so on. Hawthorne's practice is halfway between the gothic and the utopian/cataclysmic—that is, he is still aware of the symbolic significance of these doublings, but attempts to cast them in realistic form, not completely abjuring supernatural implications, but carefully building up a circumstantial basis in reality for every symbolic effect. By the time of the utopian and cataclysmic novels, such realism was the order of the day, and the symbolic meaning of events was almost totally ignored, though sometimes all the more strikingly apparent to a reader brought up on Kafka and Genet.

It was not easy for Hawthorne to maintain this balance; his favorite ambience—"essentially a daydream, and yet a fact"—was the necessary medium for the mad scientist, who was mad partly because he combined incompatible attitudes and desires, which allowed him to be a protagonist in more than one genre. The combination of realism and symbolism makes Hawthorne's plots unfold at a curiously syncopated pace. Neither Coverdale nor the reader is ever at the cutting edge of events, but is always coming in after they occur, forced to piece things together as best he can. What we always miss is the moment of decision, the choice taken and enacted. We arrive for the consequences, always a picture rather than a dramatic scene because there is no longer any choice. All that is left is meaning; but meaning divorced from choice is merely emblematic, and *Blithedale* thus becomes a strange sort of "bestiary" of the social sciences. This symbolic distancing is facilitated by heavy foreshadowing—for instance, of Zenobia's death by drowning. From the very beginning the characters are merely going through the motions (tableaux) of the foreknown end, while the narrator sits as coroner and chorus, comfortable in the knowledge that it is too late for any surprises, the conclusion too foregone for any emotions but the connoisseur's pleasure in locking the cabinet on his trophy. This is a deeply alienated vision of the world, in which everything is seen as threatening. Living habitually steeled for the blow neutralizes the anxiety, but the result is premature resignation, the belief that nothing can ever be done except to reap the consequences of already settled character and preordained event.

Hawthorne's novels are the beginning of an increasingly voyeuristic period in fiction. The manner has much in common with the spiritualist syndrome of using another person as medium for mystic visions. This, like Ethan Brand's evil investigations into sin, using other people as his laboratory subjects, is not really the aggressive, outreaching gesture it might seem. The spiritualist is a calm, passive figure, always in the background and corners of the scene, like Westervelt prowling about Blithedale or Ethan Brand brooding over his lime kiln. They are adept at fantasy, turning wishes into acts without the risk of commitment. Others live out their fantasies and their consequences, while the spiritualist, the physic experimenter, the moral scientist, and the author carefully take notes.

True realism in fiction means getting involved with one's characters, not controlling them but allowing them to live out the implications of their dispositions freely. Thus the "realistic" likelihood of a novel like *The Blithedale Romance* would be that Coverdale fall in love with Zenobia, and join with Hollingsworth in his utopian venture—for they are the attractive people and the threatening reality. And so they must be destroyed, suppressing the conflicts that might liberate Coverdale from his arbor of the sybarite imagination into a world of brotherhood and passion. This is both the plot and the method of *Blithedale*—a truly self-reflexive novel.

On the one hand Hawthorne seems a terribly reticent and defended writer, unable to bring his plots on stage, unwilling to allow his characters their action, afraid to leave a loose end, whether a sentence or a dramatic possibility. The surface is seamless, plastered over, varnished. But on the other hand, from another point of view, he is very daring and innovative. He is trying to do something with the gothic mode, to domesticate it, give it a new life. Like Melville he bursts the conventional genres and tries to write a new kind of psychological prose. No doubt this is his neurotic obsession, but from it he makes great art.

Notes

Notes to Chapter One [Pseudoscience]

[1]Harriet Martineau, *Retrospect of Western Travel,* 2 vols. (London, 1838), 2: 187–188

[2]David M. Reese, *Humbugs of New-York,* (New York, 1838), p. 21.

[3]Reese, *Humbugs,* p. 22.

[4]George Combe, *Notes on the United States of North America during a Phrenological Visit,* 2 vols. (Philadelphia, 1841), 1: 84 [October 24, 1838].

[5]Harriet Martineau, *Letters on Mesmerism* (New York, 1845), p. 7.

[6]Ibid., p. 3. Miss Martineau's experience with the cow was not so unusual. William Gregory, *Letters to a Candid Inquirer on Animal Magnetism* (London, 1851), pp. 243–244, reported experiments being carried out on snails, and John Wilson, *Trials of Animal Magnetism on the Brute Creation* (London, 1839), pp. 41–48, spent many hours at the Zoological Gardens in Surrey, working his magnetic will upon Rajah and Hadgee, two pliant elephants from Ceylon. Wilson's first successes in putting animals to sleep were with his favorite cats, who succumbed to the magnetic passes while nestled in his lap.

[7]Ralph Waldo Emerson, *The Complete Works of Ralph Waldo Emerson,* ed. Edward Waldo Emerson, 12 vols. (Boston, 1903–1904), 10: 337–339.

[8]John Quincy Adams, *Memoirs of John Quincy Adams,* ed. C. F. Adams, 12 vols. (Philadelphia, 1874–1877), 10: 345 [August 2, 1840].

[9]Ralph Waldo Emerson, *The Journals and Miscellaneous Notebooks of Ralph Waldo Emerson,* ed. William H. Gilman, Alfred R. Ferguson, et al. (Cambridge, Mass., 1960–), 5: 388.

[10]Reese, *Humbugs,* pp. 60–61.

[11]Editorial note on H. R. Schetterly, "The Millenium," *American Phrenological Journal* 8 (1846): 202–3.

[12]From a letter of William Miller to his faithful, quoted in Clara Endicott Sears, *Days of Delusion* (Boston, 1924), p. 87.

[13]John Humphrey Noyes, *History of American Socialisms* (Philadelphia, 1870), p. 615.

[14]Ibid., p. 569. Quoted from a letter of H. N. Leet in the Oneida *Circular,* November 16, 1851.

[15]Storrs wrote this avowal for *The Morning Watch,* February 20, 1845; quoted in Sears, *Days of Delusion,* p. 242.

[16]See Frank Podmore, *Modern Spiritualism,* 2 vols. (London, 1902), 1: 170. Later in his career Harris, like Mary Baker Eddy, who was also indebted to mesmerism, came to believe that magnetic influences were "malicious":

If you would overcome disease,
With Fairies wise, with Fairies wise,
Call Virtue through you like the seas:
Demagnetise, demagnetise!

(from Harris's "Songs of Fairyland," quoted in Herbert W. Schneider and George Lawton, *A Prophet and a Pilgrim* [New York, 1942], p. 170).

[17]See *Bible Communism* (Brooklyn, 1853), pp.42–43.

[18]Ralph Waldo Emerson, *The Letters of Ralph Waldo Emerson,* ed. Ralph L. Rusk, 6 vols. (New York, 1939), 1: 291.

[19]Quoted in Nelson Sizer, *Forty Years in Phrenology* (New York, 1882), p. 14.

Notes to Chapter Two [Mesmerism]

[1]*Edgar Allan Poe,* "The Facts in the Case of M. Valdemar," *The Broadway Journal* 2 (December 20, 1845): 368.

[2]Thuos Mathos [Thomas South], *Early Magnetism in its Higher Relations to Humanity, as Veiled in the Poets and the Prophets* (London, 1846), p. 116.

[3]*The Broadway Journal* 2 (December 27, 1845): 390–91.

[4]Robert H. Collyer, *Exalted States of the Nervous System,* 3d ed., originally published as *Mysteries of the Vital Element* (London, 1873), p. 55. The resurrection motif in fiction might have been borrowed from any number of sources, but Poe probably found it, combined with mesmerism, in his friend George Lippard's *Quaker City,* published in Philadelphia the same year as "M. Valdemar." In it Lippard describes a revivification, purportedly accomplished by the magnetic powers of his villain Ravoni, but in fact an effect of a mysterious drug which had suspended life in its victim for a carefully calculated period of time—not seven months, but a matter of hours. (See *The Quaker City,* New York, 1970 [1845], pp. 444–52.) Lippard's scene is decorated with numerous putrid corpses—"Better to look into the plague-pit where man and woman and babe lay mingled together, one reeking mass of quick lime and gory flesh, than to have gazed upon that corpse extended on the Dissecting table. . . ." (p. 441)—but his miracle is performed on a more palatable body—a sexy young girl. Poe might have gotten the idea of a corpse suddenly rotting from Charles Brockden Brown's *Wieland,* where Wieland's father begins to putrefy before he is dead (see Charles Brockden Brown, *Wieland* (Garden City, 1962 [1798], p. 26). The idea of combining the resurrection with the corruption was characteristically Poe's, as was the notion of attempting to bridge the gulf to the spirit world by talking to the corpse.

While a Mr. South fell for Poe's hoax, a few years later there was a Mr. North—William North, a pot-boiling novelist—who borrowed the plot for a short story of his own, "The Living Corpse" (*Putnam's,* 1 [1853]: 32–39). And shortly after that another hoax version of the material appeared, in Ferdinand C. Ewer's "Eventful Nights of August 20th and 21st, 1854." This fooled the prominent spiritualist Judge John W. Edmonds, who reprinted it in his own magazine as an authentic case of communication with the dead. (See Ferdinand C. Ewer, *The Eventful Nights of August 20th and 21st, 1854; and How Judge Edmonds Was Hocussed; or, Fallibility of "Spiritualism"* (New York, 1855). North and Ewer are both discussed in Howard Kerr's *Mediums, and Spirit-Rappers, and Roaring Radicals* [Urbana, 1972], pp. 68–71.)

As late as 1875 people were still claiming to have actually restored life through animal magnetism; see O. M. Wozencraft, "The Dead Brought to Life by Animal Magnetism," *Pacific Medical and Surgical Journal,* 17, n.s. 9 (1875–1876): 221–222, and a refutation in the following issue, pp. 265–266.

[5]These purported accomplishments, and the facts of Collyer's life which follow, may be gleaned from his various works: *Manual of Phrenology,* 4th ed., (Dayton, 1842); *Psychography* (Philadelphia, 1843); *Lights and Shadows of American Life* (Boston, 1844); *Fossil Human Jaw* (London, 1867); *Exalted States of the Nervous System* (London, 1873); and *Automatic Writing* (London, 1876).

[6]*The Pioneer,* 1 (1843): 55; only the original version of "The Hall of Fantasy" contains the reference to Collyer by name—see H. P. Miller, "Hawthorne Surveys His Contemporaries," *American Literature* 12 (1940): 228–235. On Collyer's itinerary, see Joseph B. Felt *Annals of Salem,* 2d ed., 2 vols. (Salem, 1845), 2: 82, as well as Chauncy Hare Townshend, *Facts in Mesmerism* (Boston, 1841), pp. 525–39.

[7]See John Davies, *Phrenology: Fad and Science* (New Haven, 1955), pp. 132–33.

[8]See *The Spirit World* 3 (September 27, 1851): 117.

[9]See Sidney E. Lind, "Poe and Mesmerism," *PMLA* 62 (1947): 1077–94. Lind thinks Poe used the edition of 1844, but Collyer's 1841 edition is an equal possibility.

[10]See Charles Gibbon, *The Life of George Combe,* 2 vols. (London, 1878), 2: 74; *American Phrenological Journal* 5 (1843): 331–32.

[11]*New-York Weekly Tribune,* November 18, 1843, p. 4.

[12]Charles Poyen, *Progress of Animal Magnetism in New England* (Boston, 1837), p. 45.

[13]Elizabeth Peabody to Mary Peabody, June 18, 1836, Berg Collection.

[14]*The Franklin Institute Journal* 9, ser. 3 (1845): 250–51; 37, ser. 3 (1859): 31.

[15]*The Essex Institute Historical Collections,* 56 (1910): 291; 57 (1911): 32, 39.

[16]Sophia Peabody to Elizabeth Peabody, May 2, 1838, Berg Collection. Sophia's attitude of friendly condescension toward Mrs. Fiske is apparent in another letter (April 21, 1838). Sophia brought her flowers and knicknacks: "I do not think I ever enjoyed anything so much in my life as doing these things for persons who could in no other way obtain them, or think of having them. The only solid happiness in this world, is in giving pleasure."

[17]Poyen, *Animal Magnetism,* pp. 200–1.

[18]Sophia Peabody to Elizabeth Peabody, May 2, 1838, Berg Collection. George Peabody's "hydrostatic" was a device for the treatment of his spinal ailment, which caused progressive paralysis and finally death.

[19]Sophia Peabody to Elizabeth Peabody, May 4, 1838, Berg Collection.

[20]See Louise Hall Tharp, *The Peabody Sisters of Salem* (Boston, 1950), pp. 149–50, and letters from Sophia to her mother dated from Roxbury in 1832, in the Berg Collection. I am also indebted to Professor Norman Holmes Pearson for information about Mrs. Park.

[21]Hawthorne to Sophia Peabody, October 18, 1841, Huntington Library. The passage in brackets is deleted in the manuscript (though not by Hawthorne), and was first deciphered by Professor Randall Stewart.

[22]Hawthorne's reservation, that Sophia not allow herself to be "put to sleep," was perfectly feasible in contemporary magnetic therapy, built on a theory of "effluence" and "fluids" rather than suggestion and the unconscious.

[23]Hawthorne to Sophia Peabody, April 17, 1839, Huntington Library. Quoted with slight inaccuracies, here corrected, in Julian Hawthorne's *Nathaniel Hawthorne and His Wife,* 2 vols. (Boston, 1884), 1: 203.

[24]The controversy over who first "discovered" anesthesia is still confused. Besides the two dentists, among the contenders were Emerson's brother-in-law Charles T. Jackson, Southern physician Crawford W. Long, and the notorious mesmerist Robert H. Collyer.

[25]See Sophia's letter to her mother early in 1853, quoted in *Hawthorne and His Wife,* 1: 483. Compare a reminiscence by Sophia's sister Elizabeth printed in the *Essex Institute Historical Collections,* 94 (1958): 272.

[26]See below, p. 216, for the full story of Margaret Fuller's mesmeric cure.

[27]Sophia Hawthorne to Annie Fields, February 20, 1863, Boston Public Library. Still another literary amazon was experimenting with mesmerism during these years. In July of 1844, while visiting her brother Henry Ward Beecher, Harriet Beecher Stowe described her reactions to her absent husband: "July 15. These last few days, Henry has been trying to mesmerise me. —The first session he succeeded in almost throwing me into convulsions—spasms & shocks of heat & prickly sensation ran all over me[;] my lungs were violently constricted & my mind in dreadful commotion & I was so frightened that I called out for quarter. This strange tempestuous effect was occasioned simply by our sitting opposite to each other with our eyes fixed & our thumbs in contact for about thirty minutes— & it was dissipated by making reverse passes which relieved first my head, then my lungs,.] then my lower limbs & lastly my arms, tho the thumbs remained numb & prickly for some time after. You may be sure after being thus violently possessed with the demon of mesmerism I began to have rather reverend ideas of the same[.] We tried the same experiment in the evening[.] It was less violent—more gradual but very similar—stricture across the lungs[,] burning pricking currents into the head[,] spasmodic movements of muscle with more or less numbness[.] The next time after a long conflict I passed into a semi somnolent state & quite to my surprise found my hands without any will of mine rising up & moving in various ways[.] I watched their motions with very curious sensations—for amid all the bodily effects my mind & powers of observation seemed uncommonly bright & active[.] The last time I came nearer to the *stupor & drowsiness* described in books. The sensation was precisely the same and equal in amount to that produced by laudanum when I took 140 or 150 drops last Spring—but this sleep was not consummated[.] Thus you see I have come to the verge of the Spirit land. If I meet any thing new there I will tell you the next time I write[.] It was wholly unexpected to me that I could be subjected to this power, no one else who ever

tried has produced the first particle of effect & indeed my nervous system seemed to offer gallant resistance[.] Show this account to Edward & see if he does not think there is an animal magnetic fluid[.] The first sensations were like violent & quick repeated electric shocks in the head[,] lungs & limbs[.] Those afterwards like the slow steady accumulation of galvanism—but in all this as yet my body only had yielded, not my mind[.] I came somewhere near the latter this morning & it seemed to me that a greater amount of force of the same kind would soon reduce me to entire sleep[.] Well but this is a strange business[,] this human frame[.] I should be glad to know more of it[.]" Schlesinger Library.

[28]Henry Jones, *Mesmerism Examined and Repudiated* (New York, 1846), p. 11. Jones is quoting from the anonymous *Confessions of a Magnetiser,* published in the preceding year in New York. That the results might not be invariably bad is argued by this man's account of "winning the heart of his own wife at the age of seventeen, by first magnetising her for disease, &c." (Jones, p. 15).

[29]Poyen, *Animal Magnetism,* p. 120.

[30]This and other notices in the Salem newspapers are quoted in Elizabeth Ruth Hosmer, "Science and Pseudo-science in the Writings of Nathaniel Hawthorne," Ph.D. diss., University of Illinois, 1948, p. 252, *passim.* A useful survey of the subject.

[31]Jones, *Mesmerism,* p. 20.

[32]Ibid., p. 3.

[33]T.S. Arthur, *Agnes; or, The Possessed: A Revelation of Mesmerism* (Philadelphia, 1848), pp. 26, 33.

[34]"Theory of Animal Magnetism," 5 (1839): 323.

[35]Poyen, *Animal Magnetism,* p. 29.

[36]Compare the situation in seventeenth-century Salem with Dr. Reese's warning in *Humbugs of New-York:* "The purest characters in the community may wither beneath the calumnies of these *clairvoyant* 'factory girls' who may accuse their neighbors of crimes, which they profess to witness during a magnetic reverie" (p. 61).

[37]Julian Hawthorne, "The Salem of Hawthorne," *Century Magazine,* 27 (1884): 9.

[38]Another entry for 1842 probably owes something to mesmerism: "Some man of powerful character to command a person, morally subjected to him, to perform a certain act. The commanding person suddenly die; and, for all the rest of his life, the subjected one continues to perform that act" (*AN* 226). Compare Poe's inversion of the same idea in "The Facts in the Case of M. Valdemar."

[39]John Bovee Dods, *Six Lectures on the Philosophy of Mesmerism* [in vol. 1 of the Library of Mesmerism and Psychology] (New York, 1854), p. 65.

[40]Orestes A. Brownson, *The Works of Orestes A. Brownson,* ed. Henry F. Brownson, 20 vols. (Detroit, 1882–1887), 9: 38–39.

[41]George Lippard, *The Quaker City*,p. 462.

[42]Ibid., p. 445.

[43]Ibid., p. 533.

[44]See H. Mattison, *Spirit-Rapping Unveiled* (New York, 1855), pp. 156–68. For a more detailed and personal account of temporary insanity caused by mesmerism, see John Wallace Hutchinson, *Story of the Hutchinsons,* ed. Charles E. Mann, 2 vols. (Boston, 1896), 1: 271–78.

Notes to Chapter Three [Physiognomy and Phrenology]

[1]Haynes's own nickname was "Black Hawk." A dozen years later, he served as the model for Lawyer Giles in "Ethan Brand," and some of his traits may be seen in Brand himself (*AN* 101).

[2]Samuel R. Wells, *How to Read Character* (New York, 1890), p. 190.

[3]Samuel R. Wells, *New Physiognomy* (New York, 1896), p. 700.

[4]The original list of faculties, developed by phrenology's founders, Franz Joseph Gall and Johann Gaspar Spurzheim, was limited to fewer than three dozen, largely derived from the faculty psychology of the Scottish philosophers.(See Nahum Capen, *Reminiscences of Dr. Spurzheim and George Combe* [New York, 1881], pp. 145–47.) With the advent of phrenomagnetism (see above, pp. 35-6), the catalogue tripled. Such post-Spurzheim discoveries of phrenological organs—Physiognomy, Money-making, Tattling, Love of Pets, and many others—are catalogued in the *American Phrenological Journal* 4 (1842): 226–30, and *The Magnet* 1 (1842): 107–9.

[5]From a letter written during his American tour by the Scottish phrenologist George Combe to Professor Silliman of Yale; quoted in Charles Gibbon, *The Life of George Combe,* 2 vols. (London, 1878), 2: 82.

[6]Sir Charles Bell, *The Anatomy and Philosophy of Expression* (London, 1912), p. 49.

[7]*American Phrenological Journal* 4 (1842): 14. On practical phrenology, see John Davies, *Phrenology: Fad and Science* (New Haven, 1955), pp. 30–45; and Madeleine B. Stern, *Heads and Headlines: The Phrenological Fowlers* (Norman, Okla., 1971).

[8]Letter from Hawthorne to his sister, May 4, 1823, quoted in Julian Hawthorne's *Hawthorne and His Wife,* 2 vols. (Boston, 1884), 1: 110–11.

[9]See Davies, *Phrenology,* p. 13; Louis C. Hatch, *The History of Bowdoin College* (Portland, Me., 1927), pp. 461–63; and *General Catalogue of Bowdoin College . . . 1794–1950* (Brunswick, Me.), pp. 53, 57.

[10]See Manning Hawthorne, "Nathaniel Hawthorne at Bowdoin," *New England Quarterly* 13 (1940): 274.

[11]Dr. John Bell in the *Philadelphia Medical Journal* 8 (1824): 172, as quoted in Davies, *Phrenology,* p. 15. "Playful allusion" was not necessarily incompatible with belief in phrenology, as the case of Sophia Peabody Hawthorne may illustrate. In 1830, long before she met Hawthorne, Sophia read George Combe's *Constitution of Man,* which, since its publication in Boston the preceding year, had become phrenology's best-seller in America: "I have been reading Combe," Sophia confided to her diary. "I admire the book exceedingly, and feel very much inclined to believe in Phrenology" (Julian Hawthorne, *Hawthorne and His Wife,* 1: 79). A decade later Sophia enlivened a letter to her mother with the following "playful allusions" to the science she still believed in: "Upon arriving, we found that little Alice had fallen from her crib at noon & bruised her intellect sadly. If she had struck her affections, the consequences might have been fatal, for she fell with great force, but she came plump down upon Comparison, Eventuality & Individuality from the vast Chimbosario height. These organs swelled so gave an entirely different aspect to the poor child" (July 4, 1841, Berg Collection). Compare Hawthorne's allusion to phrenology in describing the behavior of his baby daughter Una, in a letter of 1844 to G. S. Hillard: "She seldom cries except for hunger—her alimentiveness

being enormously developed" (Maine Historical Society, quoted in "Unpublished Letters of Nathaniel Hawthorne," *Athenaeum,* 3224 [August 10, 1889]: 192). As late as 1852, there is another joke at the expense of phrenology, in *The Blithedale Romance,* where a barkeeper is said to have profited by his "particularly large development just above the eyebrows" in his skill at making "gin-cocktails" (*BR* 177).

[12]See Marion L. Kesselring, "Hawthorne's Reading, 1828–1850," *Bulletin of the New York Public Library* 53 (1949): 121–122, 185, 188.

[13]See the introduction to Arlin Turner's *Hawthorne as Editor* (University, La., 1941), pp. 1–14; and Manning Hawthorne, "Nathaniel Hawthorne and Elizabeth Hawthorne, Editors," *The Colophon* 1, no. 3 n.s. (1939), not paginated.

[14]Hawthorne quoted Silliman's *Journal* 24 (1833): 326–41, in the June number of the *American Magazine of Useful and Entertaining Knowledge,* p. 410. In February 1837, back in Salem, he checked out the *American Quarterly Review* 20 (1836), which had a thirty-page article on "Phrenology." (See Kesselring, "Hawthorne's Reading," pp. 136, 173.) Park Benjamin, editor of the *New England Magazine,* published no less than seven articles on phrenology in 1833 and 1834.

[15]*Southern Literary Messenger* 2 (1836): 286. In 1838, after Poe had left it, the *Messenger* devoted over twenty-five double-column pages to George Combe's New York lectures on phrenology, and other magazines also reported liberally from similar uncopyrighted materials.

[16]See Ruth Hosmer, "Science and Pseudo-science in the Writings of Nathaniel Hawthorne," Ph.D. diss., University of Illinois, 1948, pp. 243–44.

[17]*American Magazine of Useful and Entertaining Knowledge,* 2 (1836): 337.

[18]Ibid.

[19]Ibid.

[20]Ibid., pp. 199–200.

[21]Ibid., p. 268.

[22]Ibid., p. 334.

[23]Hawthorne used the first American edition of 1829 for his extracts. His copy was borrowed from the Salem Athenaeum for him by his sister Elizabeth, who herself made copious extracts from popular works for Hawthorne's use in the magazine. Elizabeth may be responsible for the selections from Combe, but since the book was checked out from January 27 to April 6, it is possible that her brother might have excerpted it himself. See Kesselring, "Hawthorne's Reading," pp. 134, 178. Combe's passage on the American Revolution is on pp. 239–40 of the 1829 edition.

[24]*American Magazine of Useful and Entertaining Knowledge* 2 (1836): 302–4, 349–50. With some additions and transpositions, these excerpts represent pp. 119–24, 93–96, and 282–84 of the 1829 edition of Combe.

[25]Channing's remark is recorded in Gibbon, *George Combe,* 1: 221, and is cited in Davies, *Phrenology,* p. 165. Davies also quotes Oliver Wendell Holmes to similar effect.

[26]Amariah Brigham, *Remarks on the Influence of Mental Cultivation and Mental Exercise upon Health* (Hartford, 1832). This was a book that Hawthorne read in 1835 (see Kesselring, "Hawthorne's Reading," p. 175). Brigham's interest in the question was not narrowly phrenological. His work, along with other early efforts like Rufus Wyman's *A Discourse on Mental Philosophy as Connected with Mental Disease*

(Boston, 1830), and William Sweetser's *Mental Hygiene: or an Examination of the Intellect and Passions, Designed to Illustrate their Influence on Health and Duration of Life* (New York, 1843), constituted an attempt to come to grips with the mind/body problem from the viewpoint of a "modern psychology"—a phrase Hawthorne used appropriately in *The Seven Gables*. Brigham and other asylum superintendents (including Hawthorne's contemporaries at Bowdoin, Drs. Luther V. Bell and Isaac Ray) were among the thirteen founders of what is now the American Psychiatric Society, and they led the way in the investigation of medical, legal, and philosophical implications of the relations between mind and body. See J. K. Hall, ed., *One Hundred Years of American Psychiatry* (New York, 1944), pp. 54, 67.

[27]Chandler Robbins, *Remarks on the Disorders of Literary Men* (Boston, 1825), p. 19. See Kesselring, "Hawthorne's Reading," p. 189. Robbins recommended frequent baths, exercise, and the like as "means of preventing the evils usually incident to sedentary and studious habits." Perhaps the high wall-desk Hawthorne used at the Old Manse was chosen, as Ellery Channing later guessed, because "he did not wish to have the sedentary habit, which he had heard [in Robbins?] was unwholesome"—F. B. Sanborn, *Recollections of Seventy Years,* 2 vols. (Boston, 1909), 2: 535.

[28]Thomas C. Upham, *Outlines of Imperfect and Disordered Mental Action* (New York, 1840), p. 262.

[29]Hawthorne to Longfellow, June 4, 1837, Houghton Library. Quoted in Malcolm Cowley, ed., *The Portable Hawthorne* (New York, 1948), pp. 607–10.

[30]Andrew Combe, *The Principles of Physiology* (New York, 1842), p. 268.

[31]See, for example, *AN* 169, 184, 244, 251, 270, 285, and 510.

[32]See John Graham, "The Development of the Use of Physiognomy in the Novel," Ph.D. diss., Johns Hopkins University, 1960.

[33]Maria McIntosh, *The Lofty and the Lowly,* 2 vols. (New York, 1853), 2: 97. The character in question is also well endowed with "benevolence," and turns out, not surprisingly, to be an abolitionist. An earlier book by the same author contains the following description of the hero: "His person was under the middle size, and his features plain, yet command seemed stamped upon his aspect. The physiognomist declared that the secret of his power lay in his dark and deep-set eye, and in the firmly-compressed lips, which told of an indomitable will. The phrenologist placed it in the contour of his head, with its broad and high forehead."—*Charms and Counter-charms* (New York, 1848), pp. 8–9.

[34]See Andrew Combe's article, "Remarks on the Possibility of Increasing the Development of the Cerebral Organs by Adequate Exercise of the Mental Organs," in the first volume of the *American Phrenological Journal* (1838). John Elliotson, the famed London mesmerist and phrenologist, was quoted in the same journal to this effect: "Gall told me that Napoleon's hatter assured him that the head of that ruthless destroyer of human life grew to the age of thirty five." *American Phrenological Journal* 3 (1841): 288.

[35]Hawthorne to Sophia Peabody, from Brook Farm, September 22, 1841, Huntington Library. See Henry W. Sams, ed., *Autobiography of Brook Farm* (Englewood Cliffs, N. J., 1958), p. 35.

[36]See Isaac Ray, *A Treatise on the Medical Jurisprudence of Insanity,* ed. Winfred Overholser (Cambridge, Mass., 1962).

[37]William Dunlap, *History of the Rise and Progress of the Art of Design in the United States,* ed. Frank W. Bayley and Charles E. Goodspeed, 3 vols. (Boston, 1918), 1: 221–222. Hawthorne used the first edition of 1834, which I have not seen.

[38]Thompson's portrait may be examined in the Centenary Edition of *The Scarlet Letter,* where it serves as frontispiece. Though it is impossible to guess from the portrait Thompson's reading of Hawthorne's physiognomy, there is available a fragment of phrenological insight into Thompson's own character, provided by Sophia Hawthorne. In 1858, when the Hawthornes were in Italy, they saw a good bit of Thompson, who, Sophia at once divined from his countenance, "had a temper." Julian Hawthorne, *Hawthorne and His Circle* (New York, 1903) p. 262.

[39]The early history of daguerreotypy in the United States shows its similarities to the pseudosciences, thus providing a pretext for Hawthorne's rather fanciful use of it in *The House of the Seven Gables.* François Gouraud, the first exhibitor in America of original daguerreotypes taken by Daguerre himself, set up his show in Boston in 1840, turned up in New York later that same year selling medicines and nostrums, and finally ended his short career (he died before the decade was out) by inventing *Phreno-mnemotechny* (New York and London, 1845) and *Practical Cosmophonography* (New York, 1850), under the name of Francis Fauvel-Gouraud. See Robert Taft, *Photography and the American Scene* (New York, 1942), pp. 40–43; and the *New York Morning Herald,* March 5, 1840. Robert H. Collyer, who has already been discussesd as a typical mesmerist, admired Gouraud and compared him to Spurzheim, the man who brought phrenology to America: "As soon as Spurzheim caused an interest in the science of phrenology to be awakened in the community a thousand ignoramuses arose—men who did not know scarcely the difference between the animal and the intellectual regions, and set themselves up as disciples of Gall and Spurzheim, and went about to enlighten the world. As soon as my friend, Dr. Gouraud, introduced the exquisite specimens of Daguere's [sic] genius in Photography, he filled the Tremont House with admirers, and thousands applauded his merits, but nobody paid."—*Psychography, or, the Embodiment of Thought* (Philadelphia, 1843), p. 34. Collyer's *Psychography* may have influenced Hawthorne's conception of Holgrave's peculiar use of the daguerreotype to read the secret thoughts and characters of his subjects. In inventing "psychography" Collyer had anticipated his friend Gouraud by combining phrenology, animal magnetism, and daguerreotypy in a single "mental photographic process"—the embodiment of ideas which, by a *concentrated* and *undivided* effort of the will, may be depicted on a recipient brain" (p. 31).

Notes to Chapter Four [Homoeopathy]

[1]Samuel Hahnemann, *Organon of the Art of Healing,* 5th Amer. ed., trans. by C. Wesselhoeft (New York, 1876), p. 69. There is no evidence that Hawthorne ever read the *Organon,* so I have used Wesselhoeft's translation, to underscore the prominence of the Wesselhoeft homoeopathic family, who provided the Hawthornes with their pediatric care in the 1840s and 1850s. The first four American editions of the *Organon* were reprints of the original British translation of 1833.

[2]David M. Reese, *Humbugs of New-York* (New York, 1838), p. 80.

[3]Ibid., p. 105. The followers of Samuel Thomson, like those of Hahnemann,

opposed bleeding and recommended more "natural" medicines than calomel and other mineral-derived poisons. After Thomson's death in 1843 (also the year Hahnemann died), most of his disciples became Eclectics. See Alex Berman, "The Thomsonian Movement and its Relation to American Pharmacy and Medicine," *Bulletin of the History of Medicine* 25 (1951): 405–28, 519–38.

[4]Ibid., p. 101.

[5]See Oliver Wendell Holmes, "The Medical Profession in Massachusetts," in *Medical Essays,* vol. 9 of *The Complete Writings of Oliver Wendell Holmes* (Boston, 1891), pp. 9, 319, 325, 348.

[6]Oliver Wendell Holmes, *Homoeopathy and its Kindred Delusions* (Boston, 1842), p. 53.

[7]William H. Holcombe, *The Truth about Homoeopathy* (Philadelphia, 1894), pp. 8–9.

[8]Ibid., pp. 11–12.

[9]See Julian Hawthorne, *Nathaniel Hawthorne and His Wife,* 2 vols. (Boston, 1884), 1: 100; Randall Stewart, *Nathaniel Hawthorne: A Biography* (New Haven, 1948), p. 4.

[10]See Martin Gumpert, *Hahnemann: The Adventurous Career of a Medical Rebel* (New York, 1945), pp. 124–25.

[11]See Edward A. Lodge, *The Legality of Drug Provings Recognized* (Detroit, 1862).

[12]Julian Hawthorne, *Hawthorne and His Wife,* 1: 47; Louise Hall Tharp, *The Peabody Sisters of Salem* (Boston, 1950), pp. 37–38.

[13]Julian Hawthorne, *Hawthorne and His Wife,* 1: 63.

[14]Hahnemann, *Organon,* pp. 178–79.

[15]Ibid., p. 227.

[16]Ibid., p. 199.

[17]Hannah G. Creamer, *Delia's Doctors* (New York, 1852), p. 69. I am indebted to Mrs. Dorothy M. Potter, Librarian of the Essex Institute, for help in tracing Miss Creamer.

[18]Ibid., pp. 99–100.

[19]*Harpers' Magazine* 6 (1852–1853): 126, quoted by John Davies, in *Phrenology: Fad and Science* (New Haven, 1955), p. 105.

[20]Hahnemann, *Organon,* pp. 158–60.

[21]Ibid., p. 163.

[22]Gumpert, *Hahnemann,* pp. 72–77.

[23]Hahnemann, *Organon,* pp. 163–64.

[24]Ibid., p. 161.

[25]Oliver Wendell Holmes "Border Lines of Medical Knowledge," in *Medical Essays,* vol. 9 of *The Complete Writings of Oliver Wendell Holmes* (Boston, 1891), p. 245. See also p. xiv.

[26]See Oliver Wendell Holmes, "Medical Profession," p. 319.

[27]Holmes, *Homoeopathy,* p. 39.

[28]Hahnemann, *Organon,* p. 191.

[29]Holmes, *Homoeopathy,* p. 39.

[30]Louise Hall Tharp identifies the "Dr. Wesselhoeft" mentioned in Hawthorne's letter to Sophia, April 24, 1846, and other family letters, as Dr. Robert Wesselhoeft, but it is possible that his brother William was the doctor who treated the Hawthorne children for scarlet fever in 1848—(Tharp, *Peabody Sisters,*

p. 202). Perhaps both of the brothers prescribed for Sophia and her family. Robert, a friend of Charles Follen and, like him, a follower of Friedrich Jahn, advocated gymnastics as well as homoeopathy; the older brother, William, had hydropathy as *his* backup science and was the founder of the Brattleboro Water-Cure Establishment. Charles Wesselhoeft, translator of Hahnemann's *Organon,* was perhaps also a physician to the Hawthornes, for Mrs. Tharp (p. 303) reports consultations with "Dr. Wesselhoeft" on the question of Una's gymnastics class some years after the deaths of both the father and the uncle (Robert died in 1852, William in 1859). Sophia's sister Elizabeth wrote the official memorial of William Wesselhoeft, another indication of the closeness of the relationship—rather beyond a merely professional acquaintance.

31Holmes, *Homoeopathy,* p. 12.

32Ibid., p. 19.

33Quoted in Rose Hawthorne Lathrop, *Memories of Hawthorne* (Boston, 1897), p. 223.

34Ibid., p. 354; Stewart, *Hawthorne,* p. 204.

35James T. Fields, *Yesterdays with Authors* (Boston, 1871), p. 117.

36Julian Hawthorne, *Hawthorne and His Wife,* 1: 100.

37Hawthorne to Robert Manning, December 9, 1813, Clifton Waller Barrett Library, University of Virginia Library. The letter is printed, very inaccurately, in George Lathrop's *Biographical Sketch of Nathaniel Hawthorne,* included in the Riverside Edition of the works, 12: 453.

38Nathaniel Hawthorne to Mrs. Elizabeth Manning Hawthorne, March 13, 1821, Pierpont Morgan Library.

39See Tharp, *Peabody Sisters,* p. 202; and Julian Hawthorne, *Hawthorne and His Circle* (New York, 1903), p. 8. The "Boston homoeopath" was Dr. Wesselhoeft, who appears again in a letter of 1846, from Hawthorne to Sophia, during a brief separation "Thou canst not think what peace I enjoy in the consideration that thou art within reach of Dr. Wesselhoeft. It is by my feelings as to thee and Una, more than on my own account, that I find I am a true believer in homoeopathy." (Huntington Library.) The tone here is typical of Hawthorne's letters to Sophia on the subject of homoeopathy; here is a passage from another, written during Sophia's convalescence in Lisbon from bronchitis (Sophia's sister Elizabeth had sent Hawthorne a little box of medicine, apparently allopathic, to try on Sophia): "If thou wert not so very naughty—if thou wouldst consent to be benefitted by anything but homoeopathy—here in this little box is health and joy for us!"—Nathaniel Hawthorne to Sophia Hawthorne, March 18, 1856, Huntington Library.

40Julian Hawthorne, *Hawthorne and His Wife,* 2: 206.

41Ibid., 2: 207.

42Hawthorne to Fields, February 25, 1864, Huntington Library. Printed with a few omissions in Fields, *Yesterdays,* p. 116.

43See Randall Stewart, "Hawthorne's Last Illness and Death," *More Books,* October 1944, pp. 308–10.

44Hawthorne to James T. Fields, April 9, 1864, Huntington Library. Partially quoted in Stewart, *Hawthorne,* p. 236.

45Stewart, "Hawthorne's Last Illness and Death," p. 311.

46Ibid., p. 312. Quotation from Una Hawthorne, explaining her mother's change of opinion to Annie Fields.

[47]Holmes, in an account of his last meeting with Hawthorne, *Atlantic Monthly* 14 (1864): 95.

[48]Quoted from Annie Fields' diary, in Tharp, *Peabody Sisters,* p. 299.

[49]Rose Hawthorne Lathrop, *Memories of Hawthorne,* p. 478.

[50]Hawthorne to Fields, January 17, 1864, collection of Professor Norman Holmes Pearson.

[51]Oliver Wendell Holmes, *Elsie Venner,* vol. 5 of *The Complete Writings of Oliver Wendell Holmes* (Boston, 1891), pp. 322–23.

[52]Ibid., pp. ix–x.

[53]Ibid., p. 445.

[54]See Tharp, *Peabody Sisters,* p. 307; Lathrop, *Memories of Hawthorne,* p. 477.

[55]Holmes, *Elsie Venner,* pp. 226–28.

[56]Ibid., pp. 205, 323, 426.

[57]Henry C. Wright, *Marriage and Parentage* (Boston, 1854), p. 5.

[58]Andrew Jackson Davis, *Tale of a Physician: or The Seeds and Fruits of Crime* (Boston, 1869), p. 7.

[59]Holmes, *Elsie Venner,* p. 434.

[60]Ibid., p. xii.

[61]Ibid., p. 322.

[62]A. H. Grimmer [!], "The Spider Poisons," *Journal of the American Institute of Homoeopathy,* March 1952, pp. 47–51.

[63]Hawthorne seems to have read both in 1820; see G. P. Lathrop, *A Study of Hawthorne* (Boston, 1876), p. 108; Jane Lundblad, *Hawthorne and the European Literary Tradition* (New York, 1965), p. 35.

[64]Herman Melville, *Pierre* (New York, 1964), p. 344.

[65]Julian Hawthorne, *Hawthorne and His Circle,* p. 33.

Notes to Chapter Five [Social Science]

[1]Ralph Waldo Emerson, *The Journals, and Miscellaneous Notebooks of Ralph Waldo Emerson,* ed. William H. Gilman, Alfred R. Ferguson, et al. (Cambridge, Mass., 1960–) 5: 72.

[2]June 15, 1840. Henry D. Thoreau, *The Journal of Henry D. Thoreau,* ed. Bradford Torrey and Francis H. Allen, 14 vols. (Boston, 1906), 1: 140.

[3]April 14, 1839. Bronson Alcott, *The Journals of Bronson Alcott,* ed. Odell Shepard (Boston, 1938), p. 123.

[4]*Water Cure Journal and Herald of Reform* 13 (1852): 140–41.

[5]Stephen Pearl Andrews, *The Science of Society* (Boston, 1888 [1st edn., New York, 1851]), pp. 5–6.

[6]J.W. Redfield, *Comparative Physiognomy* (New York, 1852); Thomas Lake Harris, *An Epic of the Starry Heavens* (New York, 1854), p. 205. Hawthorne thought Harris's poems had "a certain light and splendor, but not to possess much power, either passionate or intellectual" (*EN* 617).

[7]See Nichols' very popular book *Esoteric Anthropology* (New York, 1853).

[8]*The Phonetic* [later *Fonetic*] *Propagandist,* 1–2 (November 6, 1850–November 17, 1852).

[9]*The Harbinger,* 3 (1846): 14.

[10]Albert Brisbane, *Social Destiny of Man* (Philadelphia, 1840), pp. iii, 29. On Brisbane's full career, see Redelia Brisbane, *Albert Brisbane: A Mental Biography* (Boston 1893).

[11]*The Perfectionist,* January 1, 1844.

[12]Quoted from *The Perfectionist* of 1844–1845 in George W. Noyes, *The Putney Community* (Oneida, 1931), p. 168.

[13]*The Practical Christian,* 8 (May 29, 1847): 2.

[14]George Ripley in *The Harbinger* 5 (1847): 13.

[15]On Modern Times, see Verne Dyson, *A Century of Brentwood* (Brentwood, Long Island, 1950). On the refugees from Hopedale, see *The Practical Christian* 13 (October 9, 1852): 3; and 19 (June 12, 1858): 1.

[16]*Brownson's Quarterly Review,* n.s. 6 (1852): 564

[17]Orestes A. Brownson, *The Spirit-Rapper, The Works of Orestes A. Brownson,* ed. Henry F. Brownson, 20 vols. (Detroit, 1882–1887), 9:29. Compare the catalogue offered in David M. Reese's *Humbugs of New-York* (New York, 1838): Animal Magnetism, Phrenology, Homoeopathy, Quackery in General, Ultra-Temperance, Ultra-Abolitionism, Ultra-Protestantism, and Ultra-Sectarianism. The list has grown in fifteen years.

[18]Brownson, *The Spirit-Rapper,* p. 153.

[19]Orestes A. Brownson, "Ultraism," *Boston Quarterly Review* 1 (1838): 381.

[20]Brownson, *The Spirit-Rapper,* pp. 1–2.

[21]See Henry James, *Hawthorne* (Ithaca, N.Y., 1956), p. 108.

Notes to Chapter Six [Associationism]

[1]Quoted in O.B. Frothingham, *George Ripley* (Boston, 1882), pp. 307–8.

[2]See Ralph Waldo Emerson, *The Letters of Ralph Waldo Emerson,* ed. Ralph L. Rusk, 6 vols. (New York, 1939), 2: 368–71.

[3]Frothingham, *George Ripley,* p. 308.

[4]Ralph Waldo Emerson, "Man the Reformer," in *Nature, Addresses, and Lectures,* ed. Robert Spiller and Alfred R. Ferguson, vol. I of *The Collected Works of Ralph Waldo Emerson* (Cambridge, Mass., 1971), pp. 147–48.

[5]See, for example, Charles A. Dana, *A Lecture on Associationism, in its Connection with Religion* (Boston, 1844), p. 26. Compare Ralph Waldo Emerson, *The Journals and Miscellaneous Notebooks of Ralph Waldo Emerson,* ed. William H. Gilman, Alfred R. Ferguson, et al. (Cambridge, Mass, 1960–), 7: 407–8.

[6]Sophia Ripley to John S. Dwight, May 6, 1841, in Zoltan Haraszti, *The Idyll of Brook Farm* (Boston, 1937), p. 18.

[7]Henry D. Thoreau *Walden,* in *The Writings of Henry D. Thoreau,* ed. J. Lyndon Shanley (Princeton, N. J., 1971), p. 46.

[8]Emerson's *Journals,* 7: 420; letter from Hawthorne to Sophia Peabody, August 12, 1841, Huntington Library.

[9]Emerson's *Journals,* 8: 38.

[10]Ibid., 8: 392.

[11]See Frothingham, *George Ripley,* pp. 116–17, and Clarence Gohdes, "A Brook Farm Labor Record," *American Literature* 1 (1929): 302–3.

[12]See Hawthorne's letter to Sophia Peabody, September 29, 1841, Huntington Library. Quoted in Henry W. Sams, ed., *Autobiography of Brook Farm* (Englewood Cliffs, N. J., 1958), pp. 43–44.

[13]Hawthorne to Sophia Peabody, September 22, 1841, Huntington Library.

[14]Emerson's *Journals,* 9: 63.

[15]Ibid., 9: 114, 163.

[16]*The Harbinger* 2 (1846): 265

[17]Bronson Alcott, *The Journals of Bronson Alcott,* ed. Odell Shepard (Boston, 1938), p. 344. Hawthorne to Longfellow, June 4, 1837, Houghton Collection, Harvard College Library. Quoted in Malcolm Cowley, ed., *The Portable Hawthorne* (New York, 1948), p. 608.

[18]Emerson's *Journals,* 7: 347; Henry D. Thoreau, *The Journal of Henry D. Thoreau,* ed. Bradford Torrey and Francis H. Allen, 14 vols. (Boston, 1906), 1: 220.

[19]Thoreau, *Walden,* pp. 134–35.

[20]Emerson's *Journals,* 9: 236.

Notes to Chapter Seven [Spiritualism]

[1]Herman Melville, *Typee: A Peep at Polynesian Life,* ed. Harrison Hayford, Hershel Parker, and G. Thomas Tanselle (Northwestern-Newberry Edition, Evanston and Chicago, 1968), pp. 48–49.

[2]Elizabeth Oakes Smith, *Shadow Land; or, The Seer* (New York, 1852), p. 18. Compare this passage in Emerson's journals: "Miss B______, a mantuamaker in Concord, became a 'Medium,' and gave up her old trade for this new one; and is to charge a pistareen a spasm, and nine dollars for a fit. This is the Rat-revelation, the gospel that comes by taps in the wall, and thumps in the table-drawer. The spirits make themselves of no reputation. They are rats and mice of society and one of the demure disciples of the rat-tat-too, the other day, remarked that 'this, like every other communication from the spiritual world, began very low'"—Ralph Waldo Emerson, *Journals of Ralph Waldo Emerson,* ed. Edward Waldo Emerson and Waldo Emerson Forbes, 10 vols. (Boston and New York, 1909–1914), 8: 298–99.

[3]See Chauncy Hare Townshend, *Facts in Mesmerism,* American Edition (Boston, 1841), p. 526.

[4]See LaRoy Sunderland, *Ideology: Mental Anaesthesia Self-induced, Miraculous Cures Self-made, Involution and Evolution in the Human Mind as in the Whole of Things,* 2 vols. (Boston, 1885), 2: 114.

[5]Georgiana Bruce Kirby, *Years of Experience* (New York, 1887), p. 161. Georgiana may have misremembered Cornelia's claims when she wrote her memoirs in 1887. There is evidence that Georgiana's first inklings of the possibility of spiritual intercourse did not occur until the early 1850s, when she was in California; see her letter to the phrenologist and feminist Charlotte Fowler Wells, asking for news of spiritualism: "If *you* have communication with those who have put off the natural body will you not enquire if the same be not possible to us in Santa Cruz. . . . "

Quoted by Madeleine B. Stern "Two Letters from the Sophisticates of Santa Cruz," *Book Club of California Quarterly News-Letter* 33 (1968): 60. It will be remembered, though, that Harriet Beecher Stowe thought to approach the "verge of the Spirit land" through mesmerism in 1844 (see note 27, chapter 2 above).

[6]Andrew Jackson Davis, *The Principles of Nature, Her Divine Revelations, and A Voice to Mankind,* 34th Am. ed. (Boston, 1876), pp. 673–76.

[7]Dozens of books on spiritualism appeared in the 1850s; for a selected bibliography, see George Lawton, *The Drama of Life after Death* (New York, 1932), pp. 631–53.

[8]Hawthorne to Pike, July 24, 1851, quoted in Rose Hawthorne Lathrop, *Memories of Hawthorne* (Boston, 1897), p. 153. On Pike's ghost stories, see *AN* 189–91, and footnote 446.2 in *AN* 656.

[9]See *EN* 154, 381, 616–17; and X 296, 376, 386–96, 411–14, 427.

[10]Sophia Hawthorne to Elizabeth Peabody, February 3, 1851, Berg Collection.

[11]See Peter L. Hays, "Why Seven Years in *The Scarlet Letter,*" in *The Nathaniel Hawthorne Journal 1972,* ed. C. E. Frazer Clark, Jr. (Washington, D. C., 1973), pp. 251–53.

Notes to Chapter Eight [Feminism]

[1]Quoted from Frances Wright's "Explanatory Notes" on Nashoba (1828), in A. J. G. Perkins and Theresa Wolfson, *Frances Wright: Free Enquirer* (New York and London, 1939), p. 193.

[2]See Arthur M. Schlesinger, Jr., *A Pilgrim's Progress: Orestes A. Brownson,* 2d ed. (Boston, 1966), p. 225.

[3]*The Harbinger* 2 (1846): 61–62.

[4]Ralph Waldo Emerson, *The Journals and Miscellaneous Notebooks of Ralph Waldo Emerson,* ed. William H. Gilman, Alfred R. Ferguson, et al. (Cambridge, Mass., 1960–), 8: 391–92.

[5]Ibid., 8: 377–78.

[6]Ibid. Cf. *AN* 176.

[7]Marianne Dwight, *Letters from Brook Farm 1844–1847,* ed. Amy L. Reed (Poughkeepsie, 1928), pp. 46–47.

[8]Ibid., pp. 57, 84, 86–87, 112.

[9]John Humphrey Noyes, *Bible Communism* (Brooklyn, 1853), p. 57.

[10]Ibid., p. 58.

[11]"Brook Farm," *Dial* 4 (1844): 356.

[12]See Lindsay Swift, *Brook Farm* (New York, 1961), pp. 113–17; Zoltan Haraszti, *The Idyll of Brook Farm* (Boston, 1937), p. 20.

[13]Marianne Dwight, *Letters,* pp. 39–40; Hawthorne, it will be remembered, had hoped to build a honeymoon cottage at Brook Farm for himself and Sophia—surely not a project likely to have prospered.

[14]Ibid., p. 134.

[15]Haraszti, *Idyll of Brook Farm,* p. 38.

[16]Dwight, *Letters,* p. 159.

[17]Ibid., p. 171.

[18]Ibid., pp. 157–58.

[19]Ibid., p. 138. Marianne, who spells the names Donelly and Westcott, does not specify which Westcott. The Brook Farm Labor Records list two Westacotts, Lewis and R. G.; the former appears in the lists only during the summer of 1844, long enough to fall in love, but suggesting by the same token an engagement of a year and half, perhaps too long for probability. Also to be noted is John Sawyer's marriage in April 1845. His bride, like Mary Lincoln, was not a permanent resident, but she joined the community with her husband. (See Dwight, *Letters,* p. 88, and Clarence Gohdes, "A Brook Farm Labor Record," *American Literature* 1 [1929]: 302.) It is hard to assess these marriages of the lesser-known members of Brook Farm, since we have so little information about their circumstances. The inner circle that Marianne gossips about, Danas, Macdaniels, Dwights and Ripleys, is probably a skewed sample too, but at least it is the inner circle.

[20]Emerson's *Journals*, 8: 393; Dwight, *Letters,* p. 41. Marianne Dwight has an instructive anecdote: "We have among new comers a Mr. Whittamore and a Mr. Curtis. John [Dwight, her brother], walking home from the woods, overheard between them this conversation. Mr. W. 'The girls here are *pretty slick.*' Mr. C. 'Yes! a very good place for a fellow to come who wants to look him up a girl.' They were very disinterested,—disclaimed all idea of wishing to be married, etc., etc. We've had a little rich fun out of this."—Dwight, p. 69.

[21]Dwight, *Letters,* pp. 115–16.

[22]Horace Greeley, *Recollections of a Busy Life* (New York, 1868), p. 178.

[23]Moncure Conway, "Modern Times, New York," *Fortnightly Review* 1 (1865): 425. On Modern Times see also Verne Dyson, *A Century of Brentwood,* (Brentwood, Long island, 1950), *passim;* Madeleine B. Stern, *The Pantarch: A Biography of Stephen Pearl Andrews* (Austin, Texas, 1968), pp. 73–86; and Bertha-Monica Stearns, "Two Forgotten New England Reformers," *New England Quarterly* 6 (1933): 60–73.

[24]Conway, "Modern Times, New York," pp. 427, 431.

[25]See John Humphrey Noyes, *History of American Socialisms* (Philadelphia, 1870), p. 212.

[26]See Dyson, *A Century of Brentwood,* p. 111; and a letter from Allen's daughter Catherine to Henry S. Borneman, July 22, 1921, Fruitlands Museums, Harvard, Mass. John Orvis was Allen's regular companion on his lecturing tours.

[27]See Mary S. Gove Nichols's fictionalized autobiography, *Mary Lyndon* (New York, 1855), pp. 309–10; and Charles Wilkins Webber, *Spiritual Vampirism: The History of Etherial Softdown* (Philadelphia, 1853), pp. 114–16, 152–53.

[28]The best edition of *Love, Marriage, and Divorce* is that brought out by the libertarian publisher Benjamin Tucker (Boston, 1889). James's review was in the *Tribune*, September 18, 1852, and the attack on him appeared in the *New York Observer,* September 30, 1852.

[29]See Orson Fowler, *Sexual Science* (Philadelphia, 1870), pp. 263–64; cf. the exchange between Austin Kent and Adin Ballou in *The Practical Christian* 15 (1854): 54; and also "Union for Life," *Nichols Monthly* 1 (October 1854): 59–60.

[30]"The Free-Love System," *New-York Daily Times,* September 8, 1855, p. 2.

[31]John Humphrey Noyes, *History of American Socialisms,* p. 94.

[32]"Fourierism in Ohio, Mrs. Gove's Crusade against Tobacco, The New Philosophy of Marriage," *The Weekly Herald* (New York), March 15, 1845, p. 86.

[33]See Mary Gove Nichols, *Reminiscences of Edgar Allan Poe* (New York, 1931), pp. 5, 7, 9; and Irving T. Richards, "Mary Gove Nichols and John Neal," *New England Quarterly* 7 (1934): 337–39.

[34]Webber, *Spiritual Vampirism,* pp. 147–48. For an illuminating contrast, compare the scene between Chillingworth and Dimmesdale that concludes chapter 10 of *The Scarlet Letter.*

[35]Ibid., p. 15.

[36]*Nichols' Journal* 1, no. 6 (1853): 45–46.

[37]G. H. Calvert wrote John Dwight, Marianne's brother, on August 26, 1855: "Fourier I see is again slandered in that trashy book Mary Lyndon, some paragraphs of which I read a year or more ago in the Nichols paper, which paper died, I presume of angina pectoris." (Fruitlands Museums.)

[38]Mary Gove Nichols, *Mary Lyndon,* pp. 310–13.

[39]Hawthorne may have known something of the Webber-Gove story. While still involved with Mary Gove, Webber had written a long piece on Hawthorne for the *American Review* (September–December 1846), under his pen name, Charles Winterfield. He praised Hawthorne rather lefthandedly, as a Whig in spite of himself, but the review was favorable. A few years later, after he had broken with Mary and lost his job on the *Review*, Webber was trying to start a plushy new magazine, and arranged with Hawthorne for the publication of "The Unpardonable Sin" in the first number. Hawthorne's letter to Webber announcing the completion of the tale still exists (dated from Salem, December 14, 1848—now at the University of Virginia). Hawthorne and Webber may have discussed the matter in person, for in *Spiritual Vampirism* Webber says he went to Boston about this time in pursuit of "some wild, distracting scheme that he had seized upon, and in which he was endeavoring to secure co-operation there" (p. 223). A number of his proposed contributors lived in the Boston area. But the financing never came through, and one of Webber's chief mainstays, J. W. Audubon, son of the naturalist, apparently backed out of the venture on account of illness. Webber was now in considerable poverty. His new wife was as penniless as he, her mother having been recently swindled out of a water-cure establishment in which she had invested her savings. Among the expedients he tried, one seems to have involved turning over (for a price?) the manuscript of "The Unpardonable Sin" to the *Boston Weekly Museum* without Hawthorne's knowledge or permission. Hawthorne heard about it, and objected in a second letter to Webber, December 18, 1849 (University of Virginia), but the tale appeared in the January issue of the *Museum* anyway. Apparently Hawthorne was sympathetic enough with Webber's plight that he did not raise much of a fuss. The story, intended from the first to help advertise a new book—ultimately *The Snow Image*—was reprinted in the May 1851 *Holden's Dollar Magazine.*

In his second, remonstrating letter to Webber, Hawthorne also mentions that Mrs. Webber has called on the Hawthornes, Mrs. Hawthorne having been ill, and further, that Webber's advice to apply water-cure techniques has been followed successfully! The tone of this letter is mild and perhaps a bit humoring, as if Hawthorne did not want to risk exciting Webber unduly. This likelihood is borne out by the next event of their recorded relationship. Edwin P. Whipple, Hawthorne's friend and one of his most influential critics, had also been a contributor to Webber's ill-fated magazine. Whipple now seems to have arranged for a review of Webber's book, *The Hunter-Naturalist* (Philadelphia, 1851), which Hawthorne wrote for the *Boston Daily Advertiser* (December 10, 1851). On December 7 Hawthorne informed Whipple that he had finished the review, "glad" to have done "this very little mite" for "poor" Webber and his wife (Morgan Library). See Randall Stewart, "Two Uncollected Reviews by Hawthorne," *New England Quarterly* 9 (1936): 508. The next day, according to his journal, the Hawthornes received another visit: " . . . came Mrs. Webber, dined, and went away in the dusk" (*AN* 313). Probably she picked up the review and the copy of the book, which had only been loaned, since it contained numerous expensive plates. Hawthorne's review was politely admiring; he made a special point of mentioning Mrs. Webber's "wood-cuts" in "some of the most spirited" of the book's illustrations.

One further contact occurred, in 1853, when Hawthorne again wrote Whipple, enclosing a letter from Webber asking for his influence with the newly elected president Franklin Pierce in procuring a political appointment in South America. As always, Hawthorne sympathized with Webber's desperate pleas, and arranged with Whipple for a case to be made. (Collection of C. E. Frazer Clark, Jr.) Webber did go to South America, not as the chargé d'affaires to Bolivia as he had hoped, but as part of General Walker's filibustering expedition to Nicaragua, where he was killed in 1856. See Evert A. Duyckinck, *Cyclopaedia of American Literature* (Philadelphia, 1877), 2: 630.

This is obviously not the story of a close friendship and therefore it seems unlikely that Webber would have told much of his seamy history to Hawthorne, whose great reserve was not calculated to inspire confidences anyway. But it is hard to be sure. After all, Webber was a volatile type, and if he had too much sense of propriety to tell his story to Hawthorne, he was unmannerly enough to blab it to the world in a book. Again, even if Webber kept his own counsel, it is possible that the story was hinted at through his wife. I have been unable to track her down past her initials (E. M. Webber—"Moione" in *Spiritual Vampirism*), and so cannot definitely say, but she seems to have been closer to the Hawthornes than Webber. Perhaps as a Boston girl and a fellow artist, she had an old friendship with Sophia (who would have been twice her age, however). Hawthorne scarcely ever speaks of or to Webber without mentioning his wife—in the 1849 letter, the letter to Whipple, the journal entry, and even the review of Webber's book. Still, it does not follow from a conjectured friendship between Sophia and Mrs. Webber that gossip was exchanged on such delicate matters as Webber's affair with Mary Gove. All in all, the chances are against Hawthorne having heard any of the scandal from the principals, though some of its aspects were probably well enough known among the literary gossips of Boston and New York. Nothing hinges on the fact anyway, for *Blithedale* resembles *Spiritual Vampirism* only in the way that it resembles *The Spirit-Rapper,* that is, as a response to a common atmosphere of bohemian ferment and decay. (I am grateful to the late Professor Norman Holmes Pearson for furnishing me with information on Hawthorne and Webber.)

40Orestes Brownson, *The Spirit-Rapper, The Works of Orestes A. Brownson,* ed. Henry F. Brownson (Detroit, 1882–1887), 9:46.

41Edward D. Mansfield, *The Legal Rights, Liabilities and Duties of Women* (Salem, 1845), pp. 270–83.

42Mary Nichols, *Mary Lyndon,* p. 135.

[43]Ibid., p. 165.
[44]Ibid., p. 214; *BR* 217.
[45]Brownson, *The Spirit-Rapper,* p. 48.
[46]Julian Hawthorne, *Hawthorne and His Wife,* 2 vols. (Boston, 1884), 1: 340.
[47]Ralph Waldo Emerson, William Henry Channing, and James Freeman Clarke, eds., *Memoirs of Margaret Fuller Ossoli,* 2 vols. (Boston, 1852), 2: 35.
[48]A passage deleted from Hawthorne's *Italian Notebooks,* quoted in Randall Stewart, *Nathaniel Hawthorne: A Biography* (New York, 1945), p. 194.
[49]Emerson, et al., *Memoirs* 2: 35–36.
[50]Webber, *Spiritual Vampirism,* p. 26.
[51]Ibid., p. 28.
[52]See Dwight, *Letters,* pp.13, 44–5, Georgiana Bruce Kirby, *Years of Experience* (New York, 1887), pp. 103, 179. Georgiana Bruce Kirby thought Maria E______ (she doesn't give her full name) was the original of Priscilla in *Blithedale.*
[53]Ralph Waldo Emerson, *The Letters of Ralph Waldo Emerson,* ed. Ralph L. Rusk, 6 vols. (New York, 1939), 3: 236–38n, 240–41n.
[54]Margaret Fuller, "The New Science, or The Philosophy of Mesmerism or Animal Magnetism," in *Life Without and Life Within,* ed. A. B. Fuller (Boston, 1859), p. 172. This is a reprint of Margaret's review of J. Stanley Grimes's *Etherology,* published in the *New York Tribune* for February 17, 1845.
[55]Ibid., p. 173. On Dr. Capron and Miss Brackett, see the Appendix to J. P. F. Deleuze, *Practical Instruction in Animal Magnetism,* trans. Thomas C. Hartshorn, rev. ed. (New York, 1883), pp. 308–15, 399–416, 477–79.
[56]The *Tribune* article is merely signed "F," but Léger reprints the letter in his *Animal Magnetism; or, Psycodunamy* (New York, 1846), pp. 394–99, and there he gives all three initials, implying that he knew the correspondent—a possibility that favors the conjecture that it was his countryman Bugard.
[57]Kirby, *Experience,* pp. 213–14. Was this sexual imagery Georgiana Bruce's contribution forty years after the fact, or was it actually Fuller's sensation?
[58]Julia Ward Howe, ed., *Love-Letters of Margaret Fuller, 1845–1846.* (New York, 1903), pp. 9, 15, 69.
[59]Ibid., p. 65.
[60]Ibid., pp. 109–10.
[61]Stewart, *Hawthorne,* p. 194.
[62]Emerson, et al., *Memoirs,* 2: 281–82.
[63]Margaret Fuller, *Woman in the Nineteenth Century* (Boston, 1855) pp. 103–4.
[64]Stewart, *Hawthorne,* p. 194.
[65]Ibid., p. 195.
[66]Julian Hawthorne, *Hawthorne and His Wife* 1: 257.
[67]Mary Nichols, *Mary Lyndon,* pp. 164–66.
[68]Greeley, *Recollections,* p. 179.
[69]Howe, ed., *Love-Letters,* p. 42.

Notes to Chapter Nine [Prison Reform]

[1]See Roy Harvey Pierce's "Introduction" to the Centenary Edition of *Blithedale,* p. xix.
[2]Georgiana Bruce Kirby, *Years of Experience* (New York, 1887), pp. 164–66.

[3]See Hawthorne's 1857 letter to Elizabeth Peabody for a hint of his complicated view of abolition—Rose Hawthorne Lathrop, *Memories of Hawthorne* (Boston, 1897), p. 335. Compare a passage in his biography of Franklin Pierce (XII 415).

[4]See John Murray Spear, *Labors for the Prisoner* (Boston, 1850–1851), and *The Prisoner's Friend,* 2 vols. (1849–1850).

[5]See George Lawton, *The Drama of Life after Death* (New York, 1932), pp. 608–23.

[6]See Merle Curti, *The Learned Blacksmith: The Letters and Journals of Elihu Burritt* (New York, 1937).

[7]Samuel May, in *Report of the Prison Association of New York,* 2d edn. (Albany, 1849), p. 126.

[8]See Howe's letter, ibid., 1846, pp. 21–22; Parker, *A Sermon on the Dangerous Classes in Society* (Boston, 1847).

[9]For Sumner's praise, see *The Christian Examiner* 40 (1846): 136; the *Tribune* articles were by Margaret Fuller (see below); on the Fowlers and Eliza Farnham, see John Davies, *Phrenology: Fad and Science* (New Haven, 1955), pp. 102–3, and Madeleine B. Stern, *Heads and Headlines,* (Norman, Okla. 1971) pp. 40–41.

[10]See Madeleine B. Stern, "Two Letters from the Sophisticates of Santa Cruz," for an account of the ouster and for the further exploits of Eliza Farnham and Georgiana Bruce as free women in California.

[11]Kirby, *Experience,* p. 194.

[12]Ibid., p. 193.

[13]Ibid., p. 206.

[14]Later Fuller moved in with the Greeleys on Turtle Bay, across the river from Sing Sing, and she went with William Henry Channing on Sunday mornings to sermonize the inmates, so she might have told her friends something of prison life at first hand. Georgiana admitted that Margaret found it difficult to "touch their level" when she spoke to the women. Hawthorne would have appreciated *that*. Ralph Waldo Emerson, William Henry Channing, and James Freeman Clarke, eds., *Memoirs of Margaret Fuller Ossoli,* 2 vols. (Boston, 1852), 2: 150; Kirby, *Experience,* p. 211.

[15]Published as *The Yarn of a Yankee Privateer* in 1926, with several missing chapters restored, by Funk and Wagnalls. The name of the actual author, Benjamin F. Browne, had been lost by this time, so the book was published anonymously. Hawthorne's friend O'Sullivan, by the way, was a strong advocate of penal reform. Margaret Fuller's *Tribune* articles appeared on June 19, 1845, and February 25, 1846.

[16]"Prison Discipline," pp. 130–31.

[17]Ibid., p. 138.

[18]Ibid., p. 139.

[19]Dorothea Dix, *Remarks on Prisons and Prison Discipline* (Boston, 1845), p. 14.

[20]Ibid., pp. 15–16.

[21]Herman Melville, *White Jacket* (New York, 1956) p. 148.

[22]Letter from an inmate dated July 6, 1844, quoted in Dix, *Remarks on Prisons,* p. 69.

[23] Quoted in Dix, *Remarks on Prisons,* pp. 71–72. Combe did, however, believe in solitary confinement for the early part of a prisoner's term, to soften him for later moral and religious influences to be applied phrenologically.

[24]Mrs. Farnham, in her edition of M. B. Sampson, *Rationale of Crime* (New York, 1846), p. 133.

[25]Kirby, *Experience,* p. 305.
[26]Dix, *Remarks on Prisons,* p. 72.
[27]May, *Report of the Prison Association of New York,* 1849, p. 91.
[28]Ibid., p. 127.
[29]Quoted in Sampson, *Rationale of Crime,* pp. 140–41.
[30]Ibid.
[31]Dix, *Remarks on Prisons,* p. 65.
[32]Ibid., pp. 60–61.
[33]Ibid., p. 62.
[34]"Prison Discipline," p. 132.
[35]*Report of the Prison Association of New York,* 1846, pp. 21–22; Samuel Gridley Howe, *The Letters and Journals of Samuel Gridley Howe,* ed. Laura E. Richards, 2 vols. (Boston, 1909), 2: 186.
[36]Albert Deutsch, *The Mentally Ill in America* (Garden City, 1937), p. 151; but by 1857 Bell had recanted—see p. 155. Moral treatment had begun at the turn of the century, with Pinel's famous doing-away with the chains at the Bicêtre and the Salpêtriere, but only in the 1830s and 1840s did it make much headway in American asylums.
[37]In Sampson, *Rationale of Crime,* p. xvii.
[38]Charles Spear, *Essays on the Punishment of Death* (Boston, 1844), p. 199.
[39]In Sampson, *Rationale of Crime,* p. xvii.
[40]Spear, *Punishment of Death,* p. 216.

Notes to Chapter Ten [The Mad Scientist]

[1]*Henry Russell* (New York, 1846), pp. 70–78.
[2]On Orvis, see A. E. Newton, ed., *The Educator . . . A Series of Revealments from Organized Associations in the Spirit-Life, through John Murray Spear* (Boston, 1857), p. 34. On Ripley, see Emma Hardinge's *Modern American Spiritualism* (New York, 1870), p. 63. Most of the others mentioned wrote books or pamphlets on mesmerism, spiritualism, or kindred subjects.
[3]Ralph Waldo Emerson, *The Journals and Miscellaneous Notebooks of Ralph Waldo Emerson,* ed. William H. Gilman, Alfred R. Ferguson, et al. (Cambridge, Mass., 1960–), 9: 323.
[4]Hawthorne to Bayard Taylor, March 2, 1864, printed with inaccuracies in Horace Scudder, *The Life and Letters of Bayard Taylor,* 2 vols. (Boston, 1884), 2: 417.
[5]John Hay, *The Bread-Winners* (New York, 1883), p. 239.
[6]William Dean Howells, *The Undiscovered Country* (Boston, 1880), 109–10.
[7]Edward Bellamy, *Looking Backward* (New York, 1960) pp. 196–97.
[8]Ibid., p. 66.
[9]Ibid.
[10]Solomon Schindler, *Young West* (Boston, 1894), pp. 195–220; like Bellamy, Schindler was fascinated by spiritualist phenomena and was an impartial observer at several seances. See his report in *The Psychical Review* 1 (1892): 41–43, and his article, "Experiment in Psychography: Slates Suspended out of Reach of Psychic," ibid., 131–135.

[11]Schindler, *Young West,* pp. 17–18.

[12]Mark Twain, *A Connecticut Yankee in King Arthur's Court* (New York, 1963), p. 128.

Index